Women, Policing, and Male Violence:
International Perspectives

Women, Policing, and Male Violence: International Perspectives

Jalna Hanmer, Jill Radford, and Elizabeth A. Stanko

ROUTLEDGE
London and New York

First published 1989
by Routledge
11 New Fetter Lane, London EC4P 4EE
29 West 35th Street, New York NY 10001

© 1989 Routledge

Printed in Great Britain by Billings & Sons Limited, Worcester.
Typeset by Pat and Anne Murphy, Highcliffe-on-Sea, Dorset

British Library Cataloguing in Publication Data

Hanmer, Jalna
  Women, policing, and male violence:
  international perspectives
  1. Women, violence; by men. Control
  I. Title II. Radford, Jill   III. Stanko, Elizabeth A.
  (Elizabeth Anne), *1950–*
  364.1'53

Library of Congress Cataloging in Publication Data

Hanmer, Jalna.
Women, policing, and male violence:
international perspectives/
Jalna Hanmer, Jill Radford,
Elizabeth A. Stanko.
     p.   cm.
Includes index.

1. Women — Crimes against. 2. Sex discrimination
in criminal justice. 3. Victims of crime — Government
policy. I. Radford, Jill, 1947– .
II. Stanko, Elizabeth Anne, 1950– . III. Title.
HV6250.4.W65H365 1989   88-18501 CIP
362.8'8'088042—dc 19

ISBN 0-415-00692-9
ISBN 0-415-00693-7 Pbk

Contents

Acknowledgements

While many women have engaged in the debates concerning particular forms of men's violence against women, few of our concerns have been taken on board in the wider academic and policy-making discussions about the nature and purpose of policing in general. This book arose from our dissatisfaction with the way policing is discussed in the wider criminological literature.

The process of articulating our concerns about policing has involved many others through the years. We would like to thank the many women who continue to keep these issues alive in their own communities by providing assistance to other women and by making demands for more effective policing. In particular, we would also like to acknowledge those who have read drafts of chapters: Pat Carlen, Cynthia Enloe, Jennifer Hunt, Peter Manning, Gloria Miraskind, Jean Osborne, Sheila Saunders, Phil Scraton, and Joanna Shapland. Many thanks to Pat Spallone for her help with the bibliography. We would also like to thank the women with whom we shared ideas about policing men's violence: Women Against Violence Against Women Groups; the Sexual Violence and the Law Group at Rights of Women; the staff of Daybreak refuge, Worcester, Massachusetts; Women's Aid groups in Britain and the Violence Against Women Study Group of the British Sociological Association.

Notes on the Contributors

Kathleen J. Ferraro is a professor of Justice Studies and Women's Studies at Arizona State University. She is a co-founder of a shelter for battered women, and worked as a staff member there for one and a half years. She has published a number of articles on battering and is currently studying legal decisions in battering cases.

Jalna Hanmer is a Senior Lecturer and Coordinator of the M.A. in Women's Studies at the University of Bradford, West Yorkshire, England. She has published widely on violence against women and is co-author of *Well Founded Fear: A Community Study of Violence to Women* (with Sheila Saunders) and co-editor of *Women, Violence and Social Control* (with Mary Maynard). She is also co-author of *Women and Social Work: Towards a Woman-Centred Practice* (with Daphne Statham), and *Man-Made Women: How New Reproductive Technologies Affect Women* (with Gena Corea et al.) and managing editor of *Reproductive and Genetic Engineering: Journal of International Feminist Analysis*.

Suzanne Hatty was until recently with the Australian Institute of Criminology. She is currently a Senior Research Fellow in the School of Social Work at the University of New South Wales. She has researched and published widely in the area of violence against women and children, particularly as this violence intersects with the law. Other research interests include the relationships between gender, deviance, and social control.

Jill Radford is active in the Women's Liberation Movement, campaigning and researching around the issues of men's violence to women. She has taught sociology and criminology at the Open University, Polytechnic of the South Bank, and the University of Keele. Her research is informed both by her political commitment to feminism and her interests in sociology and criminology. She is currently working on a Ph.D. thesis on the history of women police and their contradictory role in the policing of male violence.

Elizabeth A. Stanko's original research and interest focused on prosecutor and police decision-making. For the past twelve years, she has been actively involved in feminist issues around violence against women. Author of *Intimate Intrusions: Women's Experience of Male Violence* (1985), co-editor of *Judge, Lawyer, Victim, Thief: Women, Gender Roles and Criminal Justice* (1982 with Nicole Rafter), Betsy Stanko is currently completing a book on women's and men's relationships to personal safety and fear of crime in the United States and Britain. She resides in both Worcester, Massachusetts and London.

Olga Jozephina Zoomer graduated in psychology at the State University in Groningen, Netherlands. She has been a researcher at the ministries of Home Affairs and Justice and has published on prosecutorial decision-making, violence against women and criminal justice, and on aspects of police work. She recently complete a study on policing woman beating.

Chapter one

Policing, Men's Violence: An Introduction

Jalna Hanmer, Jill Radford, and
Elizabeth A. Stanko

This book explores the police response to violence against women. It owes its origins to the reframing of questions about the violence of men against women that began in the late 1960s when the redefinition of the problem and the process of doing something about it began to move hand in hand. Fundamental questions raised then remain important today. How are women's experiences of violence from men to be interpreted? What services do women need? How does one particular service, the police, deal with women's needs? How are violent men to be controlled? In exploring these questions we rediscovered the history of nineteenth century women's campaigns to gain improvements for women abused by men. Two major ways in which demands for reform have surfaced in the past two centuries are the subject of this volume: the demand for women police and the demand that violence against women from men be treated as crime.

As with any text, this one is specifically located in particular cultures and historical situations. In different times and places women have used various words to describe their experiences of violence from men. Throughout this volume we use the words women fashioned to define and sub-classify their experiences rather than converting these to standardized terms which reflect our own understanding today. While the experiences these terms describe, like the words used to name them, differ from each other, through the process of naming women have voiced their anger and expressed their commitment to struggle and survival. 'Men's violence', 'sexual violence', 'rape', 'incest', 'sexual abuse of women and children', 'woman battering', 'womanslaughter', 'woman killing', 'frawen mishandling', 'the male peril', 'sexual terrorism', 'outrage', 'unspeakable horror', 'sexual harassment' — these are some of the words women in several cultures and at different times in this century have drawn upon to describe their experiences of men's violence.

As with naming experiences, women also use differing terms to encapsulate an explanation of why men are violent. Just as we reject any notion that man is inherently violent, we also reject any parallel beliefs that women are incapable of resisting men's violence. The contributors to this book describe the possibilities of women's resistance, illustrating how these are partly linked to women's positions within social structures, partly to the political consciousness and support networks that have developed among women, and partly to the decisions women make regarding how much of life to share with men. Resistance and fighting back are constant features of every woman's life, but they take place in a social context of unequal power. The reluctance of the police and criminal justice system to restrain men who commit violence against women or define its perpetrators as criminal is an illustration of this.

In the early days of the present wave of feminism, terms such as 'patriarchy' and 'male supremacy' were adopted to describe societies characterized by male dominance and female subordination. This domination and subordination were seen to be located in socially constructed relations through which men maintain power over women and children (Coveney et al. 1984; Rhodes and McNeill 1985; Millett 1970; Morgan 1970; Sarachild 1975). As heterosexuality became identified as a system of social relations rather than simply sexual practice, other terms emerged (Rich 1980; MacKinnon 1987). For example, 'hetero-reality' is used to describe the world view that woman exists always in relation to man (Raymond 1986). Hetero-reality is grounded in a wide range of affective, social, political, and economic relations that make up hetero-relations between men and women. In Britain 'hetero-patriarchy' is beginning to be used to signify a system of social relations based on male dominance, or supremacy, in which men's structured relationships to women underpin all other systems of exploitation.

This book explores how the treatment abused women receive is always mediated through experiences with men, those who abuse, and those who make up the part of the state that has the mandate

2

to intervene through the use of criminal law. Terms used in this volume include 'hetero-patriarchy', 'patriarchy', 'patriarchal societies', 'capitalism', 'class', 'race', 'sexism', 'male violence', 'male power', 'male domination', 'male supremacy', 'social control'. It is not the specific names used to signify specific experiences or explanations that are crucial but the underlying relations of differential power, domination, exploitation, and oppression by men of women that these terms epitomize. These terms are given meaning through the description and analyses of the processes involved in the policing of relations between men and women. This includes both police practices and the ideologies that justify police responses.

Violence against women is a specific example of a more general failure in effective responses to interpersonal crime by the police. But this is not to argue that ineffective police action around inter-personal crime affects everyone who experiences it equally or that every group receives the same lack of or the same type of inappro-priate intervention. Research on violence against women (Bart and O'Brien 1985; Hanmer and Maynard 1987; Hanmer and Saunders 1984, 1987; Kelly and Radford 1987; Russell 1982, 1984; Stanko 1985) demonstrates the ways in which women's lives are controlled by the threat or reality of men's violence. This work shows that for many women, the primary controlling force in our lives is the ordinary, everyday men who share our homes and who work along-side women in paid and unpaid employment, in education, and with whom we spend our leisure.

Violence and its threat are ugly and crude means of securing control or dominance and may be less effective in the long run. The use of violence presumes a loss of, or an indifference to, a more resilient strategy, compliance through consensus. There is a range of mediating mechanisms through which a consensual control of women by men is reproduced; at the ideological level there is a string of beliefs about both the sanctity of the family and the inherent nature of women which are drawn on to justify women's subordination to men. The culturally sanctioned views of women and women's role are embodied in legal, economic, and financial discrimination against women and are expressed through social institutions and processes, for example in the fields of health, welfare, education, science, the military, and the subject of this volume, the police.

Violence may be used by individual men to control or punish individual women who challenge, or are seen to be challenging, their authority. Even if men do not express their power in this way, the fact that they can if they do so choose inevitably underlies apparently harmonious interactions between those who are not equal. In this way the power of men, as individuals and as a sex class, can be asserted. These interests are defined as domestic, emotional and sexual servicing in which reciprocity, to the extent that it exists, is a gift that can be withdrawn at will.

An analysis of men's violence as a form of social control of women developed from women's experiences. Women began to listen to other women with a new ear, one that accepted the view of the world as women saw it. This led to new forms of woman-to-woman assistance and to new analyses of men's violence in securing and maintaining the social subordination of women (Edwards 1987). Women challenged the violence against them and argued that power relations in which men are dominant, like all exploitative social relations, are ultimately secured by violence and its threat (Clark and Lewis 1977; Hanmer 1978; Rhodes and McNeill 1985). Men's violence against women and children is identified by radical feminists as central to the maintenance and reproduction of all exploitative social relations.

Radical feminist analyses are frequently misrepresented as biologistic. Critics persist in arguing that these rest on a belief that men are innately violent. This is not the case. Rather than resort to biology, the contributors to this book illustrate through research findings how easy an option violence is for men in male supremacist societies. The societies in which this research was conducted have constructed and continue to celebrate forms of chauvinist masculinity which not only tolerates men's use of violence, but upholds it as a virtue, whether in the promotion of war, in the defence of pornography, or in the nightly television struggles between fictional good and evil. No resort to biological explanation is necessary or even helpful to explain this reality. Further, demands that men examine and reject their misogynist construction of masculinity, and their oppressive practices would be meaningless if they came from biologistic arguments about the inherent and therefore unchangeable nature of man.

This is why strategies to confront men's violence in Western societies have actively promoted alternatives for women to escape

4

violence. In many countries women have worked to establish their own support networks, as the existence of women's refuges or shelters and rape crisis centers demonstrate. While offering new services, these women-controlled agencies compensated for the failures of the police to offer support or to act in ways which might secure women's protection. It was through these alternative responses that we began to amass evidence that the police treatment of rape and battering was inadequate and not uncommonly abusive. Another feminist response is to empower individuals and women as a group by sharing self-defence skills; developing safe transport networks for women; and engaging in collective resistance through confrontation strategies.

While these measures are all valuable, they have never reached all women. Many women have no option but to turn to the police following an attack, whether they've been attacked by a man they know or a stranger. For this reason feminists have continued to be concerned about the policing of men's violence. This concern has taken several forms, from demonstrations and protests around specific cases to police monitoring projects undertaken by women. Feminists have developed detailed critiques of the policing of men's violence and made specific demands for reform. It is within this context that we review the policing of male violence.

One aim of this book is to evaluate the demand for and intro-duction of reforms in the policing of men's violence. This requires a close study of day-to-day, on-the-ground policing, and women's experiences of this policing. In evaluating these initiatives it is important not only to learn what the police in fact do and how the women concerned feel about this, but also to refer back and locate these measures at the wider structural level. We need to question whether these reforms secure safety for all women or simply provide protection for certain women against some forms of men's violence. If reforms are geared only to curbing the more obvious excesses of male violence and to protecting women the police define as deserving of protection, then women's demands will only shore up the existing relations between men and women rather than secure the feminist aim of autonomy for all women irrespective of class, race, and relationship to heterosexuality.

Examining the individual complaints of women about violence from men raises issues about the structural role of the police in maintaining existing gender, sexuality, race, and social class power relationships. The response of the police and legal system in the control of men's violence is crucial to women's safety and survival, but as the contributors to this book illustrate, so far they have shown little enthusiasm for protecting women. Feminist criticism of police failure to deal seriously with men's violence predates the formation of the 'new police' in 1829 in Britain, and similar criticisms are a recurrent theme in contemporary feminist criticism in the four countries explored here: Holland, Australia, the United States, and England. Police failure to respond to men's violence is one of the few areas in which they are rightly, in our view, criticised for insufficient and inappropriate policing, as opposed to exceeding their powers.

As well as being of immediate importance to women who have been attacked, the police response to men's violence has a general social significance. In deciding how to respond to women reporting violent attacks, the police, and later the courts, are defining which attacks are to be criminalized and proceeded with and which are to be condoned or 'no-crimed'. The police are making a distinction between attacks they deem to be justifiable and those that are not — that is, those that require police attention. This decision-making process demonstrates that the police do not offer unconditional protection to all women against forms of men's violence. Rather, any protection they offer is conditional upon women meeting police notions of 'deservedness' and the circumstances of the attack meeting their definition of 'crime'. These notions are inevitably informed by the misogyny, racism, classism, and heterosexism of dominant social ideologies. To the extent police refuse to intervene to assist women, they are effectively legitimizing men's use of violence as a form of social control.

Male supremacy is not the only power structure in capitalist, neo-colonial societies that adversely affects women. While all women are affected by an inferior social status in relation to men, an adequate theoretical analysis must recognize other power structures based on systemic inequality, in particular those of class, race, and sexuality. These power structures are not mutually exclusive but interactive. Women can be simultaneously privileged and oppressed; for example, black working-class women are less valued in three important structured inequalities but, if heterosexual, share a privileged position through their relationship to men. The position of men and women, however, vary on the key dimension of gender, so that while some men may be less valued because of their race, class, or sexuality, all men by virtue of their gender have power as men in relation to all women.

Focusing on police racism demonstrates how women's lives are affected by the interaction of differing structures of power in contemporary Western societies. In Britain, for example, black women have borne the brunt of police targetting and surveillance strategies directed against the black community in police-defined 'high crime areas'. In Britain the death of Cynthia Jarrett and the police shooting of Cherry Groce as a result of police raids on the homes of these black women have shaped the attitude of the black community and black women towards the police. Acknowledging the differences that exist between women both in terms of the nature of the types of violence experienced and in terms of our experiences of policing, is an essential element in any response women can make to policing.

Understanding the complexity of the interactions around these power structures is an ongoing project for feminist theory. These structures are not static, but stand in a dynamic relationship with each other. The precise form of interaction between them can never be assumed but only discovered in the context of any one culture at a precise moment in its history. Women's experience of men's violence and the policing response provides one example of the structured social relations of men and women characterized by male domination.

Further, recognizing the differences between women in terms of our experiences of policing also means that it is impossible for us to work in a vacuum outside the wider police debates. From the 1960s onwards there have been important shifts in the nature of policing in most Western countries. Targetting and surveillance strategies to curb political and industrial dissent are one initiative among many in the move towards a more militaristic style of policing in an increasingly authoritarian state (Scraton 1985). Not only do shifts in policing styles differentially shape our experiences of policing — the women in the mining communities felt the harsh edge of police raids during the 1986 strike in Britain, for example — but they also have a wider impact on the climate of police-public relations. This is the context into which women may want to require a change in the type of interventions police make in men's violence.

The contributors to this volume clarify how an acceptance of gender inequality, and the ideology on which it is based, is the foundation for the present police treatment of women. It is through the articulation of women's experiences that the invisibility of women to this part of the state becomes clear. We suggest this is a glaring example of the lack of women's autonomy in present-day society. But the maintenance and reproduction of relations characterized by male supremacy require the supression of the most excessive use of violence. What is defined as excessive is culturally variable and shifts through time. It is around these margins that most feminist struggles have been conducted. Demands to outlaw rape in marriage is a key illustration of this. Another example, and one central to this book, is the demand for improvements in the police response to violence against women.

A continuing thread between these chapters is the ideological and social construction and maintenance of a division of the social world for women into public and private spheres. This division expresses the form taken by the social control of women by men. The private/public split represents who is to be policed, and how. Women's victimization patterns differ from those of men primarily in that our attackers are much more likely to be close associates and the offences are most likely to occur in and immediately around the home. Men who cross women's paths in chance encounters in public, while greatly feared, do constitute a real and symbolic threat to women, but numerically speaking constitute less of a danger. Because men are usually safe within their own homes and do not fear attack from those with whom they live, that is, women and children, assaults on men are more likely to occur throughout the community. Interpersonal assault that does not occur in or around the home is more likely to be defined as crime by the police. The central relevance of the categories 'public' and 'private' to police decision-making emerges in all the research on the police described in this volume.

This volume presents findings from research on the policing of men's violence in England, the Netherlands, Australia, and the United States within the context of changes in law and the organization of policing. To avoid over-generalization, and to facilitate comparison, women's specific experiences of men's violence and police responses are explored in four countries that share certain basic features; in particular they are Western formal democratic governments with industrialized capitalist economic structures built out of a history of colonialism. Currently these countries are characterized by cultures that are neocolonial and patriarchal; that is, the interests of men take precedence over those of women and men are organized hierarchially *vis-à-vis* each other. We regard these similarities as important, if only because policing strategies and understanding of problems and issues are shared between these countries in a variety of forms: ideological, political, organizational, and through direct collaboration in problem definition, research, and operational procedures.

Chapter 2 provides a specific historical context by exploring the demand for women police in England. While women had a limited presence and role in policing prior to World War I, it was during the general mobilization that the Women's Freedom League began recruiting women into an autonomous women's police organization. This move followed years of criticism of the failures of government, the judiciary, and the police to act against the violent abuse of women and children. It was a move that demanded a response from the state. Chapter 2 tells the story of contradiction and compromise that led to the ultimate acceptance of women police. The themes of policing for or policing of women split the feminist movements of the day and remain a major source of tension between women who demand an effective police response to male violence against women and our children, and women who believe that police intervention prior to major shifts in the power structures of class, race, and gender relations is inevitably oppressive and devisive.

Chapter 3 represents a move from a focus on women's campaigns for women police to focus on how contemporary policemen respond to violence against women. In shifting from policy to practice, the problem of policing men's violence is located in the everyday context of the organization of policing services. Many assume that to bring about a structural change in policing one must alter police policy. This approach ignores the entrenched and powerful occupational culture that exists among police. Its strength is well known, particularly at the ground level. To expect any attempt towards institutional change in policing men's violence, one must have a better grasp of this occupational culture, how it is steeped within a masculinist view of men's and women's social relations, and how resistance to imposed change is organized.

Chapter 4 examines police attitudes and practice in one

Australian state. The successes and failings of law and police reforms are examined. This chapter exposes the wide divergences between legal theory and the practices of those involved in its implementation. For example, the disparity between the beliefs of male police officers about violence against women in the home and women's reality leads to a fundamental questioning of the efficacy of state intervention in the control of male violence.

Chapter 5 begins with an overview of the rediscovery in Britain of violence against women by the contemporary women's liberation movement and describes how independent women's organizations are making demands for alterations in the policing of male violence. Police interviews in one English county, West Yorkshire, and the new organizational measures to meet women's criticisms are discussed. Here, the struggle is around the police role in defining what is a crime and preventing crime against women. This chapter suggests that hiring and promoting women is an important strategy in allieviating the problem of policing male violence.

Chapter 6 looks specifically at wife abuse, beginning with government policy and its impact on the organization and training of police in the Netherlands. Interviews with police officers and assaulted women from the fifth largest town in the Netherlands follow. The focus is on how police responses are perceived by the women concerned and how satisfied they are with current police practices.

Chapter 7 describes research into the policing of male violence in Arizona. It specifically explores the mandatory arrest policy adopted in Phoenix for its consistent application and finds not only disparities between the actions of differing officers but also inconsistencies in the actions of individual officers. In a town with a weak feminist presence, attempts to change policing practice arose solely from within the police organization itself. The significance of this for the implementation of policy is discussed.

Chapter 8 draws together the themes and issues raised in earlier chapters. A demand for police reforms, both in relation to the specific subject of violence against women and in the wider debates around policing, is a complicated strategy. It is a pragmatic response that arises from the needs of women rather than an analysis of the role of the police as defenders of existing relations between men and women in a society divided by class, race, and male domination. The contradiction is that the police are defenders of the existing order while men's violence plays a central role in upholding male supremacy within that order. There is no way the police or other agents of the state, the courts, or judiciary, can truly treat men's violence as a serious crime without undermining the social order it serves so well.

Tackling this contradiction is a complex task. Reforms that would guarantee the safety and autonomy of all women irrespective of race, class, and sexuality are unwinnable from a patriarchal state. To wait for the dawn of a non-patriarchal, anti-racist, and classless society would constitute a retreat into an idealism at the price of women's safety. Rather than try to find a path through it, feminists working around policing have engaged in research and monitoring projects. From this base informed and detailed critiques of policing practice are being produced. It may be that these continuing criticisms and critiques have played a part in spurring the police authorities into action, although other factors are undoubtedly involved in order to explain why suddenly in the 1980s the police in several countries made policy changes and introduced reforms into their policing of certain forms of men's violence against women.

However, the strategy of demanding reforms in the policing of men's violence is a contentious one for feminists. On the one hand, we are aware that men's violence against women is an extensive problem with extremely negative effects for women. Inadequate policing can aggravate the impact of the initial violence. Police failure to act positively on behalf of women can both deny women any legal redress or protection against subsequent attacks. On these grounds demands for reform can seem a reasonable strategy. On the other hand, the limits and divisive nature of reform are well known. Reform historically has been a classic method through which the powerful have dissipated protest and criticism without relinquishing control or threatening their power base in any way. Reforms may be tokenistic and divisive, but the debate is closed. In the context of demanding reforms from the police, it is essential to recognize that we are dealing with an institution known for its sexism, racism, and 'cult of masculinity' (Smith and Gray 1983).

To evaluate police-initiated 'reform' is to engage with policing both at the structural level and at the level of day-to-day policing. Some may argue that the site of the current struggle, the improvement of policing for women, is at the margins of the issues raised by the demand for changes in police practices, but it is at these very margins that the lives of women may be saved. Further, women constitute over 50 per cent of the population. Their perceptions, interests, and demands are vital ingredients in understanding today's policing issues.

This book marks a beginning in the process of opening up a field of study characterized largely by the invisibility of the needs and interests of women in relation to policing. In doing so it also identifies the relation of men to women as a problem for the police, thus contributing to the study of men and the social organization of policing that they control, as much as to the study of women. To problematize men in this way is to contribute to a developing theoretical area in gender studies as well as in criminology.

Chapter two

Women and Policing: Contradictions Old and New

Jill Radford

The history of women police in England is a subject that has been neglected by historians of all persuasions. The complex and contested origins of women police, their struggles for official recognition and their incorporation into the 'malestream' police force demonstrate that the acceptance of women as police officers was never an inevitable reform but an issue that has been struggled over for half a century, from before World War I until well after World War II. It was a struggle waged overwhelmingly by women against active resistance from Parliament, the Home Office, the male police force, and the general public.

In addition to introducing a previously unexplored area, this chapter considers a more specific concern, the policing of men's violence against women. This was of fundamental concern to feminists in the Women's Freedom League in the early years of this century and central both to their demands for women police and their attempt to establish a women's police organization. The contradictions they faced are of relevance to contemporary feminists working around the problem of men's violence and particularly to the demand made by women, from within and without feminism, for more women police to work in this area. A historical context provides a necessary backdrop to current concerns by exploring specific aspects of women's campaigns for major reforms in policing.

A Need For Women Police?

Women's concern to combat men's violence was central to an early call for women police. In the years immediately preceding World

13

War I, a group of militant suffragettes, involved in a campaign against men's violence, engaged in a political campaign for women police. Their demands had been rejected by the men at the Home Office on several occasions, but during the general mobilization following the outbreak of war the Women's Freedom League began recruiting women into an autonomous women's police organization. Although there was no simple evolutionary road from this to offical acceptance of women police, the origins of women police can be traced to the activities of the Women's Freedom League. It is this story, a story of contradiction and compromise, that is explored here. While there are problems in looking to history for solutions to contemporary problems, at the same time it is important that our current work be informed by our history.

Pre-history 1: Were the Police an All-Male Institution?

While researching the history of women police, I began to recognize a prior question: Were the police historically the exclusive all-male concern that standard police histories record? This question was informed by Enloe's (1983) discussion of the military. Her argument is that historically the military has depended on women as gendered subjects. Women, she argues, have been used as 'the military's prostitutes, rape victims, wives, widows, social workers, nurses, soldiers, defence workers and mothers' (Enloe 1983: 212). If the military, an archetypal male institution, has relied for its survival on women, it is reasonable to look to the history of the police and explore the nature of any role played by women.

As has been mentioned, any role played by women has been 'hidden' (Rowbotham 1975) or 'deliberately obscured' (Spender 1982) in most histories of the early police (Radzinowicz 1968; Critchley 1978). However, a search of less conventional and less accessible sources, from sensationalist accounts of Victorian murder trials to histories of local police forces, reveals sufficient evidence to suggest that, like the military, the police have depended on the services of women as gendered subjects to perform traditional domestic services and tasks propriety, at the time, deemed inappropriate or impossible for men to perform.

Malcolmson (1977), in a discussion of infanticide in the eighteenth century, describes the role played by midwives in the interrogation and prosecution of women suspected of this crime.

Taylor (1979), in his account of the infamous Road House Murder of 1860, provides an example of the use of a police wife as a female searcher, interrogator, and almost a pathologist. He describes how the wife of the local sergeant was required to search the servants and their clothing for evidence that might reveal who was responsible for the murder of the son of the family. Not only was the task of intimate searching of female servants considered an inappropriate task for policemen; further, in the days before forensic science, the ability to distinguish between menstrual blood stains and those of a murder victim was beyond the power of men. Women, by virtue of their sex, were considered able to perform such a task. As the investigation proceeded, the sergeant's wife was called on again when the child's nurse, at one point a prime suspect, was remanded by the court into her custody. The brief for the sergeant's wife involved both guarding and informally interrogating the nurse while the court proceedings were adjourned for a week.

Steedman (1984), researching policing in the nineteenth century, also names police wives as 'auxiliary policemen':

> In the late 1870s the experience of the young unmarried
> recruit in the northern counties was still that of the barracks.
> . . . This pattern of living made police wives auxiliary
> policemen. Prison bedding was frequently sent out for
> washing to police wives. In Cambridge, Mrs Turrell, wife of
> the head constable, earned £10 a year as 'female searcher' and
> in Radnorshire village . . . Mrs Lewis, wife of the village
> constable . . . was able to do what her husband was not; for
> example examine a little girl for evidence of her father's ill
> treatment of her. (Steedman 1984: 118)

More systematic evidence of the support services women provided for the police comes from the work of Florence Balgarnie (undated, but probably 1894) of the British Women's Temperence Association (BWTA). Disturbed by what she identified as 'scandalous proceedings in our metropolitan police department', referring to the holding of women under arrest in custody in police stations under the supervision of male police officers, she launched a campaign for the employment of women police matrons, women to guard female prisoners in police stations. As a part of this campaign, she undertook a comparative study of the availability of police matrons in London, the provinces, Scotland, and the United States. One of the difficulties she encountered was being misled by senior police officers, who confused police matrons with women searchers and housekeepers:

> At the outset, I was for a considerable time put off my guard by the replies given to me at New Scotland Yard and several police stations to the effect that police matrons had already been appointed. But on prosecuting enquiries I found the so-called police matron is nothing more than the woman searcher who generally lives away from the premises and who even if a resident sergeant's wife has in fact no standing of any kind. (Balgarnie 1894?: 12)

Similarly, in relation to the city of London, she found 'so-called matrons are employed at each of the six stations in the City; but what can the system be worth when we find their duties are those merely of housekeepers and occasional searchers?' (Balgarnie 1894?: 13). Her research in the provinces produced similar results:

> According to the information given . . . it would seem in the towns of Manchester, Liverpool, Newcastle on Tyne, Bradford, Leeds, Sheffield, Blackpool, Clitheroe, Wolverhampton. . . . matrons are in attendance, but the explanation given shows that these are so-called matrons and have no more definite position than that of woman searcher — that is although they may be resident on the spot as wives of station sergeants, they are no more actually present than if they were living off the premises. . . . At Leeds alone have I found the police matron system enforced in any practical degree and at Liverpool under very imperfect conditions. (Balgarnie 1894?: 18)

Although Balgarnie was clearly unimpressed by her findings, they do indicate the types of support services women provided as gendered subjects, and as such support the contention that 'women's skills' were essential to early policing, in both the routine maintenance of police officers and tasks like investigating infanticide, sexual abuse of children, and searching women suspects and prisoners.

Balgarnie's concern was not for the appointment of women police officers, but for women to be appointed in the more limited role of 'police matrons'. This campaign was supported by the BWTA and several MPs who raised questions in the House of Commons. Although giving support in principle, the Home Secretary argued against the immediate appointment of police matrons on the grounds of cost and the non-availability of suitable accommodation for female matrons. Towards the end of the nineteenth century more matrons were appointed, but it was not until the years preceding World War I that demands like those of the Women's Freedom League for women police officers were made.

Prehistory 2: The Police Response to Sexual Violence

The problem of men's sexual violence was identified in the discussion above as one area where women were called upon to assist in police enquiries. It was also a central, if rarely explicitly stated, motive behind Balgarnie's demand for police matrons. In discussion of conditions in Plymouth she wrote, 'I came to the conclusion that here as elsewhere, the appointment of matrons is an urgent and imperative necessity, if for nothing more than to guard the reputation of the police against, we will hope, baseless charges' (Balgarnie 1894?: 23).

However, even in the nineteenth century concern with men's violence was being voiced and demands for (male) police protection were made. Clarke, in a historical study of men's violence, noted a shift in ideology as the threat of men's violence in public was being explicitly used to underwrite a wider change in women's role in society in the early years of industrialism: 'By the 1820s the notion that sexual violence made the streets unsafe for respectable women was rarely questioned, it reinforced the burgeoning ideology of separate spheres which defined public space as male and the domestic sphere as female' (Clarke 1987: 116–17).

Clarke further identifies links between this ideology and the agitation for a 'New Police': 'Advocates of New Police accused old style constables of refusing to help women assaulted on the streets, but also of being involved with prostitution themselves, that they exacerbated the danger of the streets' (Clarke 1987: 121).

She goes on to show how those looking to the new police were disappointed: 'The police not only limited the freedom of all women to freely walk the streets; they like the non-uniformed young men found amusement in indecent assault and molested women themselves' (Clarke 1987: 122).

Clarke's account shows some of the problems of the belief, which is still dominant, that simple reforms in policing can address the problem of men's public violence against women. Further, she demonstrates that although 1829 saw a massive restructuring of policing in the formation of the New Police in London, it did absolutely nothing to afford protection to women against men's violence. Rather, the reverse was the case. The other side of protection is control. Clarke further noted that the New Police attempted to limit women's freedom by regarding women who were out at night as 'streetwalkers'. For example she notes: 'The efforts of constables to forbid women to walk the streets in a peacable manner added to the *Weekly Dispatch*'s campaign against the new police' (Clarke 1987: 122).

Although at this historical juncture the New Police were used to control women without affording any protection, the twin themes of protection and control were central to the struggle for women police.

Prehistory 3: Introducing the Women's Freedom League

It was from a concern to combat men's violence that the first feminist call for women police officers was made. In order to understand their position, some background to the Women's Freedom League is needed.

The Women's Freedom League is another part of women's history that has been overlooked. Even in their own day, many of their actions were attributed to the better known Women's Social and Political Union, the Pankhurst-led WSPU.

The Women's Freedom League was formed in October 1907 by a group of women led by Mrs Despard in a breakaway from the WSPU. The reasons for 'the split' were to do with disagreements over the internal organization of the movement. However, both organizations remained true to their original aims and objectives as militant suffrage organizations with styles of campaigning that involved marches, demonstrations, damage to property, and harassment of male politicians. These tactics inevitably meant confrontations with the police. The WFL's magazine *The Vote*, details their many actions and their experiences of police brutality, arrest, and imprisonment.

Like other suffrage groups, the WFL did not pursue the struggle for the vote as a single-issue campaign. Their analysis was that if women had the vote then politicians would not only be accountable to women, but women as politicians would have a direct voice in lawmaking. This was necessary for combating oppression and discrimination in all areas of women's lives. Their concerns included prison reform, the 'sex bias' in the laws of prostitution, conditions and pay for working women generally, and a concern with the status of women around the world, including what today would be called the third world. Their work, however, did reflect some of the racism and classism of their period, and unlike the contemporary women's movement their organization was hierarchically structured and headed by leaders who asserted considerable influence. The leaders of the WFL included Nina Boyle and Edith Watson, as well as Charlotte Despard.

Prehistory 4: The Women's Freedom League Campaign Against Male Violence

The Vote documented the WFL campaign. It carried regular accounts of men's violence against women and children and was critical of the failure of the government and judiciary to act effectively against it. In 1912 they attempted to be more systematic in this work:

How Men Protect Women

At Godalming, recently, our readers have been told how a man received a sentence of four months imprisonment — two months less than Miss Davidson received for attempting to burn letters — for repeated criminal assaults on a little girl of seven and half. 'Abominable and attrocious crime' was the language used by the magistrate. Some weeks ago 'fierce denounciation' by another presiding official was accompanied by a sentence of 3 months on a ruffian who took a semi-paralysed child of five from her mother's door to a field hard by and criminally assaulted her. The charge was so worded by the police that it only implied a lesser offence. . . .

When will magistrates learn that they must make the punishment fit 'abominable and attrocious crime'? Few people realise how many little girls are subject to these assaults. A member of our League who on a recent occasion had to wait two or three days about a court of 'justice' heard a large number of cases tried, of which nearly a third were criminal or indecent assaults on children. The cross-examining counsel in their efforts to shake the evidence of these forlorn victims of male bestiality, frequently ask questions of brutal indecency; and details are extracted and commented on that one shrinks from contemplating. It is from such scenes as these that women are excluded; one hopes, in shame that they should know the extent of the danger with which they are threatened. Common sense and humanity should exclude men.

Each branch of the WFL is earnestly invited to find members who have some knowledge of legal procedure, and who will undertake to watch the police and other courts two or three days a week. The number of cases of assault (of all kinds) by men on women and children; the nature of such cases and the sentences inflicted, would be a most valuable contribution for Branches to make to Headquarters information. Every week lists of such cases will be published in *The Vote* without comment save for the purposes of comparison with heavy sentences inflicted for lesser crimes by women and lighter for all crimes by men. (*The Vote*, 10 February 1912, p. 185; emphasis as in original)

The problems in the police and judicial response to male violence identified by the WFL in many ways parallel those identified by feminists working around violence against women in the 1970s and 1980s. These include: anger about men's violence directed against women and children; the failure of the police and legal system and concern to treat it either with the seriousness it deserved or even with the same seriousness as property crime; the humiliating inter-rogations of women and childen practised by both the police and council for the defence; and the use of these forms of questioning to discredit the woman/child abused.

Additionally the WFL had to contend with other factors, and the victories they secured in relation to some of these have withstood the passage of time. One was the male monopoly of judicial office.

Magistrates, judges, and police in this period were all male. This was aggravated by the practice of excluding women from a court when a case of rape or other sexual assault was being heard. So the abused woman or child was alone in an all-male courtroom when giving evidence. The WFL were successful in having this practice declared unlawful, but not without militant protest. In *The Vote* (24 July 1914) Nina Boyle documented how five women, who later appeared in court under the names Smith and Smythe, occupied Marylebone Court by chaining themselves to the door in an 'obstruction protest'.

The WFL also began a court-monitoring project and invited their members to monitor the treatment of men's violence. This may be the first exercise of its kind and is one often adopted by feminist campaigners and researchers today. Edith Watson edited a regular column in *The Vote* with the ironic title, 'How Men Protect Women', in which their findings were reported. The quotation below is one illustration that shows further areas of their concern:

How Men Protect Women

Suffragist and Hooligan

In the Glasgow police court, Mrs Greig of the WSPU was charged with breaking a the window of a motor car in which she believed Mr Churchill to be driving. Sentence: seven days imprisonment without the option of a fine, and seven days more in default of entering into security to be of good behaviour for six months.

At the same court, on the same day, a man convicted of persistently molesting women and girls in the street was 'admonished' and discharged. His 'excuse' was drunkenness.

The Cry of Little Children: Where Women Vote

In the Isle of Man, where women vote, a recent case of criminal assault on a little girl was punished by a sentence of seven years.

Where Women do not Vote

An old man convicted of decoying a little girl of six in the street and taking her to a common lodging house, where he made her call him 'grandfather' and repeatedly indecently

21

assaulted her. Sentence 3 months. (*The Vote*, 3 March 1912, p. 237; the article continued by citing four similar cases.)

This passage from *The Vote* again emphasises the WFL's concern with the trivialization of men's violence expressed through light sentences. Edith Watson identified a link between women's political power and the judicial treatment of male violence in suggesting that where women are enfranchised, male violence is taken more seriously. This has not been substantiated by contemporary experience, but her argument illustrates that the WFL's campaign for the vote and political power is central to their wider struggles against women's oppression rather than being just a single-issue campaign.

The next extract serves to reemphasise their concern with documenting the extent and nature of men's sexual violence:

How Men Protect Women

Since the middle of 1911 the following murders of women by men and murderous assaults on women by men have occurred:

Stewardess murdered on the high sea by man.

Mrs Hill murdered by her husband.

Mrs Eckard murdered by paramour.

Joyce Pender murdered, man acquitted on appeal.

Miss Vaughan and child blown up by man who placed lighted fuse under her bed and left the house.

Ethel Griffiths murdered in wood by her lover.

Mrs Limpus and child murdered by husband.

Mrs Philpots murdered by husband.

Mrs Norris and lodger murdered by jealous husband.

Mrs West murdered by husband.

Emmeline Churchman murdered, man confessed.

Mrs Feruson burned to death, drunken husband threw lighted lamp.

Woman murdered with her servant and little daughter, man arrested.

Woman and her two step-daughters murdered, second husband charged.

Lydia murdered by jealous lover.

Mrs Friese murdered by husband.

Annie Jennings murdered.

Dorothy Harricot Stevens brutally killed by Conrad Selby; verdict manslaughter.

Mrs Leicester murdously assaulted by husband who committed suicide.

Mrs Lawrence shot at by husband.

Mrs Owens attacked in shop by strange man.

Mrs Tennessy, disgracefully assaulted by seven soldiers at Tidworth.

Margaret Powell dangerously hurt jumping out of window to escape assault by intruder.

Mrs Scott and daughter, unconscious and bleeding, injured by Mr Scott who committed suicide.

Catherine Paterson, burnt, stripped and left for dead by paramour.

Other cases have occurred. The percentage of crimes of violence committed by men on women would appear to be far in excess of crimes committed by men on men, women on men, and women on women all put together. (*The Vote*, 16 March 1912, p. 246)

This 'in memoria' was published as an attempt to chronicle the nature and extent of male violence against women. As well as pointing to the extent of the problem, it shows that in 1912 feminists were as aware as we are today that the greatest danger to women comes from the men we are closest to, those we are taught to look to for protection from other men's violence.

The fact that the work of the WFL would not stand up to rigorous statistical or methodological examination by a modern criminologist or sociologist is not really the point. More pertinent is that the WFL identified the problem of men's violence to women as a major danger to women. Through their work in the courts, they attempted to document the problem, its nature and extent; to record and to understand the failure of the court and the judicial system to take it seriously; and to do so in an analysis that turns on the question of women's lack of political power.

Their strategy was to challenge partiarchal structures at all levels, to fight for the vote, and to fight for specific reforms. This is demonstrated in the following editorial:

Our Point of View

Man made Laws

We continue to receive from all parts of the country expressions of gratitude that every week the inequality of justice metered out to women and men under man made British law finds record in *The Vote*. Grievious and terrible as are the cases, that of Daisy Williams, sentenced a few days ago by Mr Justice Lush to eighteen months imprisonment, while the vile creature who was the cause of all the troubles goes scot-free is heart rending. Little wonder that women are driven to desperate deeds to win the right of making their voices heard in legislation when such unequal justice can exist. It is the old story: the girl compelled to fight for her existence at fourteen, trapped by a man earning £2.10s a week; she resists but is overcome by his promise of fidelity; he thrusts her down to a life of prostitution, taunts her with being there, drives her mad by associating with another woman. Then comes her revenge. She kills her rival. At seventeen, she is a murderess and Mr Justice Lush, harranging her, considers a sentence of eighteen months leniant! The majesty of law truely! The poor little victim of wretched conditions and man made law suffers in prison; the villian is scot-free to continue unhampered his deadly work of distruction. Thus is a woman's life valued. The womanhood of this nation must rise against this inequality. . . .

The Woman's March

We commend the woman's march from London to Edinburgh to our readers. . . . (*The Vote*, 21 September 1912, p. 346)

The WFL campaign against male violence continued, and in July 1913 Edith Watson became their court correspondent, providing 'first hand reports of the "justice" dispenced to men and women respectively' (*The Vote* 25 July 1913). Her reports were headed, 'The Protected Sex' and ran alongside the 'How Men Protect Women' column. Watson explained that she emphasised the word 'protected' in these titles because the notion that men protect women was central to the arguments of the anti-suffrage lobby.

The WFL's Call for Women Police

Another development in campaigning strategy occurred in June 1914 when Mrs Nott-Bower argued for the appointment of women police. It is significant that this call for women police was made by a militant feminist organization whose members had experienced the rough face of policing themselves as well as witnessing the court's treatment of women targeted for sexual violence. In view of this contradictory relationship and the contradictions currently facing feminists in relation to policing it is important to examine this argument carefully.

Nott-Bower's starting point was a recognition of the need for women to be involved in all stages of the criminal justice system — as solicitors, barristers, magistrates, judges, and jurors. She then focused specifically on the 'urgent reasons' for demanding women police. These included:

1. The need for women to take statements from women and girls reporting rape and sexual assault.

> Few members of the ordinary public realise what the present conditions are in such cases. Supposing the case be one of incest, rape or criminal assault upon a little girl, the whole story has to be taken down from the lips of the little girl by two male officers. Often she is quite alone in their company. . . .
>
> We ought to realise that in cases of incest or criminal assault upon a child we are dealing with quite innocent victims of most cruel wrong, and therefore it is doubly incumbent on the community to do nothing to add to their suffering, and above all, nothing that may further add to the original outrage by deepening its impression on a young mind . . . or further degrading them in the presence of men. (Nott-Bower, *The Vote*, 19 June, p. 136)

She elaborated on this, pointing out that having to report to male officers often deterred women from reporting sexual assault, and that this was used by abusers to their advantage:

> This unwillingness to complain is traded upon by those degenerates who amuse themselves by soliciting and annoying women, and there is evidence that often they deliberately add

some loathsome indecency to the original offence, so as to make sure that no complaint will be made to the police. (Nott-Bower, *The Vote*, 19 June 1914, pp. 136–7)

2. The need to investigate cases of abortion, concealment of birth, and other cases involving 'intimate personal investigation'.

3. The need to supervise women prisoners in police cells at night:

Clearly the possibility of supervision or inspection of prisoners at any moment must exist, but it is contrary to decency that such a power should be in the hands and at the discretion only of young men, where women and girls are concerned. (Nott-Bower, *The Vote*, 19 June 1914, p. 137)

4. The need to remove the possibility of abuse of women by policemen:

This brings us to a point concerning the appointment of women police which needs to be approached with the utmost caution, but which cannot be overlooked . . . the possibility of the abuse of their powers by individual policemen where women are concerned. . . . Very few will be ready to take the word of an abandoned woman against that of a respectable constable; but it is in that very position that the grave danger lies. The man is well aware that no one will believe a word the woman says, and if he is unscrupulous he must know that he can take horrible advantage of this immunity. (Nott-Bower, *The Vote*, 19 June 1914, p. 137)

This argument demonstrated that the aim of the WFL, in calling for women police, was to protect the interests of women, when using the law to report attacks of male violence and when charged with offences. It was in no way part of an attempt to control the behaviour of women. This differentiates the WFL's campaign from others launched by philanthropic groups at this time. Bland (1985) has argued that campaigns aimed at protecting women, not women's rights or interests, were oppressive, as protection merged into control and further constrained women's behaviour. This difference in perspective was to become highly significant in the following years.

The next month, at the outbreak of World War I, the WFL

accepted a truce with the Home Secretary. In exchange for the release of suffrage prisoners, they agreed to abandon their campaign of militancy. This did not mean that all their activities came to an end, or that WFL gave unconditional support to the war, as is shown in this extract:

The Male Peril

To women, man has always posed as protector *plus* owner. He has ignored the obvious fact that his own existence constitutes her chief need for protection. Whether he be the potential soldier who with the cry 'Woman's place is in the home' on his lips, yet claims the right if his warfare demands it, to destroy that home; or whether he be the unknown element every woman is afraid to meet in a lonely lane or in the dark; man is the prevailing danger. . . .

Greatest of all dangers to women is the unbridled passion of men. . . . Yet even now, in war time, in our own land, from our own men, the danger stalks undiminished and unchecked, always enhanced by the dislike of male judges to deal with it drastically or of other men to deal with it at all. . . . And in view of this special danger, which comes only from one sex and only affects the other, how can men be so ungenerous as to deny women the vote, and with the vote, the means of adequately protecting ourselves and punishing the guilty, in regard to these crimes. (C. Nina Boyle, *The Vote*, 27 August 1915, p. 727)

This quotation is not in the imperialist/patriotic spirit attributed to the leadership of the WSPU and by implication to other militant suffrage groups. The WFL may have suspended militant actions for the duration but did not abandon their campaign against men's violence.

This concern informed Nina Boyle's response to the Home Secretary's wartime call for special constables (*The Vote*, August 1914). Simultaneously, she wrote to the Home Secretary asking if women could become Specials and put out a call for women to enrol. Two women were actually recruited in Kent before the Home Secretary announced his refusal.

An Autonomous Women's Police Force

Not deterred, Nina Boyle with Edith Watson, her friend and colleague from the WFL, continued recruiting women into an autonomous organization, the Women Police Volunteers (WPV). Boyle explained this move:

Women Police Volunteers

It was felt by the founders of the movement that, necessary as we consider it at all times to have women police, it was far more necessary than ever at a time . . . when a large portion of the policing of the country was being made over into amateur and inexperienced hands. Without doing injustice to the bulk of these amateur special constables, it was felt also among them were most certainly to be found a number of the men from whom women and girls are at all times in danger and for whose presence the streets would be none the safer. (*The Vote*, 9 April 1915, p. 566)

The Amalgamation of a Feminist and Non-Feminist Organization

The WFL, however, was not alone. In September 1914 Margaret Damer Dawson began recruiting for an independent women's police organization. She had been a member of the Criminal Law Amendment Committee and active in the National Vigilence Association, groups which for several years had also been advocating women police. Their aims were more mixed. Dawson saw policing as an essential public service which as a matter of principle should involve women. The National Vigilence Association was primarily concerned with the control of prostitution and the 'rescue' of 'fallen' women.

This echoes a theme popular in the nineteenth century, that women prostitutes were responsible for a range of problems. The 1860s Contagious Diseases Acts were an expression of this in assuming women prostitutes alone were responsible for the spread of venereal disease. As Clarke (1987) also noted, women prostitutes were also held responsible, not only for the violence they experienced themselves, but for a presumed rise in sexual violence which, it was held, made the streets unsafe for 'decent women'. At this point in her life, Dawson accepted this view.

At the outbreak of war she joined the Chelsea Association and worked with refugees. It was her experience of losing refugee women, which she explained with reference to organized prostitution, that triggered her decision to form a women's police organization.

Dawson had never been involved in the suffrage struggles. Her interests as listed by Joan Lock included mountaineering, motoring, riding, and animal welfare. Lock describes Margaret Damer Dawson:

> Her character seems to have been an amalgam of upper class silliness and tactlessness, shyness and gentleness, high intelligence and toughness, over-confidence and utter determination. Her friends called her 'Fighting Dawson'. She had some humour and cannot have been without charm considering the vast amounts of money she managed to spirit out of wealthy friends to support her aims. Women appear to have liked her better than men, probably since she seemed unable to play up to the latter. (Lock 1979: 20)

The two women discovered each other's plans and amalgamated. Margaret Damer Dawson became the chief of the WPV and Nina Boyle her deputy. This ordering was explained with reference to Dawson's better 'connections', her lack of a criminal record, and Boyle's continuing involvement with WFL.

All those who have written histories of the WPV, namely Mary Allen (1925), an early recruit and ultimately Dawson's deputy and successor as chief, Nina Boyle (*The Vote*, 27 August 1915) and Edith Watson (quoted in Lock 1979) of the WFL, and later Joan Lock (1979), a former police officer in the metropolitan police, state the women who enrolled into the WPV were from all social classes, including women formerly in domestic service and shop workers as well as middle-class women. They were further proud of the fact that many like Nina Boyle, Edith Watson, and Mary Allen had been militant suffragettes and had experienced arrest and imprisonment as a result of their actions. They explained that after the excitement of the suffrage struggle, conventional war work seemed boring, while the WPV seemed to afford women a chance to continue to work.

The first months following the setting up of the WPV were spent in organizing, fund raising, training, designing uniforms, and awarding ranks. Boyle spent her time touring the country, publicizing the initiative, and winning recruits. Dawson was involved in organizing and training the recruits and in determining a relationship between the WPV, the government, the official police force, and military authorities. She won permission from the Home Secretary for the WPV to train and patrol in London, on a voluntary basis. Only a month before, the Home Secretary had been hostile to the idea of women police, but on this occasion accepted the WPV but voiced an aversion to Nina Boyle as an 'intransigeante and in opposition to constituted authority' (quoted from an unsigned, undated document PRO MEPO2, in Lock, 1979: 20). But reminded of the suffrage truce he gave his consent and the WPV settled down to training and to face the hostility of the press, the public, and the male police force (see Allen 1925: 21–3; Lock 1978: 42–3).

A Rival Organization

In October 1914 another organization was launched by an assortment of organizations headed by the National Union of Women Workers (later to become the National Council of Women). The aims of the Voluntary Women Patrols were unambiguous: 'to influence and if need be, restrain the behaviour of men and women who congregated in the neighbourhood of camps and to "safeguard our girls from the results of natural excitement produced by the abnormal conditions now prevailing" ' (Letter to the *Times* 13 October 1914, signed by representatives of the Mothers' Union, the Church Army, the Girl's Friendly Society, the YWCA, the National Union of Suffrage Societies, and the National Union of Women Workers).

This organization, supported by the Bishop of London, reflected growing middle-class outcry over prostitution around the army camps, a concern that rapidly grew into a panic with calls for the reintroduction of the Contagious Diseases Acts. The Voluntary Women Patrols were different in organization from Women's Volunteer Police, since the former were staffed by part-time, non-uniformed, unpaid, and initially untrained volunteer women. The fact that they were unpaid determined to a large extent the class background of volunteers: '[their] leadership was largely upper and middle class and membership mostly professional' (Lock 1978: 46). This organization was also given approval by the police authorities and in July 1916 the commissioner of the metropolitan police employed VWP in the Royal Parks to check 'unseemly conduct'. Lock explained their status: 'The women were given neither power nor uniform, but were allowed a male constable to escort each pair of special patrols' (Lock 1978: 46).

Compromise and Contradiction in the Women Police Volunteers

Feminist organizations like the WFL and the WSPU also reacted to the moral panic over prostitution and the threat to reintroduce the Contagious Diseases Acts. They campaigned immediately and effectively against reintroduction, winning a written assurance from the Prime Minister. While the VWP began patrolling London parks, the WVP were invited to send two of their members to Grantham to work with the civil and the military authorities.

Mary Allen, one of the women assigned to this work, clearly understood the nature of their expected duties: 'At Grantham it was suspected that our duties obliged us to keep watch chiefly on disorderly women' (Allen 1925: 34–5).

While Allen's writing reveals a certain pride in this work, Nina Boyle was still worried by the growing 'anti-woman' propaganda around the question of prostitution. Specifically she was aware of the danger of the WPV, established, at least as far as the WFL was concerned, to protect the rights of women, being used by the military and civil authorities to constrain and control women. These worries were realized with the introduction of the DORA (the Defence of the Realm Act), which gave extraordinary powers to the military and civilian police. Within the WPV there were divergent views about DORA. Boyle voiced her anger at these measures, which in certain towns resulted in a curfew being placed on women:

> The officer commanding at Cardiff has on the strength of the powers vested in him by the Defence of the Realm Act, issued an order that women 'of a certain class' should not be allowed out between the hours of 7pm and 8am.
>
> Those entrusted with the Defence of the Realm have put the power confided in them to the basest possible use, and are

making use of this sorrowful emergency, which has brought
so much wholesale grief and misery into the lives of women,
to strike at the dignity of the more helpless sex and to place
them in a jeopardy which will compare not unfavourably with
some of the dreaded German 'atrocities'.

The CD acts are practically reimposed. . . . Mr Asquith's
signed and pledged word has once more proved to be
valueless. (Boyle, *The Vote*, 7 December 1914, p. 409)

It was the introduction of similar powers in Grantham and
Dawson's decision that the WPV women in Grantham should
cooperate in their implementation that caused a crisis in the WPV.

Dawson described her understanding of these measures and
justified her decision in evidence to the Home Office inquiry,
chaired by Sir John Baird (1920: para. 908):

the General had issued an unhappy order . . . by which
women in certain districts were to be kept in their houses
from eight o'clock in the evening until seven o'clock the next
morning. This caused a great deal of feeling amongst women's
organizations, and we were very much criticised because we
allowed our policewomen to go to work in a town where there
was this restriction against women. My answer was that if we
found the restriction a mistake, we could easily point it out to
the authorities. . . . The General gave us an order which
granted us 'the right of access to any land or building within a
six mile radius of the Post Office. . . . This regulation gave us
the power to go into the women's houses to see the girls were
in bed, and to see who was in the houses.

In describing the order as 'unhappy' Dawson did show some
unease. She claimed that it was her report of the difficulties
occasioned by the order that led to its being rescinded (a claim
contested by feminists, who saw it as a result of their campaigning;
see *The Vote* 1, 8, and 15 January 1915).

We found that the women were getting large quantities of
drink into the houses instead of being out on the streets, and
this was doing far more harm than if women had actually
been in public houses or on the streets where people could see
them. We turned out hundreds of soldiers and girls, and
reported it to the military authority and the Chief Constable,

with the result that the order restricting women was taken off. (Dawson, evidence to the Baird inquiry, 1920, para. 908)

As her account shows, her objections were to do with the efficiency and effectiveness of the order, rather than its principle.

Mary Allen also overlooked this principle. She was more concerned with the standing of the WPV in the eyes of the authorities, and considered their involvement in implementing the order 'the first mark of confidence'. She claimed with pride: 'No order, however distasteful, could be shirked. With no sign of our inward trepidation, for the first time in history, policewomen accompanied the military on raids' (Allen 1925: 34).

Dawson's stance is perhaps not surprising, given both her philanthropic and class-based politics and her commitment to the National Vigilence Association and 'preventive work'. What is perhaps surprising, as Bland (1985) noted, is that she should have the support of women like Mary Allen, who came to the WPV from a background in suffrage politics.

In contrast Nina Boyle, upholding the feminism of the WFL, expressed outrage at the collusion of WPV with the military in implementing orders that constrained women. This anger is reflected in her account of the events:

> Grantham was one of the towns in which the illegal order as to women. . . . was copied; and the terrorism (for it was no less) instituted by this order greatly detracted from the experiment, just as conniving at or submitting to, improper police measures and methods damaged the position from the suffrage point of view. Those responsible for the carrying out of this experiment felt the value of securing this new vantage ground for women fully justified the holding a candle to certain forms of official iniquity. The founders of this Corps, however, thought differently, and felt it was impossible to be associated with any work, no matter how useful, which meant the coercion of women and girls and depriving them of their liberty, to make things easier for commanding officers, constables and recruits. (Boyle, *The Vote*, 9 April 1915, p. 567)

There was only one solution to this conflict of principle within the WPV. Boyle called for the resignation of Dawson and the organization split. It is interesting to note that both factions claimed victory at this point, a claim that is relevant to the still disputed question of the origins of policewomen in England and Wales.

Allen has presented her view of the split, which she shared with Dawson. Although in the following account she noted some of the principles involved, she attached little significance to them.

> During the first months every effort was made to co-ordinate the various activities of all those enrolled in the Women's Police Volunteer Organisation. . . . but ultimately it was decided that the views expressed were too divergent ever to make unanamity of control a working proposition.
>
> Miss Damer Dawson represented the point of view that women must, *of necessity*, work in closest co-operation with, and in staunchest loyalty to, their male colleagues; that public service is one and indivisible, that it demands the united efforts of both men and women, and that these efforts should dovetail but never conflict. The difficulty of finding common ground for any compromise brought about an inevitable crisis. . . . all members of the Women Police Volunteers were therefore requested to vote. . . . and it is an illuminating fact that, with two exceptions, the whole body of women plumped solidly for co-operation with men. . . . the word 'volunteer' was substituted. The letter S took place of the V on their badges. (Allen 1925: 17)

The points of principle noticed by Mary Allen are as fundamental to today's concerns as they were in 1915, touching on the question of separatism, the right of women to organize autonomously, as well as the question of cooperating in the control of women. Following Dawson's lead, she and the 46 out of 48 members of the WPV who voted with them accepted the view that effective organization requires working with men, even when, as was the issue here, male interests were served by restricting women's rights. In endorsing Dawson's view that 'public service' can contain no conflict between men's and women's interests, they were presuming that women's interests must be subordinated to those of men, particularly when male approval is sought. The question of official recognition was central to the aims of Dawson and Allen.

Nina Boyle, in her discussion of the split and the future of the WPV (now organized by the WFL), identified these points:

> Miss M. D. Dawson, who until recently was chief of the Woman Police Volunteers, has severed her connection with that Corps. . . . The Corps will continue its work on the lines originally laid down, i.e., for the service of women and not to assist the present authorities in carrying out laws and regulations known to be unjust and improper.
>
> The experience gained in the work so far carried out plainly points to the fact that it is impossible under present conditions to work with or under the civil or military police and use their system without in some measure assisting improperly to coerce women for the benefit of men. (*The Vote*, 19 February 1915)

Post-History 1: The Women's Police Volunteers

Although they bravely claimed to have ousted Dawson from the WPV, in effect Boyle and Watson were isolated by the outcome of the vote regarding the future of the organization. There are few further references to the WPV in *The Vote*. It appears that with the exception of a couple of groups in the provinces, this organization folded. However, it is suggested here that their stance was highly significant in political terms. It indicated their recognition that autonomy was the only strategy that did not compromise women's interests, and that if this was unobtainable withdrawal was the only political stance open to them.

Post-History 2: The Women's Police Service

Under its revised name, the Women's Police Service continued to work in Grantham, London, and other cities. They continued to train women police and in many towns worked with the police and the military, patrolling army camps and munitions factories. However, at the end of the war they were still facing the difficult question of prostitution, but by this time their position had changed. Lock suggests this was a consequence of the radicalizing impact of their work. This shift in position is illustrated in the following press statement made by Dawson: 'It's all so one-sided, so unjust to women. They talk as if men were innocent angels helpless in the hands of wicked women' (Lock 1979: 90).

Compared with earlier statements of the WFL, for example, this one could hardly be seen as extreme, but it did mark a move away from their earlier stance. What made it particularly significant was its timing. It was made at a sensitive moment for the WPS. In November 1918 the Metropolitan Police (London) announced that they would accept women as police officers, but postponed for one month decisions regarding who would be recruited. It was at this time that Dawson made the statement. Lock argued that it probably cost the WPS the recognition it had been seeking: 'It is doubly ironic to think that Damer Dawson lost this particular battle for the very same reason as Nina Boyle lost hers, the determined defence of her sex and especially, prostitutes' (Lock 1979: 91).

The leaders of the WPS were angered by the Met's decision to recruit from the VWP rather than the WPS. They had always contrasted what they saw as the amateurism of the VWP with their own disciplined professionalism.

> Amazing and inexplicable as it may appear to an unprejudiced mind, the experienced policewomen who had served their country so faithfully and efficiently, were thus completely ignored when the police force of the Metropolitan area was put on a peace footing. There were at this time in England well over one thousand trained policewomen, in or out of uniform, who had served a long and trying novitiate, having gained their experience in the hardest school. . . . It would have seemed reasonable, a matter of course, to have made use of policewomen already trained, who had won high praise for their work, rather than to face the trouble and expense of training a set of novices who would perforce have to go through a period when their contributions to the efficiency of the police force would be negligible. (Allen 1925: 128–9)

Despite their huge disappointment Allen was able to claim a degree of success: 'But though appearances seemed to militate against the Women Police Service, we had unquestionably won the battle, not for ourselvs, in the case of London, but for all policewomen in Great Britain' (Allen 1925: 133).

Privately, Allen and her companion, Miss Tagart, a sub-inspector in the WPS, had another explanation for why the WPS had been overlooked by the Met. They shared this with Margaret Radclyffe Hall and Una Troubridge, to whom they had been introduced by Miss Goldingham, a mutual friend and early recruit to the WPS who became a superintendant:

> John and Una sympathized agreeing that the authorites were against her because she was an invert (all they wanted, Una declared contemptuously were, 'fluffy policewomen'). The two couples were heartened to find they shared common beliefs on the subject of homosexuality. (Baker 1985: 267)

Anti-lesbianism may provide an explanation of why the WPS was overlooked by the Metropolitan Police and why its leadership came in for such personalized criticism. The hostility they faced seems to be something more than a simple expression of prejudice against women police. The war years 1914–1918 were ones in which women entered a whole range of occupations that formerly had been the exclusive preserve of men, and while without doubt this gave rise to all manner of male chauvinist sentiments, the specific nature of the hostility faced by the WPV/WPS is easier to understand if it is read as anti-lesbianism as well as misogyny. Criticisms of the WPV/WPS, for example, focused specifically on the personalities of its leaders, their style of dressing, and suggestions that they were other than 'normal' women. For example Ashley Brown, in a preface to an undated pamphlet written by a Captain Henderson-Livesley for the 'League of Womanhood', stated: 'the Police woman, to be efficient, must possess qualities which the normal woman of healthy mentality does not possess (Henderson-Livesley, undated: 3).

In the same spirit, Henderson-Livesley argued:

> The discussion of a lady's garments, in public at any rate, would not in the ordinary course of events strike me as being a useful proceeding, but in the present case there is justification in that the lady (Mary Allen) started the discussion herself, and moreover the matter has certain psychological implications which had a very direct bearing on the question under review. The lady in question recently visited America, and was reported, on both sides of the Atlantic, as having said that she had not worn a skirt for six years. There are some people who accept eccentricity of this

sort as being representative of the 'modern woman but it is a libel on her to do so. (Henderson-Livesley, undated: 7)

Sir Nevil Macready resorted to gossip in his attack on the leadership of the WPS:

> Another more militant organisation had also grown up during the war, adopting the title of 'Women Police', and dressing in a uniform of rather a masculine type. I was told one of them was seen wearing a sword on one occasion, but to that I cannot vouch. (Macready 1924: 399)

Mary Allen reports that when the war ended, some WPS members returned to ordinary tasks and employment, but many remained active in the WPS, working in provincial police forces and with the Royal Irish Constabulary in Ireland. Despite the rumours about their 'extremism', 'feminism', and 'eccentricities' they were hardly a radical organization, at least in the modern sense of the word. Their activities remained oriented towards prevention and rescue work, and their autonomy was a result of rejection by the Home Office, rather than a political choice.

In 1920 their senior officers were prosecuted for masquerading as police officers and as a result their name and uniform were changed again. Allen made several statements to the effect that the members of the renamed Women's Auxiliary Service were not discouraged by this change of status and second refusal by the state to allow them status as 'police' women (Allen 1925). But she also spoke of this period as 'the dark hour when even the right to wear uniform, or to use the name which they had borne with such conspicuous gallantry during the war had . . . been contested' (Allen 1925: 264).

It is this rather despairing attitude that Baker picks on in cruel satire in describing the subsequent years of this organization:

> After the war, however, despite her protestations, the Home Office disbanded the organization and it had since existed in an unofficial capacity only, kept alive largely by the efforts of Miss Allen who was never happier than wearing her uniform and highly polished boots. It seemed unlikely that the force would ever be resurrected and the dejected Commandant was reduced to hoping that coal or transport strikes might lead to call upon her services. (Baker 1985: 267)

Post-History 3: The Voluntary Women's Patrols

It should not be surprising that it was from the largely upper/ middle-class Voluntary Women's Patrols that the Metropolitan Police recruited both for leaders and members, when it finally accepted a need for women police in 1918. This organization had kept a much lower profile, content to operate within male definitions of the problem of prostitution and serve under male authority. They had the continued support of the National Council of Women (NCW) and politically remained located firmly within the ideology of protection and control, that is an ideology which held that women needed protecting from prostitution by the police. In practice this protection became surveillance and control of women by women, ultimately in the interests of men, ostensibly by protecting them from venereal diseases, which, it seemed to have been believed, were spread by women. The Voluntary Women's Patrols were implicated in this practice, in much the same way as Dawson and the Women's Police Service had been in cooperating with the military authorities in implementing the DORA regulations. The Voluntary Women's Police Patrols believed that women were better qualified than men for this moral welfare work with women and children. This definition of a traditionally gendered role for women police was ultimately acceptable to male police authorities, but not without struggle.

The leaders of the women's patrols claimed their war work had demonstrated the value of women police and led to their incorporation into the official police service.

The 5,000 voluntary patrols working in different parts of Great Britain proved the need of uniformed women to do continuous work as part of the police service, subject to its responsibilities and upheld by its privileges and authorities. In the metropolis the work done by the voluntary patrols convinced the Commissioner of Police that women should form part of the police service under police supervision and control. In 1918, Sir Nevil Macready created the Metropolitan Women Police Patrol Division, and members of the voluntary body with Mrs Stanley, their leader, appointed as Superintendent, became officially appointed members of this division. The division consisted of 100 constables, 10 sergeants, an assistant superintendent and a superintendent.

The women were very carefully selected and trained. They were not attested or eligible for pensions. (Cowlin 1937; pages not numbered)

Although the Police Act of 1919, together with the Sex Disqualification (Removal) Act of the same year, permitted the appointment of women police, their future remained insecure. In the following twenty years three committees of enquiry (the Baird Committee, 1920; the Bridgeman Committee, 1924; and the Royal Committee on Police Powers and Procedure, 1929) reviewed the appointment of women police and with different degrees of enthusiasm found in their favour. But as Critchley (1978: 215) noted: 'Few chief constables saw much value in policewomen, some suspected them of feminism, the Police Federations was openly hostile towards them and the Home Office abstained from encouraging their appointment, in spite of constant pressure from women's organisations.'

The Baird Committee (1920), for example found that there was 'urgent need' for the employment of policewomen in all large cities. It recommended that the conditions of service and status of policewomen should be standardized across the country. However, these recommendations became guidelines only and local authorities retained descretion both in regard to the appointment of women police and in terms of their status, that is whether they should be attested as full constables with powers of arrest, and in terms of their pay and conditions of service.

Two years later the struggle for policewomen was resumed in London when in 1922 the Geddes Committee on Economy recommended the disbanding of the Metropolitan Police Women. This was opposed by a coalition of supporters of women police. Allen joined leaders of the Metropolitan Women Police Patrols and the NCW, who petitioned the Home Secretary. MP Lady Astor led a debate in the House of Commons, defending the work of women police. As a result of these efforts compromise was reached and a nucleus of twenty policewomen was retained, from which the force could be reconstructed when the economy improved (Allen 1925: 178–80; Lock 1979: 135–46). These measures also had an impact on provincial police forces. In some areas further recruitment was discouraged, in others the number of policewomen were cut, and in fifteen towns women police were disbanded.

The NCW and supporters of women police continued to campaign through the 1920s. In 1929 they gave evidence to the Royal Commission on Police Powers and petitioned the new Labour government. They won a partial victory in 1931, when statutory regulations for policewomen were issued by the Home Office. Cowlin recorded that although these did much to standardise the work of policewomen, they were inadequate:

> The weakness of the position of women police lies in the fact
> that the Statutory Regulations still leave it to the discretion of
> local authorities, not only to appoint women police, but also
> to attest them. This discretion is inadequate. . . . We shall not
> be satisfied until the provinces have the advantages now
> secured for women police in the metropolis. Here women are
> chosen with the greatest care and are given a systematic
> training, as far as possible with men recruits, under the
> direction of their Women Superintendent, who now represents
> their interests on the Police Council. They conform to the
> Statutory Regulations and are assured regular pay and
> pensions. (Cowlin 1937; pages not numbered)

In 1934 the NCW and Women's Institutes, 'supported by all the principal women's organisations in the United Kingdom', organized a national petition to demonstrate the existence of a national demand for policewomen. The petition was couched in cautious language and drew heavily on the rhetoric of 'protection' consistant with the politics of the NCW (Tancred 1951: 18). The petition demanded: '(1) That certain protective and detective duties in connection with women and children be made compulsory for policewomen; (2) That a woman Inspector of Constabulary be appointed at the Home Office' (Tancred 1951: 18).

In January 1935 both demands were refused in a Home Office circular that gave unqualified support for local discretion regarding the appointment of women police officers. Edith Tancred noted that this refusal further strengthened the opposition to policewomen.

With the outbreak of war in 1939 women were appointed as Special Constables, but not before representation by the NCW. The NCW also kept up its campaign for the compulsory appointment of regular policewomen. Lady Astor again raised the issue in Parliament in 1943, pointing out that only 43 of the 158 police forces in England and Wales were employing regular policewomen, which proved the need for legislation. Once more the government reaffirmed its commitment to 'local discretion', as Tancred reported:

> The tiresome slogan of 'Local Discretion' was raised once more by the Home Secretary in replies to Lady Astor asking for compulsory appointment, and to Mr Godfrey Nicholson to whom the Home Secretary said: 'I do not think it right to interfere with the discretion of the police authorities' and at the great mass meeting for women in the Albert Hall 'local discretion' was declared to be the policy of the Government. (Tancred 1951: 27)

Campaigners for women police continued to pressure the government, calling a 'great mass meeting for women' in March 1944. This was reported in the *Police Chronicle* (25 March 1944):

> 500 women representing seventy organisations met in London on 10th March to demand the employment of more women police. There was a unanimous response to the motion.
> That the Home Secretary be asked to take immediate action to ensure that an adequate number of women police are appointed to undertake appropriate duties, and that a Woman Inspector of Constabulary be appointed to advise chief constables on selection and training.

This conference, supported by the Archbishop of Canterbury, resulted in the issuing by the Home Office of what Tancred described as a 'really strong circular' to police authorities asking chief police officers to consider the employment of more policewomen as 'a matter of urgency' (Home Office Circular of 30 March 1944: 96–194). This time a majority of provincial police authorities accepted the principle of women police. Later the same year the Home Secretary announced he would be appointing a Woman Staff Officer at Scotland Yard. These successes marked the end of the campaign for policewomen.

> A new era for the police forces — men and women alike — is opening up and the NCW are proud to think that their years of steady work have led through the findings of the Post War Reorganisation Committee to the Home Secretary's important

announcement to the NCW Conference in Hastings, 14th October 1948: 'The Law does not know policemen and policewomen but only police officers'. (Tancred 1951: 33)

So ended the struggle for the establishment of women police.

While the law may not have recognized policemen and women in the years following 1948, their roles in the police remained strictly gendered until the 1975 Sex Discrimination Act. The consequences of this Act in relation to the policing of sexual violence in Britain represents an additional contradiction for contemporary feminists. This is demonstrated both in criticisms of the responses of police-men to women reporting incidents of male violence and in mixed feminist reactions to recent police initiatives like the establishment of all women police units to investigate rape complaints. These initiatives were introduced following years of criticisms of police response to raped women by another generation of feminists campaigning against male violence. It represented a return of women as visibly gendered police officers in contradiction to the spirit of the Sex Discrimination Act.

Conclusion

Documenting government and police resistance to women police demonstrates how threatening the idea that women with authority was to the dominant class of men. Looking more closely, it is possible to see the terms on which women were eventually accorded a reluctant acceptance by the male-dominated state institutions of the Parliament, Home Office, Metropolitan and Provincial Police Chiefs, and the Police Federation, representing serving police officers. The earliest struggle within the autonomous women's police organization, the Women's Police Volunteers, in 1914, demonstrates that the idea of a feminist-inspired police organiza-tion committed to combating men's violence and the defence of women's interests was lost first. This struggle was fought out between women, the feminists and non-feminists, who had initially worked together on a single-issue campaign. Significantly though, it was fought over gender politics. On one side were Nina Boyle and Edith Watson, of the WFL, committed to campaigning for women's rights, the right of women to be treated with sensitivity when reporting male violence, and the right of all women to be free of men's control. On the other side were women, led by Margaret Damer Dawson and Mary Allen, committed primarily to the principle that women have an equal place alongside men in public service. It was the argument of this second group that won the day in 1914, on the grounds that recognition for women's work took precedence, even at the price of compromising or subordinating women's interests. In exploring the history of the Women's Police Volunteers (and after the split, of the Women's Police Service) we see how after an initial refusal to recognize an autonomous women's police organization, the male state was happy to use it in furthering its interests. Using a carrot of the official seal of approval, the state was able to usurp the commitment and energies of women in the control of other women, in an attempt to contain the problem of prostitution. Thus an organization established by women to protect women's interests was subverted by the state to control the behaviour of women in ways that would have been unacceptable for male police officers to undertake force. Feminists involved refused to cooperate in the oppression of women, recognizing that it was impossible to work with male authorities on terms that did not compromise women's interests. This conflict of principle brought to an abrupt end the first and only attempt to form a feminist police organization in Britain.

A similar recognition was imposed on the Women's Police Service at the end of World War I, when the Home Office and police authorities refused to accept into the official police, women who were not one hundred per cent behind men in their sexual politics. A women's organization that offered even a moderate defence of prostitute women and included former suffragettes and lesbians could not be acceptable to the state, despite the WVP's stated commitment to working with men on terms defined by men and their pride in their collusion in the oppression of other women.

Even the most moderate, most middle-class organization of the three, the VWP, faced a long and hard struggle for official approval. It took them more than forty years to fully convince the authorities of the efficacy of policewomen in the efficient control of women and children. This was despite the fact that they had worked consistently within the traditionally gendered roles as defined by their class and culture; that is they had never spoken out in defence of women's rights and had been very cautious in expressing their concern in relation to the problem of men's violence.

With this history behind us, I feel it is essential for contemporary feminists to be highly cautious of reforms won from a patriarchal state in relation to the policing of men's sexual violence. The history shows, I suggest, that straightforward reforms that will benefit all women are not to be and cannot be won from a patriarchal state or implemented by a male-controlled police force. Some 'reforms' may be won, after hard struggles, when arguments in their favour can no longer be resisted politically without endangering the respectable faces of 'democratic' patriarchy. Such 'reforms' need to be examined carefully, to establish whether they will indeed benefit all women, that is women of all classes, races, and cultures and irrespective of women's relationship to hetero-sexuality. Reforms, which assist men in cleaning up the face of hetero-patriarchy by making it easier for white, middle-class, 'virtuous', heterosexual women to complain of only the most obvious and excessive forms of men's violence, are not simply divisive, but by upholding the white patriarchal status quo cannot ultimately be in the interests of any women. Feminists must, I suggest, take care to avoid welcoming or cooperating in superficial or tokenistic reforms aimed at further securing hetero-patriarchy.

Chapter three

Missing the Mark? Policing Battering

Elizabeth A. Stanko

Despite the fact that women are now acceptable in the police forces in Britain, the United States and elsewhere, their numbers have remained small. Police forces remain male-dominated institutions. The policing of men's violence against women, as a consequence, remains largely in the hands of men, something which in the 1980s has given rise to feminist criticism as much as in the early years of this century.

The focus of this chapter is on the policing of one form of male violence against women in the home — battering. Under pressure from feminists in many communities, police have engaged in discussions with researchers, shelter and refuge workers, and interested community members to attempt to change their policing policy and practice towards men's violence to women. These discussions often take place outside, and unrecognized within, debates about how police can be accountable to the divergent community. To some extent over the past fifteen years, we have witnessed some changes in policing strategies towards men's violence. The reexamination of police handling of sexual assault cases is one example. Yet even these changes in police procedure have not permeated all levels of policing, nor have they succeeded in eliminating abuse of women in the police complaint process. Indeed, many women still hesitate to call police after a sexual assault.

Today, the role of policing men's violence in the home is a subject of great debate. The use of arrest has emerged from this debate as a preferred response of policymakers, police chiefs, and feminists. Many people, however, fail to fully appreciate the police as a complex institution with many divisions, staffed with officers with different responsibilities and levels of discretion. As a result of this, there are many mediating forces between decisions at policy-making levels and the implementation of these policies at the street policing level. Nor do many fully comprehend that in practice it is often the rank-and-file officer who is the one to decide which policy applies to the reality she/he faces. In terms of everyday policing, it is the street-level officer who is the major dynamic decision maker, making his/her decisions in the context of an elaborate hierarchical structure that can reward or punish its members. Far more complex than is recognized by current discussion about police response, rank-and-file police have a relationship to arrest that is not so easily resolved through organizationally imposed policy. The rank and file are themselves resistent and less responsive to change, particularly that introduced by the hierarchy within the police organization. The nature of this resistance will be explored as one significant 'problem' of policing male violence.

This chapter addresses the problem of policing men's violence against women through an exploration of the internal organization of police work and the particular response to women battering. Relying on research that examines the everyday realities and competence of rank-and-file police officers (Fielding 1984; Manning 1978; Punch 1979; Van Maanen 1978; Sacks 1972; Bittner 1967), I locate the problem of policing male violence within the occupational and organizational routine operations of police work, work which, in addition, must be viewed as a masculine, gendered activity. I focus on how police are assessed and rewarded within the organization and within their own ranks, and how, despite the call for more stringent law enforcement, the present organizational context of policing continues to be antithetical to the needs of many battered women.

Framing the Problem

Police decision making in battering situations came to the forefront of government concern in the 1980s.[1] Amid a fanfare of publicity, the findings of the so-called Minneapolis experiment heralded a breakthrough for directing police response to battering. Two U.S. researchers, Sherman and Berk (1984a), examined the effects of three policing strategies in response to misdemeanor 'simple' battering situations. The three strategies are (1) arrest, (2) some form of advice and, occasionally, mediation, and (3) separation. Results of the experiment point to arrest as the best police strategy to protect women or to halt male violence in situations of 'simple' assault between intimates or former intimates. The findings of the Minneapolis experiment were put into effect by many major U.S. police departments in the form of policies which, as the best strategy to police situations of domestic violence, encouraged, and in some instances actually directed officers to take the assailant into custody through arrest (see Ferraro, Chapter 7, this volume).

In Canada, the directive issued by the Attorney General of Manitoba in February 1983 also targeted police decision making in battering situations. This directive specified that police charge assailants in cases where there was reasonable and probable grounds that an assault had taken place. Canadian concern about policing recognized that police did not arrest assailants despite injury to the woman. This new directive required that police decisions now be based solely in evidentiary (police-controlled) rather than police-directed matters, whereby the police suggest that the woman herself charge the assailant (Ursel and Farough 1985).

Burris and Jaffe (1983), in their study of London, Ontario, police, illustrate the situation prior to changes in policy. They found that police charge assailants with assault in only 3 per cent of all family violence cases, despite the fact that they advised one in five injured parties to seek medical attention. They conclude that minimal police intervention, the standard police response in Canada as well as other countries, leads to serious and far-reaching consequences. They cite the following possible ways a minimum police response can serve to aggravate already potentially lethal situations:

1. Women become disillusioned by police response and may believe there are few options for protection.
2. The folklore about police response is widespread enough to deter women from seeking police assistance.
3. Police officers themselves become frustrated by 'domestics' and categorize them as hopeless calls.
4. Because assault rests in common law, police suggestions to a woman to bring her own charges seldom result in the filing of complaints (Jaffe and Burris (1981) found only 17 per cent of

'family violence' calls end up in family or criminal court).

5. By not arresting the male, police tacitly give to the batterer a message that it is okay to batter (the deterrence argument of Sherman and Berk addresses this point).

6. The criminal justice system is predisposed against private actions, as opposed to actions brought by the police, and therefore may take less seriously actions brought by women.

7. Women who choose to file charges must immediately become 'experts' in the maze of the criminal justice system.

8. Women who choose to file charges must be able to withstand threats or coercion on the part of their batterer in order to continue prosecution.

9. Without immediate response to a battering, the best time to inform a man of his unacceptable behaviour is lost.

The reexamination by Jaffe et al. (1986) of the London, Ontario, police department found that the introduction of policy directing police to lay criminal charges against a spouse when there is reasonable and probable grounds that an assault occurred led to a 2500 per cent increase in police use of assault charges in the handling of domestic violence calls. Ursel and Farough's (1985) report of police charging in Winnipeg, Manitoba, notes that police charging under the new directive resulted in 'a greater number' of wife abuse cases coming before the courts than in the past. This greater number, however, represents 9 per cent of the total calls labeled 'domestic'. While arrests may be increasing as argued, the decision to arrest may still comprise a small proportion of cases to which police respond (Shapland and Hobbs 1987).

Whatever they may be, police actions at the scene of a battering, according to the expectations of policymakers, police officials, feminists, and the public, are expected to somehow deter instances of future violence, stop the present violence, and reassure the woman that she did in fact experience criminal violence. Studies in other countries such as England (Edwards 1986a, 1986b), Australia (Hatty and Sutton 1986a, 1986b), and Ireland (Casey 1987) all have criticised police response to battering and have called for police to cease their benign stance towards battering. Citing the results of the U.S. and Canadian experiments, these researchers urge practitioners in their home countries to seriously consider altering their practice and lean toward a pro-arrest policy rather than one which, as each research study shows, is one of arrest-avoidance. Police practice, the researchers advocate, should treat violence among intimates as a criminal offense.

Together feminists and researchers in various countries are calling on police to adopt a tougher 'crime-oriented' approach to battering. It is difficult, however, for someone unfamiliar with the everyday task of policing to understand what a tougher stance towards battering really means for police and for police behaviour. Generally, police summoned to a 'domestic' (the police term for battering) by a threatened woman, a bystander, or neighbours, find one of a wide range of situations before them. Loud noise; threatened violence; violations of separation, divorce, or orders of protection; property damage; frightened children; or actual physical and sexual injury are but a few of the encounters lumped together as 'family quarrels'. Although each of the above situations may form a woman's particular experience within a battering relationship, to the police each call is a discrete task for the responding officer that requires some solution. Quieting the noise, 'calming' down the potentially violent individual, suggesting legal remedies to sort out court-imposed orders, or offering transportation for medical assistance to the injured woman might be, to a police officer, adequate solutions to a particular problem. This kind of problem solving is itself often difficult to do.

In an unusual coalescence of research findings, feminist pressure, and policing policy, a tougher stance is taken to mean 'arrest', and the effect of an arrest is to deter present and future violence between intimates.[2] This notion of deterrence is central to the studies of police behaviour before and after changing policy towards battering. The recommendations of studies and policy changes throughout many countries also rest on this premiss (Green 1986; Casey 1987; Edwards 1986a, 1986b; Hatty and Sutton 1986a, 1986b; Burris and Jaffe 1983; Sherman and Berk 1984; Berk and Newton 1985).

Through arrest, deterrence of the violent man is immediate. Because the violent man is removed from the situation of violence and held against his will, perhaps in some (too few) jurisdictions overnight (SANE 1987), the consensus opinion points to arrest as the best solution to 'simple' battering situations. (There is an assumption, interestingly enough, that arrest already occurs in 'serious' battering situations.) Sherman and Berk go so far as to conclude that arrest serves as an independent deterrent to future violence outside any additional effects of the court process (1984: 270).

Arrest has a variety of meanings to police. It is the assertion of a *legal* solution in the restoration of what is considered to be a violation of a private 'order'. Yet policing, as Reiner (1985) proposes, is at its very core concerned with *public* order maintenance. Arrest, one means of resolving a disruption, does fit neatly within the ideology of crime control and protection of the public. Among the police rank-and-file members, though, an arrest serves an additional function. It provides the officer with a tangible 'product' that bring status and prestige within the police organization. An arrest in a 'domestic' though is not afforded a great deal of prestige by most police officers' peers or their supervisors. It is to many police officers not 'real' crime. Additionally, as I have shown elsewhere (Stanko 1981), making an arrest may lead to police frustration with the court process. Prosecutors are still likely to decline prosecution in battering cases or reduce criminal charges to minor violations. Prosecutors' actions may in turn affect police decisions in the future simply because they know there will be little (and ineffective) court action if they arrest.

In order to examine police practice more closely, I will focus on occupational and organizational dilemmas and constraints in the routine police response to 'domestic disturbances', or as feminists refer to it, the battering of women in the home. It is best to imagine all these lower-level officers as male-oriented, with mainly male peers and male supervisors. The organizational dynamic essentially remains the same regardless of the gender of the responding officer. As Punch (1985) has suggested in his study of police deviance in Amsterdam, rank-and-file members of the police department, typically locked into organizational conflict with their bosses, have developed many ways to carry on their routine practice despite changes in legislation and policy. Rank-and-file officers can and do subvert organizational goals, constructing and reconstructing their daily realities, enforced and controlled by peer sanctions. It is to the occupational culture that I turn first.

Occupational Orientations of the Rank and File

In most requests for police assistance in battering, the officer of first response is the rank-and-file officer. Patrol work, the main-stay of the police force and the visual example of the availability of state protection, provides initial police presence. It is also the training ground for recruits into the police force. Under the wing of an older, presumably wiser veteran of the street, recruits or 'rookies' soon become inducted into the world of contemporary policing (Wambaugh 1970). Recruit training begins on patrol, where, as Van Maanen points out, recruits look forward to 'really' learning about police work, only a fraction of which they know is gained through their experiences at the academy or police training college (1978: 297). This world view treats the knowledge gained from the academy as but one — and a limited one at that — aspect necessary for survival on the street. Induction into 'real' policing introduces a rookie to a wide array of information about sex, violence, internal support, and suspicion of anyone who is not a rank-and-file police officer (Punch 1979, 1985; Hunt 1985; Skolnich 1975; Rubenstein 1973; Wambaugh 1970; Van Maanen 1978).

Rank-and-file occupational culture (Skolnick 1975) is steeped with images and expectations of a 'macho-style' masculinity (Hunt 1984; Smith and Gray 1983). Research indicates that police attitudes towards crimes such as rape, sexual assault, and battering include assumptions about male rights and female blame.[3] Police attitudes towards and about women, affected by the structural choices within the work environment, are likely to dissuade women from complaining about men's violence. And when women are attacked by boyfriends, husbands, ex-husbands, ex-lovers in their own homes, or by men known to them outside their homes, police often see the relationship or the marriage as a very important part of the violence (Black 1976). As a consequence, police scrutinise the woman's behaviour alongside that of her assailant, for both the man and the woman are each assumed to have contributed to the onset of violence.

The occupational culture of policing, particularly that of the rank and file, has been the subject of many a research project.[4] For the purpose of this discussion, I will focus on four elements of the rank and file's occupational orientation: the rank-and-file officers' definition and control over their work environment, the gate-keeping effect of police work, competence assessment by the rank and file of each other and its relationship to job satisfaction, and status and prestige and its relationship to job expectations of the rank and file. These elements of everyday police work will be explored for their possible contribution to the exclusion of violence against women from the ranks of what is considered to be 'real' crime.[5]

Defining and Controlling the Work Environment

Skolnick (1975) proposes the concept of 'working personality' to describe the effects of working environment on rank-and-file police. When the elements of danger and authority combine, he speculates, police become suspicious of many different kinds of people and categorize real police work as what they might describe as 'exciting' crime. Since their task is to solve whatever situation to which they respond, police have the power to assert a solution (Bittner 1967), particularly when they feel they or the public are in danger. One of the most interesting contradictions about policing battering is that police often complain of the danger of 'domestics'. Injury from intervention in a 'domestic' is considered by police to be pointless.

While policing does not ordinarily include confrontation with 'criminals', it does involve the mediation of conflict (Reiner 1985). In contrast to the underlying possibility of danger in police work, much of daily patrol work blends the service element of policing with the overriding goal of maintaining some form of order. Punch (1979) suggests that the police are really a 'secret social service'. Service functions are the least popular duties among the police, who, despite the mundane routine of their work, continue to focus their sights on the potential for action and excitement (Van Maanen 1978). Assignments such as caring for lost children, directing traffic after an accident, informing relatives of a death, taking complaints of unsolvable crimes (the routine burglary, car theft, or stolen wallet), and mediating a separation agreement between ex-marital partners are part of the chores of policing. These chores, however, are the bulk of police work (Shapland and Hobbs 1987).

The type and tenor of service chores, generated through citizen calls for assistance, are seldom under the control of the rank-and-file police. Despite the desire to generate their own, more exciting work, rank-and-file police — the majority of whom respond to instances of battering — may prefer to restore 'order' rather than to include as crime something they regard as a dispute between intimates (see for example Zoomer, Chapter 6, this volume). Maintaining order, as Reiner suggests, is the core mandate of policing (1985: 111–16). Conflict resolution, whether in the course of handling a dispute, a disorderly person on the street, or a battering, has the coercive power of arrest (Bittner 1967). As research on police response in battering situations indicates, even within jurisdictions that have instituted pro-arrest or presumptive arrest policies, a decision to arrest is still entirely discretionary. Attempts to remove any discretionary power from the rank-and-file officer lead to resistance. Police resistance to newly formed presumptive arrest policies could take many forms such as, for example, suspending judgement about fault when an officer is at the scene of a battering, as Ferraro illustrates in Chapter 7. She cites the example of a police officer arresting both the man and the woman. Later, down at the station house, the sergeant must make the decision about which party is at fault, thus displacing the burden of sorting who is at fault away from the patrol officer and onto the shoulders of management. Rank-and-file police, as specialists in resistance to outside intrusions (Punch 1985), cultivate resistance strategies precisely to increase their sense of control at the bottom of the hierarchy.

Resistance to department policy by rank-and-file police who resent the intrusion of policy into their discretionary yet autonomous decision making may take other forms. Rather than arrest in a battering situation, rank-and-file police may decide to rely on their age-old response: calm the man down, restore order (Parnas 1972). Sanders (1987) astutely recognizes the wider implications for this traditional stance of the rank and file. In his examination of police charging decisions for battering in the West Midlands, England, he suggests that there is an underlying structural and ideological strength to this stance. Rank-and-file police, in their capacity as upholders of public order, are merely reinforcing conventional legal requirements of law. He suggests that police are less likely to read private violence as public trouble (Myers and Hagan 1979), not because of vindictiveness toward women, blinkered awareness toward injury, or predispositions of male attitudes (although I believe many of these elements are present and do have an effect), but because of the *absence* of public disorder. Violations of public order are simply easier to prove legally than those of 'private' order.

Rank-and-file officers indeed incorporate structured, legal parameters into their commonsense, daily decision making. This decision making has a significant impact on the major task of the rank and file. As the gatekeepers of criminal matters, police select the type of crime that enters the criminal justice system.

Gatekeeping

Black's (1970) early study of three U.S. cities found that police are less likely to arrest for felony (serious) crime assailants who are family members and acquaintances of the victim. (This, however, is not true for misdemeanors.) In a more recent article, Black (1983) suggests that offences such as assault commonly involve 'ordinary' citizens who 'seemingly view their conduct as a perfectly legitimate exercise of social control'. Men's behaviour typically labelled by women as sexual and physical violations has to a large extent been considered 'normal' by ordinary citizens, the police, and the courts (Stanko 1985).

Dobash and Dobash (1979), in their examination of Scottish police, found a similar hesitancy about criminalizing violence of male intimates against female intimates. These findings are underscored by research conducted in Canada (Burris and Jaffe 1983), in Australia (Hatty and Sutton 1986a, 1986b), in the United States (Ferraro, Chapter 7, this volume), in England (Edwards 1986a, 1986b) and in the Republic of Ireland (Casey 1987).

When they are made, police decisions about including family members in the category of 'law breaker' are perfectly ordinary. As Berk and Loseke (1980–1) note, police decisions about arrest are found in their *interpretations* of particular battering situations, their prior experience, and the situation-specific rationales for decisions inherent in the policing enterprise. These rationales 'do not constitute an *abuse* of discretionary power,' they conclude, 'they are part of the *normal* exercise of duty' (p. 343, emphasis in original). In their examination of the police decision to arrest, they found police respond to such contingencies as the demeanor of the assailant toward the police, the injury of the woman, the presence of witnesses, and the willingness of the woman to sign a complaint. As Hanmer notes later, the presence of children also seems to have an effect on police officers' responses. These factors contribute to an assessment of whether an arrest is an appropriate response in a battering situation. The overall character of a domestic call, according to Berk and Loseke, affects an officer's decision to arrest.

Research by Worden and Pollitz (1984) replicates the Berk and Loseke study and extends its analysis. These researchers specify that officers differ in their orientation to the job, and these orientations in turn affect how officers read the circumstances of a battering. Battering, in many ways, resembles the kinds of work police encounter in other 'conflict management' situations. As Worden and Pollitz point out, demeanor of the assailant has significant effects on the arrest of the assailant (1984: 113). They also found that arrests were less likely for those married than those co-habitating but not married. Perhaps police perceive the actual fact of marriage as they would any 'orderly' arrangement, despite the presence of violence (see Hanmer, Chapter 5, this volume).

Gatekeeping indeed may be critically important in different stages of a battering. But even researchers cannot be assured what exactly are police responses in any stage of a battering. They must rely on police-generated information, which is, in effect, an *ex post facto* evaluation of how a police action came about. Berk and Loseke (1980–1), in their description of the methodological selection of their sample, eliminate 468 cases of the 730 total police reports sent to the family violence project. In all, 325 cases were eliminated for incomplete 'field' reports; 135 cases were excluded because they involved non-heterosexual/conjugal violence; and eight incidents were excluded where the female was classified as the sole offender in the case. While they competently address why these cases were not included in their analysis, they expose important gaps in our knowledge about what really is a 'domestic' and at what stage in a battering history do the police become involved. We just do not know what police involvement is with disputes that do not merit a police record of the event, nor do we have information that might compare police responses in situations outside the 'typical' heterosexual battering (man beating woman) with those of 'untypical' batterings.

Shapland and Hobbs (1987), in their study of policing in an English town, found that rank-and-file officers handle both 'domestic' and 'non-domestic' disturbances through arrest-avoidance. The recorded police action in most cases is 'advice given'. What kind of advice do police give to battered women?

Does it differ from the kind of advice given to individuals involved in a violent dispute between neighbours or acquaintances? The research on policing battering may reveal an interesting pattern of police handling of most fear-producing situations — ones that threaten or are occasions of violence. The police response is to 'settle' the 'disturbance'.

Research findings have also raised concern about the effect of police attitudes on the treatment of violence against women in the home, attitudes that may separate 'domestics' from other 'disputes'. Smith and Gray (1983), in their examination of the London metropolitan police, articulate a concern about the negative police attitudes towards women and the effect of these attitudes on their behaviour towards women. Similar concern is expressed by Hatty (Chapter 4, this volume) about policing in Australia; and a number of studies have illustrated the strength of this concern through examinations of police treatment of sexual assault.[6] There is some evidence, for example, that when women call the police, police are less likely to arrest (Worden and Pollitz 1984; Hanmer, Chapter 4, this volume). Berk and Loseke (1980–1) offer an explanation for this finding in their earlier work. They propose that when a woman calls the police the assault has not reached a serious level, that is, the woman is physically capable of calling. Worden and Pollitz, however, found that despite the reluctance to arrest, women are twice as likely to be injured if they are the ones calling the police. For whatever reasons, rank-and-file police do not consistently see injury within the home as evidence sufficiently serious to warrant arrest (Black 1983).

Worden and Pollitz, Berk and Loseke, along with Sherman and Berk and others tell us one crucial piece of information. The particular response of an officer is essentially *unpredictable* to the battered woman. In other words, the woman might already realize that the police response depends entirely on the particular skills and thinking of the officer who answers the call. Each situation varies, as does the weight given to crucial elements such as demeanor of assailant, injury, and so forth, but the outcome of the police intervention is unpredictable until it happens. As the research indicates, few cases that police term 'domestic' warrant serious reports. These supposedly not-so-serious situations must have some effect on the manner in which police define a 'true' domestic, one worthy of appropriate action (see Zoomer, Chapter 6, this volume). It also exemplifies the source of growing frustration for police. If the police respond to the bulk of battering that they feel is outside their jurisdiction, they may wonder what kind of battering situation the presumptive policy guidelines are supposed to address.

What kinds of cases (Emerson 1983) are 'real' battering? Decisions about 'real' battering are crucial in the gatekeeping functions of policing. Determinations about real battering reflect police competence to recognize a 'good' battering, at least one that warrants legal intervention. Frustration and anger may arise when their former categories of assessment are suddenly judged by their superiors — and prosecutors and judges as well — to be incompetent and inappropriate judgments.

Police Competence and Job Satisfaction

The competence of police to anticipate danger occurs in the context of knowing about appropriate public behaviour. Sacks (1972), in his discussion of police assessment of moral character, articulates the process whereby a rank-and-file officer learns to scour the public landscape for potential trouble. Suspiciousness of ordinary, routine scenes aids the officer in spotting danger. In viewing public space as if 'all is not what it appears to be', rank-and-file police develop a shared understanding for spotting danger. Competence, reinforced through these shared meanings of other rank-and-file officers, allows an officer to be assured that his/her assessment of public danger matches that of fellow officers.

Perhaps the more stringent assessment of competence is made by fellow rank-and-file members. Being one of the boys (and I do mean to emphasise the masculine group solidarity (Hunt 1984; Smith and Gray 1983)) requires that an officer protect his fellow officers, abide by the 'operational code' (Punch 1985) of silence, adopt similar views of serious crime, and admire the 'good' pinch of a fellow officer (Van Maanen 1978). As Radford emphasises in the previous chapter, acceptable policewomen adhere to those male definitions and points of view.

Traditionally, this competence has been confined to judgements about public space. Along with the changes towards a pro-arrest policy, at least in theory police are now expected to 'see' danger and lethal violence within the private setting as well. (Not all intimate violence occurs in private (Hanmer and Saunders 1984).)

But the guidelines are much less clear. The batterers vary by class, race, and ethnicity; their actual behaviour and deeds are seldom witnessed by the officer responding to the call. Together with the legal preference for public order violations, assessments of private order seep into new guidelines for police competence. They may be, in fact, contradictory notions of competence.

Understanding about public space, as many feminist theorists have noted, is intertwined with notions about masculinity and feminity, and the public/private spheres of each. Police officers, like 'ordinary' citizens, have notions about what battering means in the context of private, intimate relationships. Women's place in heterosexual couples, particularly legally sanctioned couples, is for the most part financially and socially dependent on men. Some officers express sympathy for this bind for women, and police resources for overcoming society's barriers for women are small. Some officers have their own personal experience with battering, whether it be in their own homes growing up or in their ongoing relationships. Some officers do beat their own wives and girlfriends (Green 1986). This personal experience also affects a police officer's own understanding of private violence, and what constitutes 'private' danger.[7]

Attempts to improve police competence to 'see' private danger come through training efforts. Now included in a limited way in the preparation of recruits, training focuses on police responses to battering. Training often consists of in-class discussions, and sometimes includes role playing and simulations of situations within which decisions about police practice take place. Resources for releasing officers to attend training may be limited, especially in times of public funding cuts and where public expenditure for law and order is likely to be spent on showpiece, technological advances such as new computers or radios. In one city in Massachusetts where training about battering is even mandated by legislation, one city responds to the problem of training in the following way. One officer will be sent to a training course and report back for a total of about ten minutes to his fellow officers. All the officers of that shift will then be considered 'trained' in the new approach to battering. When speaking about training programmes, it is essential to come to an understanding about what constitutes adequate training.

Designing training for the veteran rank-and-file officer who has been making decisions about the criminal nature of battering for years is much more difficult. One way of ensuring more successful training for veteran officers is to gear training to different styles of policing. Worden and Pollitz examine the effect of differential policing style and the response in battering situations. Using Muir's (1977) and Brown's (1981) studies, these researchers explore the potential differences among police officers who may stress varying conceptions of the proper police role (1984: 114). Those officers who adhere to a crime control model of policing may emphasise the law enforcement aspect in battering, while those who tend to see their job as assisting citizens and keeping the peace may lean toward conflict resolution apart from a legal solution. Interestingly, Worden and Pollitz find little support for differences between two types of officers ('crime fighters' and 'problem solvers') in terms of the number of arrests they make. When arrests are made, they suggest, 'the possibility that situational factors are evaluated differently by officers are reflected in patterns of arrest' (1984: 118). Each officer may be able to satisfy his or her internal assessment of competence by finding justifications for arrest that match their goals of policing.

How do the differing styles of rank-and-file police affect their general assessment of each other's competence? Do fellow officers of the same rank demand a change in each other's behaviour when responding to a battering situation, above and beyond the change demanded by management? How can we be sure that the responding officer is competent to decide the course of action in any particular situation? Officers respond to many and varied situations of battering: some are called at the onset of physical abuse, some see the resulting injuries and damage of a long-term situation, and others hear only the threats of physical abuse. Many different actions of the police are required, one of which may be to arrest. Competence is defined by the rank and file as well as for the rank and file. This lack of control by officers may lead to a lowering of job satisfaction.

Regardless of the style of policing adopted by a particular officer, his or her ability to competently attend a 'domestic' is also dependent on the information given by the dispatcher. Dispatch information about 'domestics' is often patchy and incomplete. Despite the ongoing nature of abuse in some households, there is often little or no knowledge passed on from officer to officer. In the case of the small town or rural police officer, addresses or surnames become 'known' and have an ongoing history. Officers who respond to situations of 'known' trouble have a sense of the ongoing history because these situations are part of the sharing of information in a localized setting. But in larger police departments, station house staff are often unable to locate injunction papers or to alert social workers to impending serious violence because each incident is not treated as serial violence, and therefore potentially more lethal than other situations. The accumulation of 'advice given' over months or years makes attending police officers appear incompetent because they have no idea what their colleagues did the last time they were there. Police station house file systems are notoriously inefficient; filed papers such as injunctions may fall into the wrong pile, onto the wrong desk, or under the wrong letter of the alphabet. If the competence of the police officer is to be judged by the competence of organization back at the station house, then the rank-and-file officer starts with a handicap.

But will successful resolution of a battering situation, both in terms of assessments of competence and personal satisfaction of a job well done, now place a rank-and-file officer in the precarious position of having to 'solve' a situation of battering? Even the best intentions of family members, friends, social workers, and feminist staff of services to battered women cannot solve a woman's own battering situation. Only women themselves can, with the aid of financial and emotional support and courage. Resolving an immediate crisis generally does not guarantee an escape from violence in a woman's relationship. Battering has its frustrations for the police as well as for shelter staff, social service workers, friends, and family. Experiences such as returning to the same address, witnessing a 'reconciliation' between the assailant and the woman, experiencing the court's trivial treatment of 'other cases like this', intervening in violence which is supported by the institutions of marriage or by the legalities of separation such as child access visits, as well as economic and emotional dependence, take their toll on the possibility for police to achieve job satisfaction from their work in battering situations.

Frustration, further deteriorating job satisfaction, is heightened by the rank and file's lack of control over the outcome of their work, dampening enthusiasm for any new policy. Police may be criticised for making arrests by prosecution staff, who, in the efforts to satisfy their own organizational demands of successful prosecution, typically exclude assaults between intimates and ex-intimates, as well as assaults between friends and neighbours. These kinds of cases, for prosecutors, do not fall into the categories of serious, unprovoked crime; they are perfectly ordinary events (Stanko 1977, 1981, 1982; Black 1983).

Status and Prestige: Expectations of the Rank and File

Together with competence, status and prestige are important elements within the internal culture of the rank and file. Images of the police and their work are very much a part of a shared assessment of a job well done and worth doing.

Manning (1978) suggests that prising the police away from the public and private image of the 'crime fighter' is extremely difficult. Despite the few 'good' pinches, police anticipate their possibility and work in hopes of encountering 'one' in their course of duty. Van Maanen (1978: 304) notes the importance of the 'good pinch':

> It is precisely the opportunity to exercise his perceived police role that gives meaning to the occupational identity of patrolmen. Operationally, this does not imply patrolmen are always alert and working hard to make the 'good' pinch. Rather, it simply suggests that the unexpected is one of the few aspects of the job that helps maintain the patrolman's self image of performing a worthwhile, exciting and dangerous task.

Rank-and-file officers derive a feeling of satisfaction, status, and prestige from their intervention into a special situation. That 'good' pinch, the saving of a life, or the endangering of oneself for the benefit of others brings praise from both fellow officers and the public. Routine tasks might turn into special events, but rarely. And those rare events are relished. Police share stories of exciting events, enjoying them time and time again, the description of the tension and resolution laced with a good dose of humour.

Images about 'family' fights are very strong among police. 'Come with me to a husband-wife fight,' stated one Massachusetts officer in 1987. 'You arrest the husband and suddenly she's in love again.' The scenario about battering is a set pattern. Woman gets beaten, calls police, decides she is really in love, defends the man in police presence, and reconciles after police leave. Hardly the type of call that presents any kudos, either organizationally or individually, to the responding officer. If, however, a man were holding a woman and child at gunpoint, it is likely that the excitement of intervening in a siege would overcome the tedium of intervening into the 'typical domestic'.

Despite the changes in many police departments, seldom would an officer derive organizational recognition for his/her handling of battering. Skill assessment and promotion from the police organization itself rarely recognize an officer's handling of battering. If anything, rank-and-file officers worry that these new regulations will result in more complaints filed by civilians unhappy with their handling of calls. 'If you really are doing your job,' stated a London officer in 1987, 'you'll just get more complaints.'

Rather than a source of reward, battering situations are a source of headaches and uncertainty for street-level police. The occupational culture of the rank and file indeed introduces contradictory expectations into the implementation of presumptive arrest policy initiatives. How are we to assess our expectations for social policy on battering now that it revolves around 'arrest' as a solution to battering?

Responsive Policing and Presumptive Arrest: Where Do Women Fit?

As an observer of rank-and-file police, I fear presumptive arrest policies — ideologically important in the feminists' struggle against male violence — will be undermined by the daily realities of street-level policing. Given these realities, is a presumptive arrest policy the best strategy for policing violence against women in the home? There are many complex and sometimes contradictory conclusions to be drawn from this chapter.

First, it is important to note that feminist criticism of policing practice has been heard. The accumulated effects of feminist lobbying on legislation, of legal suits charging abusive treatment (Gee 1983), of government commissions (Report of New South Wales 1985: Attorney General's Task Force 1984; Parliamentary Select Committee on Violence in the Family 1975; Report of the City of Ottawa Task Force on Wife Assault 1984), and of research (Casey 1987; Edwards 1986a, 1986b; Dobash and Dobash 1979;

Berk and Loseke 1980–1; Sherman and Berk 1984a, 1984b; Berk and Newton 1985; Burris and Jaffe 1983; and others) have pressured the police hierarchy and policymaking staff to rethink their public position on policing battering.

Second, there has been a shift in the rhetoric between police and feminists. While not every police department sees the need to change its practice or policy, departments, concerned about their image as unsympathetic to victims, have followed the suggestions of government studies. Indeed, police themselves at times sound grateful for the evidence providing grounds to initiate departmental change. Stated the community relations officer of Dublin:

> I finally came to the conclusion [after reading the recent report on wife beating in the Republic of Ireland (Casey 1987)] that this [conciliation] was not the way [to treat assailants]. The man who beats his wife deserves to go to jail, no matter what his background is. It may not be his fault, he is nonetheless guilty. That's what the criminal justice system is all about. It may be important to educate them, but in the meantime we have to stop them. (*Irish Times*, 6 October 1987)

But can we then conclude that police hierarchies have accepted feminist criticism and are setting a course to right their ways? Ellis (1987), in his analysis of U.S. and Canadian legislative and policy change towards battering, suggests that they are. He states:

> A private, interaction-gone-wrong, get-at-the-deeper-underlying-psychological-causes view of abusers and the abusive process, has been replaced by a view of wife abuse as criminal violence for which the assailant is responsible and that he should be treated the same way as any other person who commits a violent offense.

Ellis concludes that this shift of position came about because the state now sees women as an important constituency who can, through their support of police efforts, reaffirm the legitimacy of policing.

To police superiors, a presumptive arrest policy, ideologically, may be one way to satisfy feminist demands and at the same time secure the loyalty of the rank and file to the chain of command by providing them with more law enforcement options in policing battering. To what extent these policy changes penetrate the rank-

and-file understanding of battering and appropriate police action remains to be seen. The proof of any changes in policy ultimately rests with the actions of the street-level police, who are removed from the changing rhetoric of their superiors. So too presumptive arrest policies for 'domestics' may lead police to question the way they handle other disputes and disturbances. Shapland and Hobbs (1987) have observed that all types of disturbances are 'calmed down', be it a fight between a tenant and landlord, between neighbours, or between drunks in a pub. Only an attack on a police officer will provide the best guarantee of arrest. Will questions about policing battering spill over into the policing of 'disturbances' that involve violence or potential violence? How will street-level police view their policing functions if these events are suddenly re-evaluated? Will women's vulnerability to violent men be equated to other situations involving interpersonal violence, resulting in ignoring the context of gender inequality of which woman battering is part?

Do the current presumptive arrest policies therefore take woman battering more seriously than other 'disturbances' and extend police protection to women in times of acute crisis? As we will see in the next four chapters, the answer to this question is anything but definitive. It is important to note that the legal outcome of any arrest strategy rests squarely in the hands of the criminal justice system. Women may call police to get men to stop beating them, and may not be clear about what they ultimately want the police response to be. Some women, fearing retaliation, refuse to press charges against violent men because they wish to retain some control over the outcome of police intervention. Others may be quite determined about arrest as the best solution at the time. But if the criminal justice system takes total control of cases, and for example compels women to give evidence against men, as is the case in New South Wales and Britain, then women's ability to choose how police can assist them in acute crises is diminished. If we are to use policing in the process of resisting male dominance, we must insist that women's autonomy is maintained and supported.

Should we, as feminists, be endorsing, promoting, and agitating for such presumptive arrest policies? Ideologically, I think we should. But we must do so with a greater awareness of policing, its everyday tasks, and its wider function within Western societies. Calling for more policing as a pro-arrest policy does tacitly legitimize all form of policing. Fighting and preventing crime, and the strategies police use to do so, entail the use of tactics such as surveillance, which have been used differentially among segments of the population. Some theorists suggest for example that coercive police strategies such as unnecessary stop and search, used primarily in inner city areas, impede the formation of a trusting partnership between the police and the local community, including women (Kinsey, Lea, and Young 1986; Lea and Young 1984). Limiting the police use of repressive tactics, which weigh more heavily on low-income, minority citizens, will hopefully open communication and encourage the use of the police in situations of acute danger. How police conduct themselves in these tasks has far-reaching effects in the lives of citizens who may at one time or another need to turn to the police for assistance. Women's reluctance to request assistance from the police, feminists have argued, illustrates women's knowledge about the unreliability of that assistance. Women assume that police cannot or will not help them. Police now identify this reluctance as potentially damaging to their role as protectors in society (Hanmer and Stanko 1985).

Have presumptive arrest policies opened the way to promoting police accountability to divergent segments of the population, including women? Not yet, and feminists must ask questions about how all women relate to police and police protection. How could police be accountable to women experiencing battering? It depends, of course, on whether women's voices are considered the essential core of any debate about policing practice, and any efforts to monitor the practice of police, particularly at street level. To date, they have been minimally included in the political debates around policing. Few feminists in local communities have been given access to monitor street-level police practice of battering.[8]

But do all segments of the population have confidence that the police will respond in an egalitarian manner? Probably not. Public confidence in policing is likely to vary between racial, ethnic, and class groups (Smith and Gray 1983). Ultimately the effectiveness of any presumptive arrest policy rests with the rank and file as well as with the rank and file's relationship to a multi-racial, multi-ethnic, classed society. 'The pattern of discrimination [in a society] and the map of the population found in police culture,' states Reiner, 'are isomorphic. They are both interdependent and bound within the wider structure of racial and class disadvantage' (1985: 135).

Clearly, the concern about differential enforcement and policing strategies is a serious one, particularly when advocates of pre-sumptive arrest policies promise equal application of the law. Research alerts us to inequities in policing. Police have been shown to be less responsive to complaints of low-income, minority individuals (Black 1970, 1976; Hepburn 1978; Smith et al. 1984) and even less so to black women (Young 1986). There is, among some ethnic groups, suspicion of the police, and the effects of this suspicion limit their access to police intervention (Merry 1981). Certainly, in many cases police themselves have contributed to the suspicion, as in, for example, the policing of the 1984−5 miners strike in England and Wales, where the police ransacked whole villages (Scraton 1985). Police actions within low-income areas also give messages to local communities (Smith and Gray 1983), messages women hear. As one woman in London stated: 'That's what happens when we want the police to calm down, they send in the riot squad. . . . All we wanted was someone to calm him down. I know that it wouldn't have happened if we were white. We are all really angry about the police' (Radford 1984). A woman's hesitance to call the police may reflect her fear of the immigration service because of her ambiguous immigration status, or her wariness of the police because of her husband's, boyfriend's, or own, involve-ment with the law or that of her children. If police are concerned about making their services more accessible to women battered in the home, then they should also be examining what aspects of policing deter citizens from calling them in the first place.

Concluding Remarks

Police action cannot by itself stem the tide of violence against women. It can, however, stop perpetuating and reproducing it. To do so would require breaking its links with other aspects of social life that maintain and perpetuate women's subordination. Police protection within the context of male domination does not and cannot promise women autonomy. We know that the sweeping changes in legislation concerning rape and sexual assault, with for instance the law protecting women from cross-examination about their prior sexual histories, known as rape shield laws, have not revolutionized the legal stance towards women (Marsh, Geist, and Caplan 1982; Adler 1987; Stanko 1985; Estrich 1987). What feminists have observed is that too often, legal protection legitimizes the separation of women into two categories: those deserving and those undeserving of police protection. These categories, fuelled by social distinctions such as race, class, ethnicity, and age to name a few, are already intertwined within institutional decision making (Stanko 1981, 1982). More arrests of violent men — the only solution to battering available to the criminal justice system — will hopefully assist more women in acute danger.

Some women have, on their own initiative, sought out discussion with the police about their own practices and have participated in developing training programs for policing battering situations. While doing so, it is important that feminists are sensitive to police practice in multi-racial and multi-ethnic contexts and are actively confronting the use of militaristic tactics in policing. These practices may limit women's use of the police in times of crisis. But we are naïve to believe that changing police practice is just a problem of training. While 'training' is supposed to address and confront these entrenched images of women, the context of police practice — the internal organizational structure that provides the day-to-day rewards, assessments, and criticisms of police practice — remains essentially intact. So does its masculinist stance. Change within the internal structure of policing means actively confronting the stranglehold of the frustrations of rank-and-file police. It is not enough to promote legislative change, write and institute policy directing 'serious' treatment of battering, promote presumptive arrest policies, and 'train' police to be more attentive to crimes of sexual and physical assault of women. The police hierarchy must be sensitive to the concerns and the resistance of rank-and-file police. Until these supervisors find some way of incorporating their own past understanding of day-to-day policing into means of instituting practice, not much will change on the lower level.

The next four chapters will expand the ideas of this chapter by examining the policing practices around battering in four countries: Australia, Britain, the Netherlands, and the United States.

Notes

1 It was feminist knowledge gleaned from work with battered women that alerted government officials' attitudes towards the problems of policing domestics'. Del Martin's *Battered Wives*, first published in

1976, provided the groundwork for criticism of policing. Strategies to change legislation, create civil remedies, and open access to legal protection followed (see Part II of this volume).

2 The actual deterrent effect of arrest is relatively unknown in any specific case. There could be alternatives to arrest, which might constitute a 'tough' stance. Mandated anti-violence counselling might be one; mandatory community service might be another — as long as women's needs were being protected and their need for physical protection maintained. Clearly removing a violent man is the most important short-term goal, and an enforced removal through arrest, on the grounds of criminal offenses or breach of the peace, gives women some breathing space.

3 Randall and Rose 1981; Chambers and Millar 1983; Stanko 1985; and Part II of this volume.

4 See for example Rubenstein 1973; Banton 1964; Fielding 1984; Shapland and Hobbs 1987; Cain 1973; Punch 1979; Manning 1978; Van Maanen 1978; Skolnick 1975; and others. See Reiner (1985) for a summary of these studies.

5 Women themselves already exclude a great deal of their victimization from police involvement. Dobash and Dobash (1979) estimate that of the 32,000 situations reported by the 109 women, only 2 per cent of the incidents were reported to the police. A recent study of women in battered women's shelters in the United States shows that one-third of the women battered less than one year, and two-thirds of women battered more than one year called police at some point (Abel and Suh 1987).

6 See for example Clark and Lewis (1977); Chambers and Millar (1983); Rose and Randall (1982).

7 There has been concern expressed about the level of violence against women inside the police force. Armed forces personnel, often compared to police, have levels of violence against women five times higher than those in the civilian population.

8 This may be partly due to the reluctance of many men to support feminist definitions of and plans of action against violence toward women. Scraton (1985: 168) describes the dilemma thus 'Just as it is probable that men from all classes see street violence as a "problem" for them, they would not see most actions of sexual harassment as a "problem" at all.'

Chapter four

Policing and Male Violence in Australia

Suzanne E. Hatty

In your memory stretches a dark series of scenes. Your stepfather drunk and violent, your mother crouched against the wall shielding her head with her hands and screaming for you to run for the police. You can't even calculate the number of times you ran in your pyjamas to the police station, only to be left loitering in the lobby while the policeman drank another cup of tea before setting out to deal with another 'domestic'. . . .

There was always the same scene when you got back to the house; the policeman standing calm and disinterested in the hallway, while angry man and distraught woman made long and involved accusations against each other. Then the policeman would say he wasn't going to take sides, but there'd better not be any more disturbance.

The Treatment and the Cure (Kocan 1986: 44)

This scene occurred in Australia in the 1950s. It describes a child's anguish in the face of police reluctance to intervene on behalf of an abused woman. It also tells of the apparent condoning of male violence by this policeman. It is a scene that occurs on a daily basis in many Australian cities and towns — even 30 years later.

This chapter will examine the issue of male violence against women, particularly male abuse of a female partner. This examination will be located in the context of the feminist project: the redefining and renaming of violent male behaviour directed at women. Specifically, the promotion of the law as a primary means of addressing male violence will be analysed. The ideological constructs utilized by street-based police officers will form the focus of this analysis. The manifest failure of the current law reform initiatives within one Australian state will be interpreted within this context.

Conceptualizing the Violence

Within academic and legal discourse, definitions of violence — and harm — are typically derived from 'malestream' standards. There is an emphasis on the 'visible' and the quantifiable to the exclusion of the 'invisible' and diffuse (Hatty 1986). Apparent physical injury takes precedence over psychological injury, which must be inferred and may be manifested over long periods of time. These definitions of violence are consistent with the classic mind/body duality in which men are constituted as mind, that is, reason, objectivity, and affective restraint, while women are constituted as body, that is reproductive agents devoid of rational intellect. This duality implies that if physical violence is to be directed at any target, women can properly be regarded as that target. Furthermore, the identification of women with the body legitimizes physical violence against women; they are designated as the carnal ground upon which men may tread. This is a privilege enshrined in the dichotomous ideological constructs defining gender.

Feminists have found it necessary to deconstruct these definitions of violence and create, in their place, a feminist discourse based on the totality of women's experience. As the dichotomous relations of male/female, mind/body, and subject/object are reproduced within the structure of scientific method, feminists have also found it necessary to develop more appropriate research methodologies. Traditional approaches to studying male violence against women are eschewed in favour of approaches born of a collective understanding of women's experience of male violence. Feminist research methods thus repudiate the spurious devision between the 'researcher' and the 'researched'. Moreover, in recognition of the scope and range of male victimization of women, feminists reject the distinction between victims and non-victims (Kelly 1987). There is an acknowledgement of the functional significance of the male abuse of women, irrespective of whether this abuse encapsulates physical or psychological violence or the threat of such violence (Dobash and Dobash 1984). It is an explicit acknowledgement of the benefits accruing to the male from

71

violence: on an individual level, a compliant, available partner; and on the social level, a validation of the patriarchal order of gender relations.

In an attempt to link theory and practice, and hence dissolve oppositions, the search for appropriate method has become paramount. Feminist research is based on an identification with the reported experiences of other women, the researcher becoming the filter through which these experiences are revealed, untainted by 'malestream' constructions. Feminist researchers assert that it is vital to allow women to define the meaning and impact of the violent experience (Kelly 1987), thus displacing the hegemonic views of male violence consistent across the academic, legal, and therapeutic domains (Hatty 1986, 1987a; Edwards 1987; Radford 1987).

Responding to the Violence

In the course of redefining the experience of male violence against a female partner, feminists have sought to expose the deficiencies in existing legislation and its implementation. Indeed, research conducted with women who have invoked the law has vindicated feminist claims, especially with regard to the police (Pagelow 1981; Bowker 1982; Pahl 1982; Hatty and Knight 1986; Knight and Hatty, in press). Within these studies, specific criticisms of police performance have focused on the reluctance to arrest the male partner, the inappropriate use of crisis intervention techniques, and the neglect of referral agencies. Research on the police response to violence against a female partner indicates that these criticisms are justified (Berk and Loseke 1980–1; Smith and Klein 1984; Worden and Pollitz 1984; Hatty and Sutton 1986a).

Feminist concern over the manifest failure of the criminal justice system to protect or assist women has been translated into reformist efforts (Hatty 1987b). Feminists in many countries have centred campaigns on the issue of legislative change. These campaigns have been based on the need to recognize the inherent criminality of such male violence against women (Hatty 1987b).

In several countries the state has apparently cooperated with feminist demands for law reform. A multitude of Task Force reports on 'family violence' have been produced within the last five years (for example, the Attorney General's Task Force on Family

Violence 1984; Report of the City of Ottawa Task Force on Wife Assault 1984). Seven of the eight Australian jurisdictions have published government reports since 1981. The main theme of these reports has been the criminalization of male violence against a female partner. This approach has been strengthened by the results of the Minneapolis 'domestic violence' experiment. The findings of this experiment lent tentative support to the idea that arrest of male batterers would reduce the likelihood of further violence (Sherman and Berk 1984a, 1984b; Berk and Newton 1985; Sherman, Garner, and Cohn 1986).

In Australia, state-based activity in the area of male violence against a female partner has been most prolific in New South Wales, a populous state located on the eastern seaboard. In 1981 the premier of New South Wales established a task force to investigate the issue of 'domestic violence', that is, physical and psychological violence directed at a female partner. Following the recommendations of this task force, the government introduced legislative reform to the Parliament in 1982. These reforms were passed and subsequently proclaimed in April 1983. Further amendments were passed in December 1983. The philosophy of this legislation has been described as follows (Report of the New South Wales Domestic Violence Committee 1985: 5):

> The Domestic Violence reforms, both legal and procedural, mark a turning point in the treatment of this problem in New South Wales. They demonstrate a clear determination to make the Police and the Courts more effective in dealing with domestic violence.

The new legislation defined the range of offences constituting 'domestic violence' in New South Wales: all assault offences, including sexual, committed by one spouse upon the other ('spouse' covering both legal and *de facto* marriages, and separated or divorced couples). The legislation clarified police powers of entry, providing for a radio telephone warrant to be obtained from a magistrate when entry was denied. Spouses became compellable witnesses in criminal prosecutions for domestic violence, with limited judicial discretion to grant exemption. The legislation also provided for the issuing of a protective order in cases where a person reasonably feared violence or harassment from a lawful or *de facto* spouse. In addition, complainants living with or separated from a spouse could seek an Apprehended Domestic Violence Order under civil law to protect them from future violence. The police could also act as complainants for such orders. These orders, valid for six months, carried the power of arrest following breach.

Accompanying this legislative reform were a number of significant policy and procedural changes relating to police performance. These were introduced 'with the objective of encouraging police action against domestic violence and enhancing the protection available to women' (Report of the New South Wales Domestic Violence Committee, 1985: 6). In internal circulars, police were instructed to lay a charge of assault whenever the evidence permitted, thus removing the onus of action from women. Police training in the area of 'domestic violence' was also expanded and altered. Feminists working in refuges and government departments regularly participated in in-service training courses, and several seminars on the new legislation were organized. A Programme Co-ordinator for Family Violence was appointed within the police department and Domestic Violence Liaison Officers were introduced throughout the state. The duties of these officers included establishing contact with refuges, legal centres, and counselling and interpreter services, to name a few, and investigation of complaints of police performance in the field.

Evaluation of the effectiveness of the 1983 legislation has been conducted regularly by the New South Wales Domestic Violence Committee, a committee operating under the auspices of the Premier's Department. The brief of this committee is to monitor the use of the new legislation, investigate women's satisfaction with the law, and assist in the implementation of programmes in various government departments. Most importantly, the function of the committee is to co-ordinate the state response to male violence in the home. As such, the committee is mainly composed of government representatives, working in conjunction with feminists within the Women's Co-ordination Unit of the Premier's Department.

Employing a combination of official statistics supplied by the police and the courts and anecdotal evidence from various sources, the Domestic Violence Committee has monitored the progress of the new changes. In 1985 they reported that there were very few matters reaching court as a result of police action; that is, proceedings were generally commenced by way of a summons taken out by the woman rather than a warrant issued by a police officer. Apart from indicating a reluctance to arrest a violent male offender, this situation carries several serious implications for women: first, a summons cannot provide interim protection, as the provisions of the Bail Act restricting the offender's access to the home do not apply; and second, proceedings undertaken by way of summons are subject to lengthy delays before reaching court.

In the 1985 document, the Committee also reported that Stipendiary Magistrates were excusing spouses from giving evidence on the basis of their own criteria. Reasons cited for exemption from giving evidence included the reconciliation of the parties (56.7 per cent), the trivial nature of the offence, a lack of previous record, and the interests of children and family. While the last is not defined, it is reasonable to assume that it is synonymous with the interests of men. Thus, the compellability provision of the legislation was being seriously undermined by the magistrates' action.

More recently, the Law Reform Task Force on Violence Against Women and Children, established in New South Wales to recommend legislative changes, testifies to the manifest failure of the law to assist women abused by violent lovers or husbands. The Consultation Paper issued by the Task Force (1987: 85) notes that the 1983 Crimes (Domestic Violence) Amendment Act 'required a particular commitment from the police'. Specifically, it was envisaged that the police would make the necessary applications for the Apprehended Domestic Violence Orders designed to protect women from future violence. However, the Committee noted (1987: 85): 'Despite the legislative intention, departmental instructions, training and increased resources, police have been slow to respond and take responsibility for cases in the way the Government had hoped.'

The Committee further described this as a 'disappointing response by police' (1987: 87), perhaps negating the buoyant optimism of the 1985 (p. 5) statement: 'The establishment of special provisions under the *Crimes Act* and concomitant changes in police procedures to deal with the problem of domestic violence [are] thus significant changes for women.'

The remainder of this chapter will tell the hidden story behind the failure of this 'legislative intention'.

Police Constructions of Violence Against Women

> Certainly in conversation with men inside the job, there are
> jokes about the 'maddies', the stupid ones, the gullible ones,
> the 'naggers' and so on.
>
> Male police officer, Metropolitan Sydney

While there is a dearth of research on police attitudes towards male
abuse of a female partner, recent Australian research has established a comprehensive database in this area (Hatty and Sutton
1986a, 1986b). This research was carried out in Sydney, Australia's
largest city. Approximately 500 general-duty officers from
Australia's largest police force were interviewed in a random
sampling of the various districts of metropolitan Sydney. In
addition, police intervention in a random sample of 'domestic'
incidents was observed and police officers were interviewed following each incident.

The research was undertaken in the context of feminist concern,
manifested both within and without the bureaucracy, over existing
legislation and its implementation. The research received generous
financial support from the Commonwealth government and the
New South Wales state police. Interviews were completed during
1986.

The observed 'domestic' incidents could be divided into violence
between couples (abuse or assault of a female partner in all but one
case) and disputes or violence between other family members or
neighbours. Partner incidents numbered 106 cases. The remainder
of the 132 incidents were family or neighbour disputes.

The police responded in different ways to the two categories of
incidents. Despite the fact that injuries to the woman or the
presence of weapons were more likely to be associated with partner
incidents, arrest of the offender was far less likely to occur. In
partner incidents in which women were injured, arrest occurred in
36 per cent of cases. Moreover, while the Crimes (Domestic
Violence) Amendment Act of 1983 makes provision for arrest on a
specific 'domestic violence' charge, police officers were far more
likely to use other legislation to deal with the offender. A common
response was to apprehend the violent male as an intoxicated
person and detain him overnight, thereby avoiding the use of the
domestic violence legislation. Instead, police officers resorted to
legislation applying to the public domain (public drunkenness).

The offender was more likely to be arrested if he threatened the intervening officer with violence or if the couple was separated or unmarried. Physical injury to the woman, previous police intervention, or previous arrest on a domestic violence charge were not significantly related to the arrest of the offender in the current incident. These responses are consistent with the police role, espoused in contemporary police training, of maintaining public peace and order.

Interviews with police officers immediately following intervention in 'domestic' incidents indicated several problematic attitudes and behaviours in connection with female partner assault. Police officers tend to divide the community into 'deserving victims' and 'hopeless families'. The former were women who either had attempted or intended to leave their violent partner. 'Hopeless families' were defined as those who were dependent on government assistance. These families usually lived in housing estates to the west of Sydney.

Within these categories, police often attributed responsibility to the woman for the violence, or displayed disrespect for her position. In one incident a police officer described how he had been called to an address because a woman was afraid for her safety. The woman's *de facto* husband had been drinking heavily and was threatening to kill her. The woman stated that she had been assaulted on previous occasions. The officer concluded that no action was necessary because 'she'd been stirring him up'.

In another incident, a woman begged the police to arrest her husband. She lowered her jeans and lifted her top to show the officer her bruises. (She had previously been told that the police would not arrest without visible signs of injury.) The officer declined to arrest, claiming the woman was exaggerating. However, he commented, 'Not bad legs, though!'

Police officers also trivialized the violent episodes or identified with the male perpetrator. One officer interviewed after intervening in an incident in which a woman had sustained cuts and bruises at the hands of her boyfriend concluded, 'She's quite big enough to look after herself.' In another incident, an officer listened to the accounts provided by both the female and male parties regarding the violent epidosde. The officer resolved the serious discrepancy between these accounts by rejecting the woman's version and accepting the male's explanation that 'she went berserk for no reason and ended up with cuts all over'.

Problematic police behaviour included the failure to arrest the violent male, or placing the onus on the woman to initiate legal proceedings. A police officer described how in one incident he had instructed a Vietnamese husband 'not to smack his wife around again', and in another had asked an Aboriginal woman who had visible signs of injury if 'she wanted any further action taken in relation to the matter'.

Clearly, observation of police practices, particularly the circumstances surrounding the resolution of each incident, lends support to government claims that the police are not acting in accordance with the provisions of the new domestic violence legislation.

Interviews with the 500 general-duty police officers investigated attitudes towards existing training, intervention in 'domestic' incidents, and beliefs concerning male violence toward a female partner. It is possible to identify, on the basis of these interviews, a dominant set of beliefs concerning male violence.

This set of beliefs is held by the majority of officers irrespective of sex, and constitutes a powerful ideological climate shaping the police response to violence against a female partner. Moreover, beliefs are reproduced within the police force, with young officers quickly adopting the dominant views on male violence. There is very little opportunity for young officers to seriously challenge accepted ideas and practices. Conformity thus becomes the vehicle ensuring continuity of attitude and behaviour over long periods of time.

Police Constructions of Male Violence: Women's Role

Three separate ideological constructs comprise police beliefs regarding the role of the woman in the production of violence.

The first of these is the degree to which the woman adheres to traditional gender-based behaviours. The police conceptualize any departures from the accepted standards of mothering and housekeeping as contributory factors towards violence.

From my experience, I think the woman should do more around the house. The woman demands a lot, but doesn't do her bit — and he retaliates. I'd feel the same.

Some of these women behave like animals. Some sink so low,

they become animals. They leave their kids on the floorboards with nothing on. They're really bad mothers. The old man just snaps. Usually he's only thinking of his kids.

I feel that a lot of women could've avoided the violence by being a bit more generous — doing a better job of the housework and taking better care of their appearance.

Moreover, behaviours that violate the norms of feminine sexuality, such as infidelity, going out alone at night, or drinking alcohol in male company, are seen to warrant particularly harsh measures on the part of the husband or lover.

There's a certain kind of woman involved in 'domestics' — the sultry types, the ones who hang around bars. These women go out to meet men. They put an enormous strain on relations. I've seen men go berserk with worry.

I see a lot of women who are drunk all the time. They're just sluts. They should be looking after their kids. They're just low women with no morals. They drink in pubs.

You see a lot of tramps in this business, women who'd screw anyone. They've just got that look about them. You can't really blame the men.

Some police officers also believe that women are inherently inferior to the male, and that it is women's physical vulnerability that determines the effects of men's violence. This belief in the biological inevitability of women's physical and social dependency underscores concern over women's failure to conform, providing the violent male with a justification for his behaviour. It also provides the police with a rationale for non-intervention.

Women are just inferior — physically and mentally. Intervening in 'domestics' has confirmed this. You push a woman and she falls in a heap.

Men are so much stronger. Women cling to them. It's natural. The man is definitely the boss. There are privileges attached to this; men have the right to keep the woman in line.

Females are definitely the weaker sex! Men have always dominated women — just like in the animal kingdom.

The second ideological construct determining police beliefs regarding the woman's role in the violence is her perceived degree of responsibility, that is, the degree to which she is seen to have 'provoked' the man. Provocation is conceptualized within narrow terms and relies on misogynist notions such as 'nagging', 'taunting', and 'mental torment' of the man. It is entirely consistent with the male offender's perspective, and does not seek to understand the behaviour from the woman's viewpoint. Some of the officers also subscribe to the idea that the men are simply responding in kind to women's aggression, that is, are engaging in self-defence. Hence, the archaic concept of the violent, dangerous woman is in evidence here.

> Women in 'domestic' situations often contribute to the violence. They are nagging bitches. They go on and on, and the guy can't take the torture any longer. He uses violence to put an end to it.

> Some of the women involved in domestic violence are a problem. They continually nag. If they're dissatisfied, they should go, not cause trouble.

> Lots of these women push the guy to the brink. It's all their fault. The men are really provoked.

> Females can be very violent. They'll often attack the husband physically, and he just hits back. He's often just protecting himself.

The third, and perhaps most potent, ideological construct concerns the woman's psychological instability or psychopathology. Many officers not only believe that women subjected to abuse are psychologically abnormal, but are psychiatrically disturbed. The officers freely offer many different diagnoses of these apparent psychological illnesses. Many consider such illnesses to be biologically based. None consider these apparent conditions to be the result of the abuse; most consider them a catalyst to it.

> I tend to believe that women are very unstable creatures, not capable of rational thought or action. A lot of them are schizophrenics. It must be their biology or something.

> The women are really screwed in the head. You've got to be to like all that pain, haven't you?

Most of these women are hysterical, slack, dirty and untidy. Who'd want them? They're classic nut-cases. I often think that we should be locking them up.

Police Constructions of Male Violence: Men's Role

While there is some perceived similarity in police attitudes between the role of each sex in the production of the violence, there are notable differences. These refer particularly to the significance accorded to biological and social factors in men's use of violence.

In constructing the male role in violence against a female partner, police usually believe that stereotypical masculinity involves some degree of aggressive behaviour towards others. Such masculinity, according to the police, is biologically based, not socially constructed. The police thus believe that maleness itself confers the power of physical dominance over women.

It's basically natural. Violence is instinctual to all men.

It's the nature of the beast. Men are just aggressive. It's just part and parcel of being the dominant sex.

The majority of police officers maintain that substance abuse, especially alcohol abuse, transforms the character of the male, often rendering him violent. In this construction, alcohol consumption results in violence. Although this is one of the most pervasive social myths about violence against women, it nevertheless serves to greatly reduce the responsibility of the male partner. It becomes the substance, rather than the individual, which is in control. Police officers often construct elaborate rationales for the supposedly aberrant behaviour of the violent man in the grip of alcohol.

These guys are clean-living, respectable people who are under lots of stress. Maybe they're unemployed. They take solace in the drink. They become completely different characters — belligerent, violent, and abusive. They wouldn't normally be like this.

I blame all this domestic violence on alcohol. The wife nags. The bloke drinks. It's a fatal combination.

I've seen blokes really change under the influence of alcohol. They're capable of doing things they'd never normally do — like violence.

Consistent with the above, many police officers believe that violent men are simply reacting to a cluster of social stressors; these might range from employment difficulties to problems with the management of finances. Invariably the reaction to such stressors is considered rational and justified. Male violence against a female partner is interpreted, within this construction, as indicative of the stress associated with the male role.

> I've developed a great sympathy for men in general. I see a lot of good blokes affected badly by the pressures of life — and by the drink.

> The violence is an escape valve from the pressure they're under. The stress is there and something or someone pushes it too far. They're usually frustrated at work — the boss might be giving him a hard time — and they get home and the wife starts on him. It's too much for any reasonable man.

It is worth noting, at this point, the disparity within the police belief system between attributions of responsibility for the violence to the female and male partners. Responsibility is firmly vested with the woman; misogynist beliefs concerning the nature of women, appropriate gender behaviour, and the fragility of women's mental health underscore this notion. Indeed, it is instructive to contrast these negative views of women abused within relationships with the extreme sympathy extended by the police to children in violent homes (Hatty and Sutton 1986b). Exaggerated beliefs in the relationship between maleness and violence, and the stressors associated with the male role, effectively minimalize men's responsibility for violent behaviour. The police, then, construct and perpetuate a dichotomous set of beliefs in which women are cast as failures or oppressors, and men as heroic victims.

Women's Response to the Violence

Police beliefs concerning women's response to the violence are largely derived from ideas about its production. Again, police beliefs hinge on the degree of role conformity exhibited by the female partner.

Police understand a woman's decision to call the police to be motivated by the following: the woman's desire for revenge on the male partner; a wish to manipulate either the partner or the police; a need for immediate cessation of the violence coupled with an unpredictable or inconsistent intention towards the abuser; and a pronounced reliance on external authority to solve individual problems. The police, thus, often express a good deal of cynicism over women's motivation to invoke the law.

A lot of them are hysterics. Some are purely malicious. Some use the police as a tool against their husbands.

Most times they want us to do everything — arrest, charge, draw and quarter him. The next day, it's a different story. They're hostile toward us because they've made up with their spouse. They only used us to get even. It hardens you against the women.

I've realised that there are certain types — the 'schemers' — whom I detest. They use the police to get back at their husbands. They're too weak to do anything about the situation themselves.

Police interpret women's decision to remain in a relationship according to a fixed cluster of beliefs. These include traditional devotion to the ideal of wife and mother, a lack of intelligence, a lack of psychological strength, masochism, and psychopathology. Obviously, most of these beliefs can be characterized as misogynist.

I now see women as stupid. They cop the beating but don't want us to gaol him.

Often they're just dumb, or perhaps a weak character, a character you can't respect in any way.

My experience with domestic violence has led me to form certain opinions about women. I believe that they're basically masochistic, and that's why they stay through the brutality and violence.

Women only stay in these situations because they're mad, insane. Also, I'm convinced that they get a lot of pleasure out of the violence. Perhaps it turns them on.

Police beliefs regarding the production of male violence are organized around the central premiss that a certain amount of violence within relationships is 'normal'. Furthermore, the vast majority of police believe that such violence — being acceptable — is not criminal. Indeed, this is consistent with the offender's reaction to police intervention; police officers report that most offenders are very hostile towards intervening officers.

> When you first arrive they try to con you. A lot of them are just irate and aggressive. They want us to know what the hell you're doing in *his* house. It's a private matter.

> Usually they say, 'It's my business and nothing to do with the police.' They say, 'It's my privilege to hit my wife.'

Police tolerance of 'domestics' is limited. They maintain that particular characteristics of the situation, for example a history of police intervention, colour their response. Frequently, if male officers take any action in such a situation, it will be in line with an extreme masculine stereotype. Within the context of their institutional authority, the officers often resort to individual strategies such as threatening the offender with physical violence.

> It's the same old story. Sometimes you have to be aggressive to make them see reason. Sometimes you have to outdo his aggression.

> I'm more savage than I used to be. I used to look for a way out of using physical force. Now I know it's going to happen. It's a better alternative to arrest.

> If he's going to give you trouble, you have to sort him out — physically, if necessary. You can't have him telling you what to do. It usually does the trick.

A Survivor's Perspective

It is vital that police constructions of male violence against a female partner be subjected to scrutiny. Arguably, the most effective way to do this is to compare these constructions with women's experiences of male violence. While a good deal of research on violence against women in relationships has been undertaken in Australia (see for example Knight and Hatty, in press), it would seem appropriate to present women's testimony, unmediated by the researcher's interpretation.

An Australian survey of women's experience of physical and psychological abuse within relationships was undertaken by the author in 1985. A comprehensive questionnaire was placed in a national magazine with a large female readership. Responses were anonymous. However, hundreds of women identified themselves and attached lengthy case histories to their completed questionnaires. It is possible to extract information from these questionnaires which directly challenges police constructions of male violence against women.

In contrast to police beliefs regarding this violence, women consistently report that the physical violence is unprovoked. While the sequence of male behaviours leading up to a violent episode can often be identified, women contend that the instigation to violence often comes from an internal source, such as an irrational desire to control the woman.

> He would instigate an argument without any reason and then become violent.

> I walked past my de facto and sat on the couch. On the way past he asked me a question. I answered with 'I don't know.' He then got up and repeatedly hit me on the head. I will say this much — on the worst occasion, there was definitely no provocation on my part as I was sleeping when he attacked me.

Further, women typically employ a series of well-considered tactics to placate the violent male. Women attempt to manage the volatile situation through diffusing tension, by being excessively compliant or passive, or simply deflecting the male's attention. Whatever the tactic chosen, women frequently take emotional responsibility for the violent behaviour of their male partners.

> He came home one night with 'that' look on his face. He was spoiling for a fight and I knew that no matter what I did I would be bashed. He spent the night picking and trying to get a reaction out of me. With great difficulty, I stayed calm and pleasant, but every word I uttered was twisted. I went to bed early to avoid him, but it wasn't any good.

> After he'd had a go at me, he'd get depressed. I would coax

him out of it by being nice to him, offering him cups of tea, giving him a kiss, and telling him I love him. This way I'd know he wouldn't get violent again.

In conceptualizing women as either manipulative, vindictive, or masochistic, the police effectively deny the sadistic behaviour of the violent men and the degree to which women abhor the abuse. Police constructions of violence against women do not generally recognize the sexual or psychological abuse meted out by violent men. Within their misogynist belief system, the police only acknowledge the existence of visible injuries, while also distorting the events prior to the infliction of these injuries.

My self-confidence was so low. No matter what I tried to talk to him about, he said I didn't know what I was talking about. He constantly had to put me down to make himself feel big and a man. He hated women really and anyone who showed any strength was a slut or a bitch.

It always seems that when I am happy in myself and feel life is OK, he cannot wait to bring me back into depression. It's as though he is only happy when I cannot cope.

I've had a lot of support from a girlfriend. If it hadn't been for her, I would not have made it through the last six months. It's truly been a living hell. I just hope the pain, the guilt and the humiliation will disappear — and the nightmares.

While police officers proffer cynical interpretations of women's motivation to summon police, women tell a different story. Women report a pronounced distrust of the criminal justice system and deep disappointment and frustration at police performance.

The police were called and I was told that because we're legally married, nothing could be done. At the time I was very confused and bewildered, so I didn't pursue it further. Now, eight weeks later, I know my rights, and would have demanded them.

The police don't care about your problems and are very unsympathetic towards you. They don't tell you what your alternatives are and generally act as though you're a nuisance to them. Once they've left, your husband hurts you again.

Even if he is arrested, the police can't protect you from him 24 hours a day.

The police were not interested when I tried to report the violence I was experiencing. I tried several times and they wouldn't even listen. One actually told me, 'Good. It's time women are put in their place.' I gave up my attempts to report the violence after that!

Women also report serious conflict and ambivalence over remaining with an abusive man. In confirmation of existing research (Kalmus and Straus 1982; Strube and Barbour 1983; Knight and Hatty, in press), women cite financial and social dependency, protectiveness towards children, shame, and fear as factors that deter them from leaving the relationship.

I didn't leave home because of the children, and of course, I had no money because I'd put every penny into the house; and he wouldn't let me work.

I attempted suicide for the first and last time. I then started to plan my escape. It took another year to leave. It's not easy when you are hunted.

Clearly, a comparison between police constructions of male violence and women's experiences of this violence indicates that the two are, in fact, diametically opposed. This antithetical relationship between ideology and reality ensures that women who seek police intervention are effectively introducing a second assailant (Stanko 1985). The dual victimization of women reverberates through a number of facets of life, entrenching the power of the abuser, confirming the inevitability of women's vulnerability, and compounding the effects of the initial abuse.

Conclusion

With the advent of feminist activism in the 1970s, male violence against women was designated as a social problem worthy of the attention of bureaucrats, academics, and service providers (Struder 1984). Feminists had already reframed this violence, labelling it 'a crime of momentous proportion' (Ellis 1984: 56). However, with the legitimation of the issue, governments began to respond to this new definition — feminist claims for law reform received state attention.

Subsequent analysis of the success of this manoeuvre indicates the existence of several difficulties, some associated with the philosophy of the law itself and some with its operation (Hatty 1987b).

Conceptual difficulties include a failure to consider the implications of the form of law (Smart 1986; Stang Dahl 1986). This has led to a naïve engagement with the legal system divorced from its historical and socio-political roots. Other conceptual difficulties include the symbiotic relationship between the criminal justice and social welfare systems. The likelihood of diverting violent men into counselling programmes is increased within this relationship. Arguably, these diversionary tactics do not necessarily benefit women (Hatty 1986).

Practical difficulties include exaggerated expectations of a criminal justice system that is slow, cumbersome, and unable to provide long-term protection (Ford 1983), an almost exclusive emphasis on the gatekeepers of this system — the police — and a neglect of decision making within the court (MacLeod 1986). Further, women's reluctance to involve the police has frequently been overlooked (Berk, Berk, Newton, and Loseke 1984; Bowker 1984; Hatty and Knight 1986).

Underpinning these difficulties is the ideological consistency between the structure and function of the law, on the one hand, and the attitudes and practices of those who implement it, on the other. This has the effect of rendering irrelevant the intervening discourses articulated by feminists, irrespective of whether these feminists are working within or without the bureaucracy.

This chapter documents the significance of the ideological constructs held by police officers at street level, and demonstrates the similarity between these constructs and the ideology evident within judicial discourse (Edwards 1985, 1987; Radford 1987). A juxtaposition of police attitudes and women's experiences reveals an enormous disparity between male belief and female reality, and signals the futility of promoting the law as a primary solution to violence against women. It highlights the failure of the law at a very fundamental level: the nexus between ideology and practice.

Clearly, strategies other than those based on state intervention in women's lives must be developed. Indeed, the role of the state, as interpreted by male liberal or left theorists, has continued to generate controversy among feminists (Mackinnon 1983; Davis and Faith 1985; Hanmer and Stanko 1985). As a first step to the development of viable alternatives there is a need for ruthless appraisal of current state-based manoeuvres, rather than an uncritical acceptance of options offered by the state or its agencies. Such viable alternatives might include collective efforts among women to label violent men and deprive them of social power, while providing increased support and protection for women who will no longer tolerate male violence. Passivity is, after all, incompatible with the feminist project.

Chapter five

Women and Policing in Britain

Jalna Hanmer

Women's demands on the police for improvements in their response to requests for help from women are becoming more widespread.[1] For over a decade the role, if any, for the criminal justice system has been under constant discussion within women's helping agencies. The issues move from a recognition of the unsympathetic treatment of women to the need many women and children have for an appropriate police response. Civil law remedies, in particular injunctions, with and without divorce and other proceedings, are often cumbersome and ineffectual in curbing violent men. The first British survey to concentrate solely on improving policing services to women was initiated by the West Yorkshire County Council which, until its abolition by central government in 1985, had responsibility for the West Yorkshire Police Authority. This chapter draws on the interviews with police officers and welfare agency personnel.[2]

The recent history that has lead to a growing focus on policing begins with refuges for abused women started by groups of women in the women's liberation movement. Women's Aid, the refuge movement for women and their children who need to leave home because of physical, sexual, or mental abuse, grew from two refuges in 1971 to almost 200 in the United Kingdom (England, Wales, Scotland, and Northern Ireland) by 1977. The British Parliament established a Select Committee on Violence in Marriage which reported in 1975, firmly establishing the abuse of women in their homes as a social, not just an individual problem.

The Parliamentary Select Committee located intervention into violence in the home in welfare services to be provided primarily by Women's Aid and in the civil law remedy of injunctions. The

Home Office took no interest in this newly rediscovered social problem, and neither Women's Aid not the Parliamentary Select Committee saw the police and criminal justice system generally as a part of the state able to offer a helping service to women.[3] The attitudes of the police at the time partly explain why this was so. Their evidence to the Parliamentary Select Committee on Violence in Marriage was unequivocal on the inadvisability of intervening in matrimonial situations.

The Association of Chief Police Officers of England, Wales and Northern Ireland explained their position like this:

> Whilst such problems take up considerable police time during say, 12 months, in the majority of cases the role of the police is a negative one. We are, after all, dealing with persons 'bound in marriage', and it is important, for a host of reasons, to maintain the unity of the spouses. Precipitated action by the police could aggravate the position to such an extent as to create a worse situation than the one they were summoned to deal with. The 'lesser of two evils' principle is often a good guideline in these situations. (p. 366)

Their memorandum accepted the need for temporary shelter for abused women, but went on to say, '*Every effort should be made to re-unite the family*' (emphasis theirs; p. 369)

This may seem a simple case of concern for the institution of marriage overriding the legal rights of one of the marriage partners, but embedded within this response is an understanding of the status, and thereby the individual and social power, of women. 'It is submitted that the equal status of women in society today precludes any preferential treatment for them; otherwise the law could fall into disrepute' (p. 378).

In addition to these ideological statements, Women's Aid were experiencing problems with policemen who abuse their wives. Trying to assist women whose husbands could call upon an extended network of officers to locate 'their women' was extremely difficult, particularly when officers had served in more than one force area. Women support workers in Women's Aid were also experiencing difficulties in obtaining effective police help when men discovered the location of the refuge and tried to forceably enter the premises to gain access to women who did not want to see them. While responses from the police varied between towns, districts, and individual officers, there was a marked tendency for the police to underestimate the violence of men and the need for police assistance by women and by refuges operated by women.

A role for police involvement focused on the enforcement of the civil law remedy of injunctions. The Parliamentary Select Committee recommended legislation, and the Domestic Violence Act 1976 enabled County Court judges to attach a Power of Arrest to injunctions in certain cases. This power was subsequently extended to magistrate courts. Over the past decade solicitors acting for abused women have gathered a wealth of experience in attempting to protect women through this civil law remedy, much of it negative as the most commonly issued injunction is not backed up by power of arrest and therefore is particularly useless (Hanmer and Saunders 1987; Meredith 1979; Women's National Commission 1985).

Action around rape, the next issue of violence against women to be taken up in Britain some five years later, had a very different starting point. From the beginning rape called into question the criminal law, its administration, and the nature of police intervention (Chambers and Millar 1983; London Rape Crisis Centre 1984; Toner 1982). Rape, with its implication of stranger attack, was seen as a criminal law matter, although the advisability of reporting to the police was hotly contested by women providing services to sexually assaulted women and girls. The disbelief and lack of sympathy shown to women by the police and the humiliation experienced in court led Rape Crisis to provide a full description of what might happen if the offence was reported while leaving the decision to the woman concerned.

Rape Crisis was responsible for establishing some of the first incest survivor groups (the first in London in 1980). Many women who phoned them wished to talk about violence from known men and often in their childhood. Rape Crisis found themselves talking to women who had never told anyone of experiences that may have taken place twenty or more years ago. As the emotional pain had never been addressed, support groups for survivors were set up. A shift occurred from conceiving rape as a stranger attack to recognizing that it is far more likely to be an assult from a known man who is likely to be a family member.

Women's Aid estimates that between 20 and 33 per cent of the children of women coming to refuges are physically and/or sexually abused by the mother's husband or cohabitee. But the remainder are not untouched by what has happened. Abuse may be observed by children and they may fear that they, too, will be attacked. When physical and sexual attacks on women take place in front of children, how can they be sure that their father, having turned on their mother, might not move on to them as well? Terrified and distressed children accompany their mothers to refuges. Today both Rape Crisis and Women's Aid find themselves providing services to women abused as children and to women and children currently being abused.

In the late 1970s and early 1980s pornography and sexual harassment at work also became issues for women, and their relationship to other forms of violence experienced by women began to be understood (Mackinnon 1987; Rhodes and McNeill 1985). As with other forms of directly experienced violence, abuse through the use of pornography is more likely to involve men known to women and children than strangers. Sexual harassment at work also often involves men known to women.

Restating the Problem by Focusing on Policing

Through offering help to women the separation of different forms of violence into specific offences was exposed as artificial at the level of women's experience. The research question became how to explore the different forms of violence experienced by women over their lifetimes. And this needed to include the impact of pornography and sexual harassment at work as well as childhood and adult physical, sexual, and mental abuse on the lives of women. Victimization surveys of women's experiences became a way into a further critique of policing.

Small-scale neighbourhood research projects aimed specifically at women have had greater success in providing information on other crimes against women (Hanmer and Saunders 1984; Radford 1987), than the government-sponsored national incidence surveys (Hough and Mayhew 1983, 1985; Chambers and Tombs 1984). These government surveys have been remarkably poor at gaining information from women, while non-random surveys give a tantalizing taste of the magnitude of sexual and other violent crime against women (Bains 1987; Hall 1986).

The reason the critique of policing in Britain has surfaced through victimization studies is because of the difficulty in gaining access to records or police officers for interview or systematic observation. In Britain it is not possible to begin directly with the police as they are insulated from investigation by a state that restricts access by researchers and others who are critical of their performance. Research on the criminal justice system is largely controlled by the Home Office directly through its own research unit and the university research groups it sponsors. However, the police are sensitive to public opinion, and elected officials, councillors, and members of Parliament can have influence in particular circumstances. This is the origin of the West Yorkshire study.

This recent history of women's agitation, service provision, and critical research has led to increasing concern by the British government about issues of violence against women. Significant documents on violence against women in the home are the England and Wales Home Office Circular 25/83 which issued guidance to police forces in 1983. This was followed by the Women's National Commission Report on Violence Against Women in 1985. The Home Office responded to this Cabinet Office report with Circular 69/86 in 1986. There has been a flurry of interest in London. The Metropolitan Police Force, the largest in Britain, set up two working parties, one on rape in 1985 and one on domestic violence in 1986. The London Strategic Policy Unit, in monitoring policing in the capital, produced a report on violence against women in the home in 1986. That year also saw a report on research in London by Susan Edwards.

By the end of 1987, however, only three special interview and examination rooms, known as rape suites, have been created in London for sexually assaulted women and children, and women police surgeon numbers have only been increased marginally. Manchester, the second largest force, has established only one rape suite. In Birmingham the rape suite was destroyed in the uprising in the black ghetto. To date the reports calling for major changes in police policies and practices have led to little practical change in virtually all policing areas in Britain.

West Yorkshire, the third largest police force in England, has made more progress than most with the establishment of a section of the Major Crimes Support Unit staffed only by women officers in the two largest urban centres, Bradford and Leeds. Their brief is to interview and offer appropriate support to women and children who report rape and other major sexual crimes. During the period of the research this unit was expanded in size and a third urban location established. The Unit received positive publicity locally and, given a system of automatic referral by police officers of complaints of sexual assaults deemed serious in law, the number of women and children processed by the police increased dramatically.

In addition, in areas of high referrals of child physical and sexual assault local stations responded by setting up special squads of men and women officers, uniformed and CID (Criminal Investigation Department), to process these reports. Interagency coordination, particularly between statutory social service departments and the police, is increasing.[4] For example, a neighbourhood network of local men receiving sexual servicing from under-age girls who were paid with small items such as cigarettes or pocket money was exposed by the concerted cooperative efforts of the Leeds Social Service Department and the police, resulting in the prosecution of over 100 men. During the research period another similar investigation was under way in another area of West Yorkshire.

The last part of the package, the response to violence against women termed by the police domestic disputes, was under review at the time police officers were being interviewed. The Force Order (specific procedures regulating how officers are to respond to domestic disputes) was superseded by another immediately after the interviewing of police was completed. These orders are confidential to the force and were not revealed to the researchers, but the chief constable subsequently received local publicity about a tougher line to be taken with domestic offenders, which may reflect the direction of change.

The area for research conforms to the old West Yorkshire Council boundaries, and currently the district council areas of Bradford, Halifax, Kirklees, Leeds, and Wakefield. West Yorkshire is a county of contrasts, with both rural and urban areas. Sheep farming and wool manufacturing dominate the area even in this period of economic decline. The wool industry has brought a number of immigrant groups into the county, most recently those from Pakistan, Bangladesh, India, and a smaller Afro-Caribbean population.

Consciousness of violence against women is particularly heightened in West Yorkshire, given several infamous serial murders, the Moors murders of children in the early 1960s, and more recently the so-called Ripper murders from 1975 to 1980.[5] Peter Sutcliffe, the 'Ripper', was a local man, and almost all of the thirteen murdered women and attempted murders of seven others took place in West Yorkshire. These killings and the threat all women lived under during those years profoundly altered the consciousness of women about personal safety and policing.

There is an active women's movement in the larger urban areas in West Yorkshire. There are seven Women's Aid refuges, two Rape Crisis groups, and one incest survivor's project in West Yorkshire. In addition, Leeds City Council's Women's Committee sponsored two conferences on violence against women, the first local authority in Britain to do so. This led to regular meetings with the police on the policing needs of women and finally, in 1985, just prior to this research project, there was a so-called domestic killing of a Bradford woman, Julie Stead, which led to national television time critical of the police. West Yorkshire has also seen the most militant activity against pornography in Britain, beginning with the slogan 'Angry Women' or 'Women Are Angry' appearing as graffiti on billboards and so on from 1979. Much of this activity has been illegal, particularly arson attacks on sex and video shops selling pornographic goods.

West Yorkshire has a local police force, with the substantial majority of officers born and bred in the county and even in the subdivision in which they were working.[6] We were struck by the diversity of opinions and general life experience of the randomly selected 46 males (including two Asians) and nine female officers interviewed, even though there are important similarities between them. The force is drawn almost exclusively from the working class, and older officers, even those in high positions, may have a lower educational attainment than demanded for recruits today. Officers joined the force for a variety of reasons; almost none had 'always wanted to be a policeman/woman' and, more recently, the current economic recession has led skilled workers to change their career path from industry to the police.

Of the various forms violence against women and children can take, officers were more likely to have responded to incidents of violence against women in the home, and more likely to have done so recently, than to any other interpersonal crime against women (Table 5.1). The home was also the place officers visited most frequently when called to all types of violence against women. Two-thirds of the interviewed officers could recall attending an incident within the past few months, and all had this type of police work experience.

Table 5.1 Attendance at incidents of violence against women in the home

Within past year	Over a year ago	Cannot remember/NA
37 (67%)	13 (24%)	6 (11%)

Source: Compiled by the author

The second most frequently dealt with type of violence is sexual offences against children. Almost half of the officers have dealt with or were currently dealing with, an incident that occurred within the last year, but just under a third said that either they have never done so or that it is not relevant to their present postings (Table 5.2). In West Yorkshire child sexual offences are now referred to the Major Crimes Support Unit, where both men and women officers take the statements from victimized children, but they do not pursue the offenders. This role is reserved for CID officers in the relevant geographical area.

Table 5.2 Response to incidents of child sexual abuse

Within past year	Over a year ago	Never/not applicable
23 (42%)	15 (27%)	17 (31%)

Source: Compiled by the author

The third most frequently dealt with type of violence is rape and sexual offences other than rape against women. A quarter of the officers have dealt with a case within the past year, while a third have never done so or are not certain if they have (Tables 5.3 and 5.4). These type of incidents also are now referred to the Major Crimes Support Unit, where women officers are available to take statements and the CID pursue the offenders.

Table 5.3 Response to incidents of rape

Within past year	Over a year ago	Never	No answer
14 (25%)	16 (29%)	19 (35%)	6 (11%)

Source: Compiled by the author

Table 5.4 Response to incidents of sexual offences other than rape

Within past year	Over a year ago	Never	Not sure	NA
16 (29%)	13 (24%)	8 (14%)	17 (31%)	1 (2%)

Source: Compiled by the author

Thus in West Yorkshire it is only with incidents defined as domestic disputes or sexual offences legally defined as less serious that the investigation and decision on appropriate courses of action may be undertaken by any officer. All crime legally defined as serious will involve the CID and/or the Major Crimes Support Unit and may be taken over completely by these sections of the organization.

Factors in assessing violence in the home

Officers generally agreed that the initial assessment of the situation is crucial. They said that they have to go in and find out exactly what has happened, that is, who has done what to whom and why. The factors in assessing the appropriate response are multidimensional and officers usually mentioned more than one, although officers used different combinations. For example, 'If a man and wife have just had a row and she is claiming assault, the officer must (a) establish the general situation and whether it can be sorted out straightaway, (b) the extent of injuries and (c) take into consideration if there are children.' Another officer gave a completely different list, while describing his approach as the 'same as with anything else. You ensure either party definitely wants to make a complaint, that they won't just withdraw it once they see daylight and that the correct evidence is there.'

Many factors, in addition to whether a criminal offence had been committed, influenced the police response. Factors mentioned were located in the individuals themselves and their lifestyle, their past and present interaction, the cause of the dispute and who is judged to be at fault, the extent of injuries, whether or not there is corroboration, who phoned for the police, the involvement of children, how easy the situation is to sort out, whose name the house is in, the safety of officers and those in the house, whether anyone wants to complain, whether the complainant will withdraw, the assumed effect of the police response, and whether a criminal offence has been committed.

The Individual and Lifestyle

One officer felt that one must take the parties' lifestyle into consideration before taking any kind of action. For example, if the family is on a low income, perhaps unemployed, then all they have is each other and one cannot be responsible for splitting them up. Another officer felt that the mental state of both parties has to be considered before deciding a course of action.

Past and Present Interaction

Other officers put the emphasis on 'getting the story of previous assault; how long they've been together, if there have been problems in the past, the cause of the dispute that evening'. Drink is said to play a major part, followed by money problems and sexual jealousy and infidelity.

Children

The majority of officers said that they become extremely concerned when children are either directly involved or are in the house at the time of the incident. The safety of children is considered to be of prime importance. Some officers said that if they feel the woman is in danger then they will remove both the woman and her children to a place of safety. The one officer who admitted personal experience of violence said, 'If there's children involved I tend to try and arrest, having been through it myself. It's not very nice when you're a child seeing your father hitting your mother.' Another reason for the importance of children in making assessments is a belief that 'they don't choose to be in the situation they are in, unlike most adults.'

Who Phoned?

Officers said it is important to find out who has called the police. 'It may be neighbours who have called you. The parties involved may not want you in and you can do more harm than good.'

Officers said you have to be wary when interfering between man and wife. 'From expereince I've been to incidents where a woman has been assaulted yet she's not called the police. It's been the neighbours because of the noise and my appearance has been regarded as interference by both of them.'

Has an Offence Been Committed?

Officers drew a distinction between assaults in order to decide how they should intervene. This involved incorrectly identifying some assaults, and particularly common assault, with the civil law. Officers said they must 'assess situation in my own mind and decide if an offence has been committed. If an offence has been committed. If an assault, what degree is it; the civil law offence of common assault or a criminal one?' Another officer felt that unless there is 'something criminal involved it is nothing to do with us. Unless there is some future danger these are civil disputes.' These remarks appear to pinpoint the heart of the matter. Most officers seemed to regard marital violence, or disputes between women and men who have a close personal relationship, as almost always resulting in a civil rather than a criminal offence.

Safety of Officers

Officers said that among the many considerations must be the safety of the officer. The concern seems to be that when intervening in a domestic situation it is likely that the neighbours have called for the police rather than the injured party and that 'you will incur the wrath of both sides'. This outcome was deemed especially likely when one or both parties were drunk or had been drinking.

The use of a number of these factors in making an assessment is illustrated, for example, in this typical account:

Neighbours called us because of the rowing of a couple. We got a report of a disturbance in the street. When we got there a woman about 24 years old was holding a very young baby in her arms. The husband was there, the worse for drink, and they were rowing. He kept slapping at her head. The sergeant and another officer took the woman and child into the house and two other officers talked to him. The root of the problem was that they were skint, and he'd been boozing all day so she'd gone off at him.

This assessment affected the action taken by officers.

We told her to get some things for her and the baby and we took them to a neighbour's for the night. We told him that if he created any more trouble we would lock him up. If these neighbours hadn't taken her in we would most certainly have locked him up for the night as she or the baby could have been hurt.

The assault to the woman was defined as non-criminal because there was a reason for a domestic row between a married couple to get out of hand that made sense to the officers, that is shortage of money for the household. However, something had to be done because there was a child, and the possibility of future injury. But the intervention needed was short-term because the offender's attack was judged temporary because he would sober up by the next day.

The Family Fight View

Most officers interviewed felt that 'normal man-and-wife arguments are nothing serious', and that usually 'just a warning will work'. Officers generally felt that they should 'listen, but not interfere', because 'in a lot of cases all they need is a referee'. The primary police role is to 'cool a situation out' or diffuse it. One officer said, 'We are told to keep it quiet.' Some officers thought it was totally inappropriate to call in the police 'when you are arguing'. They related this to their own experience, for example: 'Well, me and the wife go at it hammer and tongs and I may lose my temper and give a quick crack sometimes, but I wouldn't have the police come in and sort it out for me.' Male police officers showed an implicit understanding of the husband's point of view, that is many thought he had been provoked. One officer wondered, 'Why had it ever started? Why had it ever got to that peak? Why do police have to sort out marital problems?' However, there was also a recognition that violence in the home can have serious results. 'Any domestic could be murder and it is important to give time and attention.' 'If necessary I arrest the man, rather than go back later and find someone stabbed.'

The desire to know something about the background is a clear deviation from normal policing practice. The desire to find the cause ('drink, money, unemployment, stress in marriage, breakdown of relationship') is not the usual policing procedure. It would seem very strange if officers thought it necessary, for example, to find out why a youth in the inner city has just mugged a passerby in order to decide on the appropriate action to take. More than likely the youth will have a continuous history of poverty and unemployment or have suffered some other social or personal deprivation, but for the police attending the scene of the crime this will count for nought. Similarly, it is unusual for an officer to empathise with a mugger, but not at all unusual for a married man to identify with a marital dispute. As one officer said, 'I relate it to my own circumstances and it's not the way to carry on when there's children in the house.' The question that is begged here is, do officers on the basis of their own experience over-identify with the situation they are investigating to the detriment of law enforcement?

How Officers Decide on What to do

The assessments of the situation made by officers were a mixture of legal, practical, and personal factors. The responses showed no uniformity of approach, no obvious set of procedures to be followed. The area of discretion revealed by their answers appeared to be vast. Experience was seen as fundamental to assessment and decisions on action to be taken. More senior and experienced officers were particularly likely to refer to their experience as a key factor: 'I always do what I think best at the time and that only comes with experience of dealing with people.' Another officer identified the man as the most important person to assess: 'Trying to read a man's mind; this is a question of experience.' Other officers referred to more intuitive qualities: 'Instinct is the most important quality'; and 'You deal with each job individually by the feel you get when you are there. You can feel. If you go in and apply the same spiel to each dispute it doesn't work.' The reason situations have to be approached through feelings and intuition was explained in this way:

If you are good at your job you might have to spend two hours. It doesn't matter how long you spend as long as you've got some solution which is agreed by both sides. Whatever the solution, if you leave one disgruntled it will fester and you'll be back in an hour.

Views on Women

The understanding officers have about women is fundamental to their decisions on appropriate action. Many officers felt that a woman may wish to have the man arrested there and then as 'she will agree to anything as long as the attack stopped and the situation diffused'. But the following morning, or even a few days later officers said she is likely to withdraw her complaint or is willing to try again to make a go of the relationship. Police officers and women complainants were said to have differential interests:

> Great difference between women and the police is that what happened to the woman now and her decisions are made on her feelings at that particular moment, whereas a police officer has to consider what the climate will be like in some months' time when it all goes to court.

While theoretically the possible outcome of complaints and cases should not influence the decisions of officers called to the scene, in practice this was a frequently mentioned factor affecting police actions.

The general feeling of officers about why women behave in this way is summed up by the inspector who said, 'Partnerships do not just break up on the odd assault as there are more family ties, etc., to consider.' While this view applied to all women, officers said it applied even more strongly to Asian women: 'Asian women are less likely to complain and when they do the extended family gets them to withdraw. For white women there is less interference from the extended family.' Asian families are said to 'sort their own problems out'. Religion also is seen as a factor:

> You don't get much around here because it's an extended family network and the women being mainly Muslim are subservient to the men. The woman isn't as isolated because there is usually someone else in the house, usually the mother-in-law she can talk to. The Muslim families don't mind if a husband hits his wife, but if he goes 'womanising' then it can turn into a feud.

This officer went on to give an example of a wife who did complain:

> He had a girlfriend and she, the wife, was upset. He hit her. Wife phoned via a neighbour but he wasn't there when we arrived. She wasn't upset about him hitting her, but rather the shame he'd brought on the family by going with another woman. He was taken aback because she had brought in someone from outside. I don't ever recall going to a domestic with an Asian family.

While these remarks and views are racist when made about Asian women, not only because it is assumed that this behaviour is legitimated by religion and culture among Asians, but also because of an implied assumption that the dominant culture and religion in West Yorkshire are not like this. There is a lack of recognition that the same processes and beliefs can be found in white families in the dominant culture and religion. Patriarchal social relations are dominant in Western as well as Eastern culture and religions. The issue is hetero-patriarchy as, by and large, male officers do not identify with women victims. Their response is rooted in their gender experience as males in cultures and religions in which men dominate and are deemed superior to women.

These views may also be a rationalization for why few Asian women call the police. The effect of limited calls from Asian women means that police racism, and the racism inherent in the Nationality laws and the fear these generate among Asian people, need not be recognized by police officers. In some districts the first response officers make to Asian calls for assistance, whether complaints of violence in the home or racist assaults, is to investigate the status and rights of the complainant to be in Britain (Radford 1988, personal communication).

Officers occasionally claimed to understand a woman's reluctance to either leave or take further action against her husband. Asian women were said not to know their rights under British law. Financial dependency was another explanation, but the majority of officers placed the responsibility on the woman to deal with the situation. For example, officers felt the woman should 'leave her husband and find suitable accommodation elsewhere'; 'the action is hers, she has to do something for herself'; 'use their own common sense to avoid repetition'. Failure to do so was interpreted as proof either that women do not want to be helped or are incapable of being helped. As one officer said of victimized women, 'Eighty per cent never go to court and the remaining twenty per cent would complain if the sentences were stiffer.'

Mediation

The majority of officers considered that their main function in attending domestic disputes is to mediate between the parties. Some felt that their very presence is enough to cool the situation out: 'When you go into a domestic dispute you are dealing with years of history. All you can do is defuse the situation at the time, it's all you can hope to do.' When asked about the advice offered officers said they 'calm them down' or that they 'chat for 5 or 10 minutes' or 'sit and talk to both parties separately and then bring them back together again'.

Who is to be advised can present a problem to officers.

> How do you define the victim? Sometimes the woman sets him up and pushes him until he loses his bottle and then all she has to do is call the police and we'll arrest him. You can't tell. I always advise both parties.

The advice this officer offers is:

> Firstly I say wait until the morning. They are fully mature adults and they know what they want to do. The civil law and injunctions are open to them and if they feel that the situation is getting out of hand again, they ring us and we will come.

Some officers felt that if the situation is really heated then the couple should be separated at least until the next day when tempers have cooled and, in many cases, the man has sobered up. Officers advocate talking him out of the house and suggest that he should go and stay somewhere else, or if he will not leave then the woman and children should go to their family, neighbour's, or what the police described as a battered woman's hostel.

Civil Law Remedies and Marriage Counselling

When officers felt there was a problem that could not be dealt with in these ways, the advice offered is to see a solicitor and possibly obtain a non-molestation injunction, preferably with power of arrest. To seek help from the Marriage Guidance is another type of advice when officers decided there were obvious marital problems. Prosecution was advised less frequently than civil law or counselling remedies. The advice offered was said to depend upon the circumstances: 'If it is the first time it comes to police attention and it is not particularly vicious in my view, I place the emphasis on smoothing things over.' This officer went on to say, 'But I do mention options.' Another, a woman police constable, summed up the extent of police help as follows:

> The only help that the police can give is short term. It is a matter of referring to other agencies. I may offer advice to women or offer helping agencies, but if they want to make a complaint, I will act on that.

Defining 'Domestics' as Crime and the Use of Arrest

Arrest may be used as a threat or as an action. Officers said they warn the parties about what will happen if a complaint is made and that they can arrest them both. This is particularly likely to happen on repeat calls: 'If we keep being called back, we'll arrest you both.' The alternative threat to arrest used by officers is to withdraw help: 'We may slow down how quickly we come'; or 'We won't come anymore if you won't do anything.'

Almost every officer said they would arrest 'as a last resort'. They justified this decision because in the end the woman would not be prepared to be a witness in court and she would withdraw her complaint. Officers felt it had to be 'blatantly obvious that the man had done it', and that the police should always calm the situation down and 'not make a mountain out of a molehill'. However, all officers agreed it depended the severity of the crime. How severe a crime had to be to justify arrest varied between officers. Some said they 'only deal with a Section 47 upwards', as it is 'not in the public interest to prosecute for domestic violence'.[7]

Officers said they assess the immediate effect arrest will have in solving the problem: 'If he is actually beating her up there and then an arrest is an effective way of dealing with it. Not always but quite often.' The caveat expressed by this officer was that 'You've got to consider if you arrest someone are they going to remain under the same roof. If they will exacerbate the problem.' Officers fear making unlawful arrests and think no matter what they do, it does not help, but simply causes more tension. But another officer referred to the use of arrest as taking positive action:

> I was brought up in the old school. I like to take positive action and if that means locking him up, or both of them up, I will. I'm confident enough to do it. In the old days you took positive action and it was called positive policing.

Other reasons for arresting both the man and the woman reside in the allocation of blame and the relative difficulty of producing calm. For example:

> When we arrived there was a large scale argument in an extended form taking place. The father had a small baby and he was trying to strike his wife and she him. The whole family were in an excited mood. The woman had been beaten because she had been out with someone else. Arrested them both for breach of the peace as there was no complaint of assault and both were bound over to keep the peace by the court.

In this example the woman was seen to have brought the attack on herself and therefore she, too, was arrested.

A process sergeant, responsible for assessing the volume of evidence in the file prepared by an officer after an arrest is made, explained the procedure for processing a complaint through an example:

> If it's a domestic we have to look at whether there are any problems of the women withdrawing. For example, in a case where there was constant trouble between a woman and her boyfriend, he seriously assaulted her and she complained. The police got medical assistance for her and the boyfriend had to be arrested to get him away. No statements could be taken that night and when officers went back she didn't want to proceed. The charge was actual bodily harm. I sent the papers down for a breach of the peace in relation to the man's behaviour towards the police. This wasn't a one-off assault. I thought it would happen again. We have him bound over now to keep the peace so we have some control over him.

This example illustrates an action other than 'no-criming' (i.e. dropping the prosecution when the woman withdraws), but the charge is significantly reduced and not based on the man's behaviour towards the woman. In this instance, the man was thought to need controlling. It is not obvious how this conclusion was reached as injury and repetition of assault do not inevitably lead to this outcome. It is likely that there is a complex interaction between the actual behaviour of the man and the attitudes of particular police officers towards specific groups of people. Officers said that knowledge of a man's previous criminal behaviour and his attitude towards the police when they call are both relevant in defining men as in need of control, while general factors that involve value judgements about groups of people, such as racial groups and social classes, are probably relevant.

How Common is Arrest?

Officers varied considerably in their use of arrest in situations defined as domestic disputes. Although this is a frequent demand on officers, a small minority had never made an arrest while others had done so infrequently. 'I don't think I've ever arrested a man as a result of a domestic. The whole objective is to get in, separate them and cool them down' (constable with six years in the force). 'Few and far between' (constable with thirteen years in the force). 'Normally unless it is a violent assault it wouldn't be normal practice to arrest. The majority are not real assaults' (inspector with thirty-two years in the force). 'I try not to get involved. If there is a dispute of a minor nature I try to resolve it with the family because of my knowledge of the community' (constable with twenty years in the force). 'Nine out of ten times we pick up the pieces the next day' (woman officer with eleven years in the force). Several officers said that on odd occasions they have locked up women. Officers, however, were more likely to have made at least one arrest for an offence defined as arising out of a domestic dispute than for sexual assaults against women and children (Table 5.5).

Most officers had arrested a man at some time for violent crime in the home. Violence in the home is a frequent reason for police to be called to the scene; any officer on duty can find himself dealing with this type of call, and a range of minor charges can be made by any officer. Charges used range from being drunk and disorderly, to

Table 5.5 Officers who have never arrested a man for physical and sexual assaults against women and children

Violence in the home	7%
Child sexual assault	40%
Rape	42%
Other sexual offences	20%

Source: Compiled by the author

criminal damage when the house is in the woman's name only, to breach of the peace, as well as the more serious assault charges. If a warrant has already been issued for the arrest of the man on any charge, this too is used.

One officer gave an example of persistence on behalf of a woman that equals the best work of women's agencies and their solicitors. As with many cases of repeated violence, the man had legal access to the children. Rows developed on access visits which culminated in an attempted strangulation. As her neck was badly damaged he was charged with attempted murder and held in jail but against the advice of the police the judge granted bail. While there were bail restrictions limiting his access to her, the police believed he would return to her house and kill her. The officer then rearrested him the moment he was released for breaching an injunction and the Crown Court judge gave him four and one half month's custodial sentence. By the time this was up the other case reached court and he received five years.

More officers had arrested for violent crime in the home than for child sexual assault or rape. These differential percentages partly reflect the different organizational response to crimes deemed major when referral to the CID after the initial visit or complaint is compulsory. They may also reflect the frequency with which the police come across specific crimes and their attitudes when they do. For example, the view that rape is 'easy to allege and hard to prove' was widespread. In describing cases in which women complained of rape, a third were said by officers to be malicious allegations or were withdrawn by the woman. The majority were sceptical when talking generally about rape and seemed to feel that it is a weapon that women can always use against men rather than a serious threat to women's safety, although this view was not shared by a substantial minority.

Effect of Repeat Visits on Officers

Most officers said attending an incident between the same people on more than one occasion was likely to affect their attitudes, and to do so negatively (Table 5.6). This is because officers are likely to interpret repeat calls to be the result of women not taking their advice. Ignoring the advice given can lead officers to withdraw help.

> If it is a situation that has occurred before on a number of occasions and the victim has either made a complaint which was withdrawn or been advised to contact a solicitor and has not done so, I would consider that the victim is prepared to accept the situation as a normal part of their married life.

Another response is to feel that there is little one can do, particularly when the cause is seen to be drink, except remove the man or the woman until its effect wears off: 'If it's a regular you know the danger signs; one drunk, one sober, the look of fear.'

Table 5.6 Do repeated calls for assistance from women have an effect on police attitudes?

Yes	No	Not sure	Sometimes	NA
43 (78%)	2 (4%)	2 (4%)	1 (13%)	7 (13%) = 55

Source: Compiled by the author

Officers described their emotional responses to women who seek police assistance on more than one occasion as annoyance or exasperation or anger or being used.

> Sometimes annoying. Same advice every time and no notice is taken. Sometimes nice lady and trying hard. Husband might be sole cause of what is going on. Can never decide fully about this but can tell sometimes.

> You can become exasperated by keeping on telling them to go to an agency and they don't, but keep calling us back. I say, 'If you don't help yourself how can we help you?'

> Who is at fault? If it's 50/50, we've given advice earlier, and if they are not compatible it is up to them to separate. I

wouldn't deal with them quietly. I'd be looking to her to make a complaint and stick with it. It makes me angry.

You can get women who cause as much trouble as men. Women do use us. 'Will you see it through?' 'Yes.' Then they don't turn up for photographs the next day and a week later withdraw. We have arrested someone and process started. Women just using us. They know all along they are not going forward.

These emotional responses stem from a belief that women can control the situation if they want to. This last officer went on to say, 'Why do they get themselves in these messes? I can understand stranger attack, but a lot here are repetitive offences/call outs. Why doesn't she leave if she doesn't like it? It goes on over and over again.' He then related this to his own marriage: 'My marriage, no problems. I have a good'un. I can't understand why we should be expected to sort out their problems.'

Two women officers gave contrasting views. One responded exactly like male officers ('I have no patience with people who put up with it time and time again. I can't understand it.'), while the other gave a woman-centred response:

The first time you go you consider it fairly serious and then you go the next week and feel, 'What am I doing here?' But really in all the years there's only been one woman I've been exasperated with and in the end I took her up to a refuge and she left him.

Several officers made positive comments about repeat visits.

I am not going in as blind as the first time. If the reason for the call is related to the last time then people will recognise me as being there before. This develops trust between myself and the complainant and accused. I give the same options, but in stronger terms. I say, 'Can't tolerate this.'

However, this officer said he had returned to the same house twice only once in the last two years, which reflects the random way calls are allocated.

Only one officer said he tried to arrest when calls are repeated.

You check to see if it's a long standing thing and if it is you advise her to prosecute. I'll take him away at least for that night so she can make her mind up. If it's a one off, perhaps I will advise Marriage Guidance or something. I'll still arrest if I can.

Child Sexual Abuse

Child sexual abuse has implications for women in two ways. It can be an experience in a woman's own childhood and/or in that of her children's lives. When her children are being abused she may live under threat or experience violence herself. But less than half of the officers (40 per cent) were aware of a link between child sexual abuse and violence against the mother. Two officers explained that while evidence of violence against the mother may well come out during a case conference with the social service department, it does not always come to light during the normal course of police investigations. One officer felt that when there is child sexual abuse by the father, a 'high percentage of mothers are in physical fear of their husbands' and that the mother may 'have a tacit knowledge that something is going on but he uses violence to deter her from telling anyone'. But because the mode of work is to substantiate a particular offence, 'This is not developed in an investigation.' An example of where this happened was given by an officer:

> I dealt with a case of a husband buggering his wife. Began with the investigations of alleged assault on a 3-year-old boy in the family. The boy told the mother and the mother told a social worker. Then it came to light about sexual conduct with the wife. She says it is without consent and he denies this. There is a history of violence towards the mother. He is pleading not guilty and is on conditional bail not to go to the home. He denied indecent assault on the child so we could not bring a case against him.

Another officer working in a child abuse team explained,

> The law as it stands at the moment has been described in the media as the child molester's charter. The main reason for this is because the law requires the evidence of a young child to be corroborated. I have come across only one case where I had corroboration other than the admission of the defendant. This means that offenders go unpunished.

Another officer, a detective chief inspector, monitored the referrals of child sexual abuse in one month during the summer of 1987. There were 17 children and 234 hours of investigation, but cases involving only two of these children went to court, a typical outcome.

The implications of the problems experienced in prosecuting men for child sexual offences for women with children who have been abused are dire. For example, in one case monitored during the research a woman's child was taken into local authority care because the father, who did not live with the mother and child, sexually abused the girl on legally granted access visits when she was taken to his home. When the mother told social workers that she did not think she would be able to refuse entry to the abusing father who was out on bail, the child was removed from the home. The father was charged with rape and incest but because the girl was under seven years of age she could not give evidence. Ultimately the father was found not guilty for lack of suitable corroboration. In the civil law care proceedings hearsay evidence of rape and incest was admitted and acceptable as conclusive proof that the child was not safe in the care of her mother, with whom she had a close and loving relationship. The welfare agency concerned regarded this as a suitable outcome, as the man is free and the mother cannot guarantee the safety of her child. Cases like this illustrate the further harm that is done to women and children by state services that hold women responsible for the behaviour of men. In this instance it is not policing practices, but the legal process in which policing is embedded that determines the outcome.

The reality is that when interpersonal crime and its consequences are being adjudicated, men and women are routed through different legal systems. Administrative and civil law is for women and criminal law is for men. When charges are made of criminal offences, the rights of the accused receive much better protection through a fair trial in which the rules of evidence are much more demanding and all allegations in relation to the accused must be proved for conviction. Administrative law, in particular, offers women substandard protection in relation to the admissibility of hearsay evidence and the standard of proof required generally. While the usual justification is that a man may lose his liberty and therefore greater care must be taken, for a woman the loss of her children can be a life sentence equally as grueling.

113

Women are being advised to use the civil law remedy of injunctions to stop men from molesting them or entering their homes, along with divorce or separation and the regulation of access to children. These civil law remedies do not offer immediate relief even though in theory, and occasionally in practice, emergency injunctions can be obtained and served on the offending man. This routing of women through the civil law along with the lack of application of the criminal law to men, means that women must depend on professionals and agencies outside the criminal justice system for assistance, if the classic strategy of moving away does not work or is not seen as an option. The police, however, showed little awareness of this.

How Can Other Agencies Support the Police?

Officers were asked how other agencies could support the police. The most frequently mentioned agencies were the local authority's social service departments, particularly when children were involved. It was generally agreed that social workers are in a position similar to that of the police. They are all overworked and attend situations only when a crisis is under way; the best solution may not be forthcoming under these circumstances. It was lamented that the police and social workers only have contact when a crisis occurs and that there should be other forms of contact to discuss methods of working between the two agencies.

While the old antagonisms between social workers and the police have abated over recent years, possibly because of the necessary contact when children are abused, some officers still remain sceptical about social workers seeing them as 'too soft'. Officers who felt that the police are having to deal with situations that are outside the realm of policing and more in the sphere of social work would like to be free of this as soon as possible. But social work and probation services are not always seen as competent.

> I think as far as domestic situations are concerned it's a counselling role for people who have time to to it. It's not the police role. We don't have the time. But it's not for young people in Social Services or Probation. You need people with a bit of wool on their back. It needs somebody who can command respect in a position of authority with legal backing.

Counselling and advice giving are understood by this police officer in a way completely different from that of social workers. Other officers gave a more distanced explanation.

> The social service department looks at it from a different angle. This is not a bad thing, but we do frown on some of their methods and decisions. Police want to take steps quicker than other agencies and this stems from being there when it is happening.

Several officers mentioned the need for more refuge provision so that women can get away until the situation calms down, 'even if it is only for a night'. Victim support schemes, sponsored by the Home Office and receiving referrals from the local police, are firmly established in West Yorkshire as elsewhere. But only one officer mentioned this scheme, because 'Only burglaries are notified to them, we never send them into domestic situations', although referrals of rape victims were to begin in West Yorkshire during 1987.

A frequently expressed view was that there is not much an agency can do if the woman does not intend to take any advice.

> No use bringing in independent agencies. Majority of wives don't want to know. If you brought in welfare or social agencies they'd say, 'Get on your bike.' You might aggravate the situation. If you kept in touch like that you'd be accepting guardianship of them.

Can the Police Respond More Effectively to Violence in the Home?

Over one-half of officers thought they could not be more effective when attending domestic disputes, while a third thought they could be. The changes needed to become more effective were located in law and court procedures, but not their own behaviour, except for two officers who mentioned the need for more training in talking to people and information on suitable advice to offer. One justification for complacency arises from having developed a particular technique for handling violence between men and women known to each other, while another is the knowledge that a senior officer can be asked for advice if necessary.

Most officers felt they were doing everything that they could. As one officer put it, 'I wouldn't be doing my job right if I didn't do everything possible first time.' However, a woman constable summed it up with her immediate response, 'I'd like to think that if I was being beaten up someone would come and rescue me.' She went on, 'But it's very difficult to know what people want.' Officers felt that 'It's difficult to visualise what more a police officer can do.'

Another officer said,

I wouldn't know what else to suggest. We shouldn't spend hours and hours with couples who fall out. We have other things to do. That also has an effect when we attend if we've got other jobs to do. If you have the time you spend it, if the circumstances warrant it.

A chief inspector said that he felt there are no effective measures that can be used by officers.

I could issue instructions to officers at this station to treat each case of domestic violence seriously and remove the male. I won't do that because I may be instructing officers to make an unlawful arrest on some occasions. I would give instructions to treat the whole area as a serious matter, but I hope they do it anyway. Nothing effective can be done.

A detective constable reiterated cynical feelings:

Better not to arrest as there will be eight hours of paperwork. We do 80% paperwork now and it doesn't help the wife or the child. Bind over to keep the peace might help. Fines are counter-productive. No matter what we do it doesn't help but causes tension.

One officer suggested that 'a back-up service would be beneficial in very nasty or ongoing situations'. The Major Crimes Support Unit, staffed by women officers, was referred to as a way of offering a specialist service and its expansion would be welcomed by some ('Should be advertised more including where women police unit can be contacted. There should be a number to ring for sexual assault and domestic violence.'). This was the only internal organizational suggestion made by officers.

The Views of Welfare Agencies on the Police

The responses of women-centred welfare agencies take a very different line about what women want, how will they respond, and what constitutes relevant policing. They also adopt a very different approach to women seeking help. Interviews were conducted with 44 women and 4 men staff at 48 agencies in West Yorkshire that women are likely to turn to in times of crisis. The agencies offered one or more of three services; advice, counselling, and accommodation, and consisted of community centres, advice centres, Rape Crisis, Women's Aid Refuges, housing services, marriage guidance, telephone help lines, victim support schemes, and included agencies specifically for Asian and black people generally.

Only a minority of agency workers thought the police were helpful to victims of violence. The majority thought they were not. For example one advice worker said, 'There is usually a big resistance to going to the police.' And another said, 'I have heard of cases where women say the police won't interfere in domestic disputes.' The views of agency workers on the response of the police to requests for help from women corresponded closely with those of the interviewed police officers. The considerable differences between their views arose out of their understanding of the needs and wishes of women and what constitutes effective help. Two Women's Aid workers who had suffered violence in previous relationships explained how these differences are rooted in gendered life experiences. 'Men never experience that kind of terror, so how can policemen understand how women in violent situations actually feel?'

But the police response is not uniform. Both the welfare agency personnel and the police agree that they are more likely to respond in some situations than in others. Violence against women in the home was seen as the crime least likely to elicit a positive police response. Agency workers agreed with the police that the presence of children makes a difference, but not always in the desired way. 'They'll remove kids to a place of safety, but not women.' A Women's Aid worker explained that policemen (and she emphasised 'men') have a vested interest in not treating violence in the home as a serious crime. 'We've had two policemen's wives in here recently. If a policeman is battering his wife about and a woman goes to him for help, well I mean!' A woman's counsellor said,

'Men don't want to look at their own violence. They look upon it as "provoked". They have sex and violence all mixed up.'

Age is another important variable. Not only was the involvement of children as victims said to evoke immediate police intervention, but also crimes against the elderly were said to elicit more response. The very young and the very old are treated differently because the police believe that 'Youngsters [i.e. young people] can look after themselves.' Age is also the personal quality of the police officer said to make all the difference: 'Young policemen don't know what domestic violence is, and when you ring that's who they send. Older policemen have more knowledge of what goes on.' Being married with children was seen as facilitating understanding as well as a further reason for not responding positively to women in need.

Agency workers agreed with the police that visible signs of injury also make a difference, as do court injunctions with the power of arrest, threats and violence against police officers who attend the scene, and a decision by officers that the woman does not deserve to be treated violently. If a man is already known to the police, perhaps even wanted for another crime, agency workers thought the police are more likely to take an interest in any crime he may be committing, including those against the woman he is involved with. The crimes of violence police are most likely to respond positively to are those that involve strangers to the woman.

In the view of agency personnel the primary reason women report to the police is to receive safety and protection, 'to receive help and in the hope that something will be done about the situation'. Women are said to report out of fear and as a last resort when unable to deal with the situation. Retribution was offered as an explanation ('to see the culprit punished'). Another reason for women reporting to the police was because they think they should and to protect other women. The police can be seen by women as the only form of intervention available. One view of agency workers was that women are more likely to report child abuse than crime against themselves. Anger and a hope that reporting will act as a deterrent to future assault were also mentioned.

Agency workers thought the major reasons women do not report violence against themselves relate to their views of the police. Women may worry that they will be blamed for the crime or will not be taken seriously, or the police will be reluctant to believe them. The police response may be unhelpful, unsympathetic, lack interest in the woman's situation, or be incompetent ('a waste of time to report as no action will be taken; nothing will be done'). Women were said to be frightened of the police, will not report rape, and their own experiences and those of other women were said 'to put women off reporting'. A perception of the police force as male was said to be a reason for not reporting ('Women do not want to deal with male police.').

Another reason for not reporting was said to be women's views on the unhelpfulness of courts. The type of crime can affect women in another way, especially when suffering abuse in the home. Agency workers said women are too frightened to report as more, and perhaps even worse, violence will be the result ('Fear keeps women quiet.'). Loyalty and protectiveness to their partners was another reason given. Women also have views on proper ways of living ('Violence can be an accepted part of daily life.'). Women also were said to turn the blame on themselves.

Improving the Responses of Police Officers to Women

Agency workers made many suggestions for how the police could be more helpful to women. These can be grouped into three major areas; improving communications between the police and women in the community, changing attitudes, knowledge, and behaviour of the police and capitalizing on present positive aspects of their own organizational structure and practices.

Improving communications included believing what women tell them, reducing their bias towards the man, 'In any situation they will be on the man's side, thinking she must have done something.' Officers were said to need to learn to listen and be trained in issues affecting women and about women's position in society. The aim of improving communication was to enable police officers to 'treat women with respect'. This means finding ways of behaving that do not 'treat women complainants as criminals' or make women feel guilty by the way officers question their version of events, and by officers 'stopping trying to get out of doing the man'. Improved communication would give victimized women information on police progress in their investigations and actions. Agency workers would like the police to have good relationships with people, to be approachable, friendly, and sympathetic.

Attitudes, knowledge, and behaviour of the police need to

change in order for communication with women in the community to improve. One attitude said to be in need of change is the division officers make between respectable and 'unrespectable' women: 'If only there was some feeling that the police protected us and not just "virtuous women".' 'The old stereotype of women, that they must be chaste, only go out with a man otherwise stay at home, be demure, polite, not angry, is outmoded. You have to behave like that to get help.' Views of certain crimes and women generally were other attitudes in need of change: 'Get rid of biased views on rape, that rape is a joke. Accept that when a woman says no, she means no, and not yes.' 'They could stop going round saying, "It's a domestic dispute!" It makes my blood boil!'

Knowledge of local agencies that help women, in particular Women's Aid refuges, was seen as important, as was a better knowledge of the law in situations affecting women. The behaviour changes needed are to 'treat violence in the home as a crime' and to give out information about other agencies, 'tell women that refuges exist', and to offer more practical help, for example, in getting a woman's belongings and children out of a house. Other changes needed are to 'respond more quickly to calls from women', 'keep in touch when someone is injured', and 'have a more alive presence on the streets at night'.

The most frequently made suggestion for capitalizing on present positive aspects of police organization and practice in West Yorkshire is to appoint more women police officers. Women officers were described as more sympathetic and helpful than policemen. A second reason for making this recommendation is that women find it easier to talk to other women. While the Sex Discrimination Act applies, at least in theory, to the appointment and promotion of women police officers at the present time, West Yorkshire employs 91 per cent male and 9 per cent female officers. The percentage of women officers employed throughout Britain ranges from 7 to 13 per cent. Regarding women's position within the force hierarchy, the highest-ranking officer in West Yorkshire is at superintendent level, the rank needed for taking charge of a station in a subdivision. West Yorkshire has one superintendent, several inspectors who will be in charge of smaller units of officers and the workload within a station, and 17 sergeants out of over 500, the first rank after constable. This pattern is replicated throughout Britain and does not compare unfavourably with any of the other

43 force areas in England and Wales (Jones 1986).

One agency worker thought the extent of change needed is so great that we are discussing a revolution: 'When they start putting people above property, and the poor on the same level as the rich, and consider women to be equal to men, then the police will be helpful to women.' The revolution being called for is in inter-personal relationships. The standard being called for is that of any high-quality professional intervention. Good police officers put themselves out to help, respect the women who turn to them, take time, for example in taking statements, and show through their behaviour that they understand what has happened from the woman's point of view. If the police could make these changes in attitude, behaviour, and organization of their service, then they would be more helpful, not only to the woman herself, but also to agencies working on her behalf.

These views contrast sharply with those of police officers of all grades in West Yorkshire. While this research offers more detail on responses to women complainants, these results seem to be in line with other work on the police (Chambers and Millar 1983; Chatterton 1983; Smith and Gray 1983; Reiner 1985). The changes in focus in policing proposed by women's welfare agencies are major and involve new policies and procedures in a number of areas including the internal status system, the orientation to training and training priorities, job priorities, skill assessment, promotion assessment, and operational organization, and in police culture.

We also suggest it involves change in the proportion of women to men in the police and the criminal justice system generally. Women need to be in managerial positions as well as in positions where they respond to the calls for assistance from women because, while women are supervised and controlled by men, it will be difficult for women officers to behave differently from their male colleagues. The macho image of police officers and of policing cannot be dis-mantled solely by the introduction of more women in basic grades. As Chapter 2 demonstrates the women who gain acceptance within the force are those who are more accepting of male authority and behaviour. This makes the number of women relative to men in the various grades particularly important.

Men have greater difficulty in understanding these issues because by and large they are not in danger from the opposite sex whether known or unknown to them. Women police officers share with women generally the same structuring of gendered social relations. But as long as women are recruited in small numbers, are isolated from each other within the organization of policing, and are disproportionately in the lower ranks, the masculine culture and practices of the police can more easily be maintained. With the best will in the world change cannot occur if the voices of women are silenced. Women in research, in providing helping services to women, and in the police all have important roles to play in creating a new understanding and practice. But until the proportion of female to male officers is altered it is unreasonable to expect the gendered nature of women's experience to have more than a very limited impact on the delivery of policing services to women in the community.

Controlling Men

Many officers are at a loss to think of how safety for women can be improved. As one officer put it, 'Boils down to being biological. Women are weaker than men; generally men don't fear women.' Officers who believe human relations are based in biology view social change as unrealistic ('You can't change human nature.'). Others who see society as constructed by the people who make it up focus on the need to make violence against women socially unacceptable. But how is this to be done?

It is unhelpful to simply portray women as the most vulnerable and fearful in the population, as there is a sense in which this further victimizes women. Amazingly, women survive against all odds. To stop victimizing women, attention must be turned on men, in the community *and* in the police. The emphasis on the real problem, how men are to be controlled, rather than how to make women safer, will make the struggle for women less victimizing. An emphasis on men as offenders and law enforcers also gives a positive focus to the discussion on needed changes.

But this discussion is only possible because women themselves as individuals and in groups are demanding change in policing practice. The experience gained through helping women that is concentrated in women's welfare agencies, and in women in welfare agencies, undoubtedly will continue to be the basis for a challenge to existing police policy and practices in West Yorkshire as elsewhere in Britain. This remains the most hopeful sign on the horizon.

Notes

1 This chapter does not discuss police attacks on women, although this is a major issue for certain groups of women in Britain. In particular lesbians continue to be harassed by the police at lesbian bars, discos, conferences, and demonstrations, that is anywhere there is an obvious lesbian presence. The political activity around Parliamentary action in 1988 to limit local government funding of welfare and other activities for the lesbian and gay communities (Clause 28 Local Government Bill) provides the most recent example. Police attacks on women who demonstrate about their social conditions have a long history (for example the suffrage campaigns; Morrell 1980). More recently among political demonstrations by feminists that have led to arrest and other harassment, are those organized by Women Against Violence Against Women, Reclaim the Night, Greenham Women's Peace Group, and various feminist conferences. Prostitutes, another group of 'unrespectable' women, also experience problems with the police and this, too, has a past. Particularly well known is the agitation around the Contagious Diseases Acts. As discussed in the introduction to this volume, black women also experience coercive policing.

2 The research into women. violence, and crime prevention was funded by the West Yorkshire County Council in 1985. This two-year project obtained the cooperation of the West Yorkshire Police, enabling interviews to be held with officers (see Note 4). Women in the community were randomly sampled in the areas where the interviews with police officers took place, and interviews were held in the county with lawyers and welfare agency personnel. A few court cases were attended and three daily papers serving West Yorkshire were monitored over a year for their reporting of violence against women. The aim of the project was to research into why women do not report crimes of violence to the police and what happens when they do. The final report contains the experiences and views of respondents with recommendations for changes in police policy and practice, the law, and its administration, and improvements in and for supporting welfare services. The complete report and the summary version may be obtained from the West Yorkshire Police Authority, County Hall, Wakefield, West Yorkshire, England (Jalna Hanmer and Sheila Saunders, *Women, Violence and Crime Prevention*, November 1987).

3 While violence against women was recognized in earlier centuries in Britain, it was during the latter part of the nineteenth century that understanding about violence against women was used successfully to secure improvements in the civil status of women (Cobbe 1878). Legislation resulted in important changes in matrimonial and family

law, and criminal law changes included the raising of the age of consent and legislation on incest in 1908. In the United States Elizabeth Pleck has charted 300 years of American social policy against family violence from colonial times to the present (1987).

4 Effective coordination between the police and social workers is not happening everywhere, however. An example of exceptionally poor relations is provided by Middlesbrough, where in 1988 a national inquiry took place into the handling of child sexual abuse cases by hospital pediatricians and social service workers involved. In this instance social workers and pediatricians were seen as too likely to diagnose child sexual abuse and to remove children from their parents' care by the police and their medical staff, the police surgeons.

5 Four children were sexually and physically tortured to death by Ian Brady and Mira Hindley. Their bodies were buried on Saddleworth Moor, a countryside area of outstanding natural beauty in the Pennine Hills, overlooked by part of the area in which the interviews with police officers and women took place. Only two bodies were recovered in the 1960s, and in 1986 the Greater Manchester police began digging again for the missing children to widespread publicity. This case illustrates that living in the country is no protection from the knowledge of crime in one's own area, however remote. As one woman interviewed said, 'I can never look at the moor without thinking of those murdered children.'

6 A randomly drawn sample of 55 uniformed and non-uniformed officers stratified by rank and type of work currently being undertaken were interviewed in four of the twenty-six policing subdivisions in West Yorkshire: one urban, one rural, and two with higher than average Asian populations. Officers were asked for their views on violence and on policing in relation to violence against women in the home, child sexual abuse, rape and sexual assault, other physical and sexual violent crimes; how other agencies can help them with their work; and how safety and protection for women can be improved. They were also asked about personal and work experience, including job satisfaction.

7 The Offences Against the Person Act of 1861, amended by the Criminal Justice Act of 1925 and the Criminal Law Act of 1977, is the most frequently used legislation for assault and wounding offences. The least serious offence under this Act is common assault. The next most serious offence is Section 47, actual bodily harm (ABH), which can be an injury from a slight bruise to quite severe injury. Different sections of the Act are used for wounding without intent to harm another person and, where intent is present, the charge is grievous bodily harm (GBH).

Chapter six

Policing Woman Beating in the Netherlands

Olga J. Zoomer

How far is he allowed to go? What is the end? That is what I wonder. Yes, I really wonder what must happen before they can detain such a person. Aren't these all crimes he has committed?

A woman

The question is, what does the judicial system do with such an assault? I don't know. I think often dismiss it. Because of lack of evidence. And what have you been doing then? A lot of work in vain, yes, a lot of work in vain. Then shouldn't you say, wouldn't it have been better to talk about it, and maybe enlist another agency who takes it over? Maybe you achieve more that way. But then we don't have time for it. There is not enough manpower for it and then we're moving into the domain of social work and that's not what we're for.

A police officer

We're fed up with hearing that several organizations 'find it so good that there are refuges' and use this as an excuse to do nothing.

Blijf van m'n Lijf (women's refuge)

Introduction

Over the last fifteen years in the Netherlands, as in many other countries, the police have been criticised over the way they deal with instances of woman beating. Women who turned to the police for assistance felt that they were not taken seriously and that they were put off by the police while their abusive husband or lover got away with it undisturbed. They began to demand a less reluctant attitude of the police.

For the police, however, violence against women, especially in the home, was never a matter of great concern. Along with the general public they thought that it does not happen often and that, when it does, it is a private matter anyway. However, the first refuge for battered women, which opened in 1974, filled up so quickly (as did the twenty other refuges that have opened since then) that it became increasingly clear that woman beating is not the problem of a few couples whose bad relationship had got a bit out of hand, but rather a large-scale phenomenon affecting many women's lives. In the process of redefining this violence as a social problem and a matter of political concern, feminists reproached not only the police for apathy and inappropriate reactions, but also the criminal justice system, the traditional helping professions, and the government. This resulted in a growing awareness in these bodies of the seriousness of the problem and of their own responsibility to take action.

The Government's Response to Violence Against Women

The first move toward an integrated government policy on violence against women was a study conference on this topic — a meeting of feminists, researchers, politicians, and policymakers that took place in June 1982 (Acker and Rawie 1982). In 1983 and 1984 this was followed by government papers in which a policy to fight (sexual) violence against women and girls was unfolded. The recognition of the relationship between violence against women and the position of women in society led the government to adopt a two-pronged approach in which measures were to be taken to improve and support emancipation of women as well as to offer protection from male violence. A stronger position of victims of violence was sought through legislation and through better police performance combined with a more active prosecution policy. The use of civil law procedures (for instance to obtain an injunction against a violent man) was also put forward in this respect. Further, the need for adequate services was emphasised. In particular when the violence happened in the home, provision of services was also seen as an alternative to criminal proceedings. In fact, where it came to practical implications a distinction was maintained between 'public' and 'private' violence. Public violence was to be treated as a criminal offence, but in cases of private violence concern for the right to privacy prevented the government from taking the same clear stance. Notwithstanding this, the police were assigned an important role, whether as law enforcers or as providers of social services. In addition to the outline of policy the government stressed the need for more research. Since then several studies on male violence against women have been granted.

What else has been achieved? Although the intentions to improve the position of women in society — and especially their financial independence — seemed promising, the government has not shown much determination in accomplishing their stated objectives. In fact, over the last few years several measures have been taken ('justified' by the need to cut government expenses) which could achieve only the opposite effects. Measures that affected police and public prosecutors' practices concerned in the first place sexual assaults. In 1986 guidelines were issued on how to deal with victims of rape and indecent assault (a committee to develop these guidelines was already established in 1979 by the ministers of Home Affairs and Justice). At the same time comparable guidelines were issued concerning victims of other serious (violent) crimes, but no special attention was paid to woman beating. Police practice in these cases has probably been more influenced by direct contacts with the refuge movement (Blijf van m'n Lijf) and by a national campaign in October 1984, during which attention was once more drawn to the need for more adequate police performance in instances of battering.

It should be noted that within the feminist movement this appeal to the police is subject to debate. It has been argued that women can expect nothing from the police or from a criminal approach generally, and that the alternative of civil lawsuits against abusive (ex-)partners is a better means to protect and empower women (Hes 1984–5). Indeed, an increasing number of women appear to find their way into the civil courts.

The Police and Woman Beating

In spite of the attention the police obviously received, not much systematic research has been carried out in the Netherlands on policing woman beating. Nevertheless, the data that exist show that in this country not many arrests are made or formal statements taken in cases of domestic violence against women (Blijf van m'n Lijf 1978; Beyer et al. 1983; Van Lierop 1985; Wöstmann and Van de Bunt 1987). According to the Penal Code of 1886, beating one's wife (or husband, parent, or child) constitutes an aggravated circumstance within the context of assaults in general, but this does not imply that it is practically considered to be a criminal offence. Unfortunately, where the police (and the criminal justice system) do not see reasons to enforce the law in these cases, it does not necessarily mean that assistance is provided in another way. Punch (1979: 139) observed, in a study on the Amsterdam police and their peace-keeping practices in interpersonal disputes, such as 'marital problems': 'These often unedifying private squabbles were rarely seen as social problems to be solved but more likely as inevitable frictions requiring a ritualised intervention, a few stereotyped phrases, and an avoidance of deep involvement.'

Yet, in recent years this practice of non-involvement has changed somewhat and woman beating seems to be treated more as a social problem deserving police assistance, while improvements in police performance are sought through better use of social skills. Although the criticism that the police 'do nothing' may have had some influence, this should be seen mainly as part of a general trend to give more substance to the social welfare aspect of the police task. Since the end of the 1960s there has been a growing interest in the social role of the police. This did not in fact mean the introduction of something new, since the police had always spent considerable time on keeping the peace and providing services (Punch 1975). They only preferred to think of themselves as crime-fighters and to consider law enforcement as their primary task, even though this represents only a small portion of their daily work (Van der Zee-Nefkens 1975; Junger-Tas 1977). In the Police Act of 1957 it is explicitly formulated as a police duty 'to give help to those who are in need of it', just as it is to enforce the law and to maintain public order. So, to bring out the social task of the police, many police departments installed specialized (units of) community police officers. The presence of community police no doubt has advantages: as peace keepers and problem solvers these officers assume different attitudes towards those duties that many others think are second rate or 'not real' police work. However, a negative effect could be that these other officers feel encouraged in a hands-off approach to social problems and leave this so-called soft domain to their colleagues, who are often referred to as the 'wet nurses'.

In the same period police training underwent a change. The training at the time for lower-rank officers was basically a one-year course in legal knowledge. Not much time was spent acquiring insight into social problems and developing skills to deal with them as a police officer. Thus, it could hardly be seen as an adequate preparation for the realities of police work. The prevailing wisdom was that these skills can only be learned on the job and that training cannot replace experience. It is therefore not surprising that the social role of the police was not always performed so terribly well. However, with the recognition of the importance of this part of police work, the need to adapt the training was also recognized. As for 'family crises', it was suggested (Vredeveld 1978) that the police could do a better job if they were trained in the use of verbal crisis intervention techniques, according to the U.S. example described by Bard (1974).

In 1983 a revised training program for lower-rank police officers was introduced. Although legal knowledge is still by far the most important, in the current course more attention is paid to problems of present-day society that the police may encounter, and the use of skills to deal with them, such as conflict management and dispute settlement techniques. Woman beating is treated in this context, that is, as a dispute. Although this can obviously lead to better police performance, it is questionable whether mediation and negotiation techniques, implying the avoidance of arrest, are appropriate in situations where violence has been used. In fact, according to Loving (1980), the crisis intervention techniques that Bard taught the police to use in domestic disputes were never meant to be used in situations involving violence. Yet, in these situations the police provide referrals to other agencies to avoid taking proper law enforcement actions (Bell 1984). Both Bell and Loving advocated that the police should act sooner to arrest the offender. In the same way Brown (1984) pointed to the need for reforming the terminology usually employed in these cases. Indeed, whereas the police use euphemisms such as 'domestic problems' or 'conjugal discord' to register incidents of actual assaults in the station diary, a greater emphasis on the criminal aspect of this violence is suggested. In short, woman beating should be taken as a crime.

As noted above, this approach is not popular in police circles and the criminal justice system, where the Penal Law is still seen as the last resort in these cases. Probably to justify the current practice of avoiding legal action, doubts have been expressed about the effectiveness of arrest and punishment. Although effectiveness is usually not a criterion for the decision whether or not to inflict punishment, it is argued that criminal prosecution will not help in cases of woman beating, if not make things worse, and therefore it would not be in the interest of the battered women themselves. A reserved attitude is preferred, it is said, to allow the parties to solve their own problems. Of course, we should not disapprove of the fact that officials in the criminal justice system and the police show interest in the effects of their proceedings, but the very fact that the police are called should probably be seen as an indication that the parties apparently could *not* solve their own problem. Moreover, a study on the prosecution policy of the Public Prosecutor in the Netherlands revealed that the reservations about entering 'family disputes' were at least somewhat selective, in that cases concerning violence in the family were more often dismissed when a woman, rather than a man, was the victim (the study included only male offenders). This could not be explained by a difference in serverity of the injury (Van Straelen 1978; Zoomer 1979).

Finally, much less is known about the effectiveness of a more assertive approach by the police (and of a possible prosecution) than is suggested by the eagerness with which it is claimed that 'it does not help'. U.S. research in fact suggests that the contrary might be true (Sherman and Berk 1984a; Berk and Newton 1985). As yet there are no indications that a practice of calming down the situation and mediation is more fruitful.

It is not uncommon when the police detect a crime that they would rather keep the peace than enforce the law. In many cases this meets with no objections. However, when a specific category of violent crimes is systematically overlooked, it is time to start worrying about this selective use of police discretion. This holds true even more since police training appears to emphasise the use of social skills rather then coercive power as a general approach in these cases. Even when it is taken into account that in certain situations the possibilities to take legal action are limited and a non-criminal approach is justified, it is questionable whether this implicit policy of decriminalization is appropriate, given the fact that woman beating often constitutes serious violent crime. It is clear that a correct assessment of such incidents is important for both the sense of justice and the safety of the women who call the police for assistance.

A Study of Policing Woman Beating

The main reason for initiating a study on policing woman beating was the obvious dissatisfaction with police services in these cases. The purpose was to find better ways for the police to assist and protect women who are abused by their male partner. The study, which was financed by the Ministry of Home Affairs, was designed to get answers to the following questions: How frequently are the police in this country called on to intervene in incidents involving woman beating, what do they actually do in these cases, and what are the rationales underlying their actions (or lack of actions)? Is advocating more arrests in accordance with what battered women actually want?

The study was carried out in Eindhoven, the fifth largest town in the Netherlands, with a population of nearly 200,000. The police force in this town is about 650 strong, which at the time of the project included fewer than twenty policewomen. The workforce is divided into a CID and a uniformed branch consisting of general patrol officers and a smaller number of community policemen.

Eindhoven has one of the Netherlands' twenty-one feminist-oriented refuges for battered women and their children (a Blijf van m'n Lijf-huis), staffed by women volunteers. There are two more institutions to which battered women can turn. These are run by professional workers, and are meant for women who need a place to stay also for reasons other than being abused. The relationship between the Blijf van m'n Lijf refuge and the police is a little uneasy. Since late 1984 there have been several meetings in which the police were informed about the background circumstances of woman beating, and police practices were discussed. It is difficult

131

to say whether these meetings actually improved mutual under-standing. During the project several police officers said that they did not like dealing with the refuge. They complained that the women staying there get brainwashed and are set against men (!) and, probably most important, they sensed a hostile attitude towards the police. Some had doubts about the self-help approach employed in the refuge. For that reason, one of the other institu-tions was quite popular among policemen. It should be said, however, that not all officers had such strong (negative) feelings towards the refuge, and maintained a functional, businesslike contact.

The project consisted of an analysis of the police files regarding incidents of woman beating and related 'domestic problems' (to use a police term), observations of police actions in these cases, and interviews. The interviews were held with forty-seven patrol officers, community policemen, and detectives who had recently dealt with an instance of woman beating (or a 'domestic dispute'), as well as with twenty-two women who had recently applied to the police for assistance or to press charges.

The incidents under study included assaults and threats of physical violence by (ex-)husbands or (ex-)lovers. Incidents that were registered in the station diary as disputes, domestic problems, and so on were included as well, as far as they involved intimida-tion by the man. These could be a quarrel in which 'the man became aggressive', or cases where a man smashed furniture, or where he kept coming back to harass the woman or disturb the domestic peace after their relationship had finished. These incidents were included because their description in the files was often not very explicit and in many cases it was uncertain whether or not a 'dispute' was actually limited to a verbal disagreement. Sometimes it became clear from other sources that in such a case violence had been used. During the project it happened for instance that incidents initially registered as 'domestic problems' were re-qualified as 'attempted manslaughter' after the woman brought an official complaint. But above all, by including these nondescript 'disputes' and 'problems', it was possible to gain a better insight into the history of serial incidents and police responses when the police had been called in to the same couple more than once. For that could be for a battering one time, but for verbal threats or a broken window the next time.

Policing Woman Beating — the Police Files

The results of a pilot study, which comprised an analysis of police files, disposed of the misconception widespread among the police that they seldom have to deal with woman beating (Zoomer 1984). In a period of three months more than 260 cases of physical violence and related 'domestic problems' were registered, that is twenty-two per week, of which at least five per week certainly involved actual assaults. Since the police don't make a note in the station diary of every incident they come across, the real number of police responses in these cases may well have been higher. In all these cases only thirteen arrests were made and nine formal statements taken.

A year later, in 1985, the police files were analysed again, this time covering a period of six months (Zoomer and Vossen 1986). Although the total number of incidents under consideration was small compared with the year before (341), the number of incidents in which physical violence was used (according to the station diary) was about the same. It is remarkable that ex-husbands and ex-lovers were responsible for half the total number of these events.

When the police were called to the scene they were most likely to either calm down the two parties or mediate or do nothing at all (or at least not something that was considered worth a mention in the station diary). This could mean that the man had left before the police arrived or that the situation had already quieted down. Yet the number of formal statements taken and the number of arrests (forty-nine and forty-eight respectively) were considerably higher than in the previous year. Although we do not know whether the incidents concerned were also more serious, this is more likely the result of a different approach by the police and a greater willingness of the women to press charges. The local refuge workers probably played some part in this. They have insisted that police officers should point out more often to the women the possibility of making a formal complaint. For many women this may have been a totally new option.

The arrest of the man is not necessarily the first step in criminal proceedings. If the situation is such that the police feel justified in taking a man to the police station, they often actually do it only after the woman had promised that she will sign a formal statement. If she does not want, or dare, to do this the police may leave the man behind with the woman, but they could also arrest him 'for his own or another person's safety'.[1] This latter tactic was used to let the man cool off or sober up, and it could happen in a threatening situation, where difficulties were likely to start again, or when the man, being drunk, could not be made to promise that he would 'keep it down' for the rest of the night. In these cases arrest was used as a last resort to restore the peace, and the man was usually released the next morning without being charged. He would instead have a talk with an officer of the community police unit. When community police officers got involved it was usually in a follow-up stage, after colleagues of the general patrol branch or the CID had dealt with the case first. They would talk to the woman, or to both parties, and give advice or information. However, according to the station diary, they did not come into action very often. This is somewhat surprising, considering the fact that in 40 per cent of the cases in the study the police had previously been called to the scene for the same reason.

It has been argued, and there are data to support this (Steinmetz and Van Andel 1985), that the police treat woman beating in much the same way as fights or conflicts between other members of the family, neighbours, or friends. In general, the arrest rate in interpersonal disputes is low (Smith and Klein 1984). In our study a comparison was made with the way the police deal with interpersonal disputes and assaults involving people other than spouses and lovers (incidents where instrumental violence was used were not included). In these cases it also appeared that the police mostly aimed to restore the peace without taking legal action. However, differences showed in more serious cases, where this approach apparently was not deemed appropriate and some coercion had to be used. Then, in instances of woman beating the offender was more often told to leave the premises whereas in other instances of assault the offender was more often arrested.

Although the police files showed that not many arrests were made *and* that social work remained somewhat underutilized, it cannot be held that the police always 'do nothing'. They do all kinds of things: send the man away, bring a woman to a friend or a refuge, or give the couple (or the woman) advice. What is lacking, however, is a well-considered policy. For, while the police are strikingly unanimous in avoiding the use of coercive power, in their peace-keeping activities they can, unhampered by any guidelines or control, put their private views into practice. This can be especially painful when the police have to go to the same address more than once, for it can happen that on one occasion the officers advise to press charges and get a divorce, while on the next occasion other officers warn against doing so and advise 'to give it one more try'.

Policing Woman Beating — the Officers' Views

According to the police there are several reasons for their reluctance to instigate legal actions (Loving 1980; Davis 1981). They have argued that women would be worse off if they did, or that women are unreliable complaintants. They also find a justification for avoiding an arrest or discouraging a woman from making a formal complaint in the fact that these cases are often dismissed by the prosecutor. In the Netherlands 'domestics' do not have a reputation of being dangerous for the police, and concern for the police officers' own safety is not mentioned in this respect.

Police assumptions about domestic violence are not necessarily supported by the facts. As mentioned before, it is not so certain that arrest (or generally a more assertive approach) will only have negative effects, and the willingness of the women to press charges might be greater than the police think (Oppenlander 1982). In fact, by anticipating a presumed lack of cooperation from women, the police are likely to actually *cause* this lack of cooperation. The expectation that legal actions taken by the police often do not result in prosecution and conviction is probably realistic, but less because women want the case to be dropped than is generally assumed (Wasoff 1982).

However, it is not only the concern for the women's interests or for police efficiency that is important, but also the views that police officers hold about woman beating, and their attitudes towards woman beating as police work (Walters 1981; Edwards 1986a). The basic reason for police unwillingness to actively intervene in these cases should be sought in the belief (which is not limited to police circles) that violent 'conflicts' are a more or less natural outgrowth of marital relations and that they are therefore acceptable to a certain extent. It is argued that the tradition of wife beating as a legitimate means of control for a husband is still mirrored in the attitudes of police officers who don't disapprove, or even approve, of it, as long as certain limits are not exceeded. Thus, police intervention is not seen as appropriate as long as the injury is not too serious and the public order is not disturbed (Field and Field 1973; Straus 1977–8; Dobash and Dobash 1980).

Police views of woman beating

First impressions suggested that the police officers in the present study were different from the ones Dobash and Dobash, and others, had in mind. They generally stated that beating one's wife is not justified and many of them expressed disdain for men who use violence against their female partner. However, they also often thought that it was understandable in certain situations. What, then, did they consider woman beating? From their answers to this question it appeared that a distinction could be made between two categories of incidents: 'just arguments' and 'real woman beating', respectively. An incident was considered 'real woman beating' when a woman was severely beaten, or terrorized mentally and physically by her husband or lover over some time. A few times sexual abuse was also mentioned. Several police officers referred to the position of the woman in these relationships, where they saw the man as the boss who apparently needs to demonstrate his physical power now and then to keep his wife in her place when she challenges his authority. One such situation was described by a policewoman as follows: 'For me, this was a typical case of wife beating, this was typically again an example of a family where the woman is subordinated to the man and where the woman therefore is in fact the loser.'

Most officers, however, considered these situations exceptional, and mostly found among immigrant workers and their families from Muslim cultures like Turkey or Morocco. This cultural factor played an ambiguous role in the assessment of violent events and the role of the victim: on one hand abuse was considered a 'normal' part of the assumed hierarchical structure of these families, and some officers felt that they should not impose their own Dutch standards and intervene in a situation that is 'accepted' by the people involved. On the other hand officers expressed more understanding for the difficult position of these women and the specific problems they would encounter if they wanted to leave their abusive husband.[2] Compared to Dutch women, minority women were held less responsible for the fact that they (still) lived with a violent partner.

Several officers said that they had never encountered such serious cases of 'real woman beating', but from what they told about their experiences it became clear that they certainly must have had.

More often the officers considered the instances of woman beating they responded to as mere arguments that had got out of hand, as incidental and accidental abuse that can happen in any relationship. These were also the situations where they could imagine somehow that a man hits his wife, for instance after she provokes him (by nagging or making him jealous), after he has had too much alcohol, or out of frustration.

Although some police officers said that they could not see how a woman could be blamed for being beaten up, most of them saw her at least as partly responsible, if not for the beating, then at least for the 'conflict' underlying it. Sometimes her presumed responsibility was only derived from the fact that she maintained a relationship with the man who abused her. What is striking here is that excuses for the man's behaviour are quickly found, even if his behaviour is seen as unacceptable and unjust, whereas there is much less understanding for the woman's behaviour. Where she is seen as having provoked, or at least as having set the conditions for the man's violence, it is not taken into account that her behaviour may just as well be a reaction to his unpleasant demeanor. In most situations that the police encounter, the man's behaviour is at least somewhat excused and the woman is at least partly to blame. In other words, he is not really seen as an offender and the woman is not seen as a victim of violence and is not taken seriously as such. One (male) detective admitted:

> We probably assess that very badly, eh, this abuse. A woman who is assaulted has to come and make a formal statement to a man. Then I will, and I suppose others will too, empathize with the man. That is . . . we always play it down a little.

The fact that the two parties have (or have had) a relationship was essential in the assessment of the incident. A few officers stated this clearly:

> Well, it is just a disturbance in the relationship, and apparently she has received some blows. I don't know if I would really call this woman beating.

Eh, woman beating as you say, I'm never really conscious of it that way, that I am on my way to intervene in an instance of woman beating. I have never had such cases, as I see it. They are all marriage problems, and then it does come to blows sometimes. And by marriage problems I also understand times when people get half beaten up. But for me that is not woman beating.

He admitted that he *might* see it as an assault when a woman gets 'half beaten up', although he considered it different from an assault on someone, somewhere in the street. The privacy of one's own house made all the difference.

Police views of woman beating as police work

Considering the fact that police officers, when responding to instances of woman beating, usually assess the situation as a 'family dispute' rather than as a physical assault, it is not surprising that they see their own task in these situations as mainly to provide services and not to arrest. Further actions to actually solve the problem are beyond the scope of the police and should, they think, be left to other agencies. The police task is thus confined to first aid, to calm down the parties, to attempt some mediation, and to leave when the situation appears to be quiet again.

When the officers claimed that 'the police can't do anything here', they often referred to their limited legal power to arrest the man. The key problem, as they saw it, is the 'unwillingness' of the women to take the initiative to criminal proceedings and sign a formal statement. However, besides the fact that this is not always needed for the police to take legal action themselves, it is also somewhat in contradiction with the fact that they often *discourage* the woman from doing so. They may advise her to press charges 'if she wants the police to do something', but one woman with several disappointing experiences with the police noticed that they also did nothing when she followed their advice. Some police officers said that they advise the woman to make a formal complaint as a sort of test to find out if she really needs help. Obviously, when a woman does not want or dare to do this, this may all too easily lead to the conclusion that the situation was not so bad after all. In these cases the lack of cooperation of the woman may serve for the police as a convenient excuse for their own unwillingness to take action.

138

Conserving police resources is generally an important motive for the police to do nothing towards starting criminal proceedings (La Fave 1969). This is certainly true for the way they respond to calls for domestic violence, which have often been described as 'rotten jobs' and as a lot of work for no results (Punch 1979). In the present study, officers (not all of whom, by the way, disliked this kind of work) seemed most concerned about this when they perceived the incident as not too serious or when they thought it was the first time and when the woman had no definite intentions to finish the relationship. In fact, the officers made an assessment of the chance that the incident would cause serious damage to the *relationship*. If they expected that the couple would make up without much intervention by the police they would rather get involved as little as possible. Of course, in many cases the couple did make up sooner or later, although it is naïve to expect real changes for the better in a relationship as a result of such a police intervention. Most officers, however, saw a 'reconciliation' (for as long as that would last) as a proof that they were right in their approach and that any action to invoke the law would have been a waste of time. In fact, maintaining the relationship was not considered compatible with taking legal action against the aggressive man. A woman who nonetheless wanted to press charges was certainly not encouraged and warned of the negative effects, or sent home with the advice to think it over and come back if she really wanted it. This was often sufficient discouragement for women to leave it at that, thus confirming the preconceptions held by the police that women who do not give up their marriage are unlikely to follow through with a complaint (it should be noted that during the interviews it appeared that several officers did not speak from their own experience but from general hearsay). Other arguments for not supporting a woman in invoking the law in such situations were related to court proceedings. The chance that the man would be prosecuted was deemed very small. However, if the case were brought before the court, the whole process was likely to take several months and the eventual sentence would be lenient and, according to the police, hardly worth the trouble, while it would certainly have a negative effect on the relationship. One cannot avoid getting the impression that here there is not so much a concern for the interests of the woman as there is a keen awareness of the amount of paperwork involved, together with the chance that it would not lead to a follow-up in criminal proceedings.

As a result of the assumption that a woman who does not give up her relationship with the assailant cannot possibly seriously want to press charges, it is often seen as a defeat and a waste of time when legal action is taken and it is found out later that the couple — after all — stays together. This could lead to the warning that she need not call again next time she was in trouble. Such warnings were also given by police officers as a means of compelling the woman to follow their advice. Here again a possible waste of effort seemed to be the prime concern.

To tell the woman that she should not count on the police next time she needs help obviously ignores the emotional and practical problems that may stand in the way of her taking action which, in the opinion of the police officer concerned, might lead to a solution. It also ignores the fact that she may be right in not doing what the police think she should do. For there is not only the problem of threats from her husband when she wants to leave him, or non-cooperation from his side when she wants counselling to keep the marriage together, but also the fact that even if she does follow the advice given by the police, this often does not help. We only have to look at the high number of ex-husbands and ex-lovers that were responsible for the incidents in this study to realize that finishing the relationship does not guarantee an end to the violence.

Police views of the women's interests

The police officers often referred to the interests of the women when explaining their actions, or avoidance of actions. By not arresting the man or by discouraging the woman from invoking the law, they sought to avoid giving the man another reason to assault her. It was also said that prosecution and punishment would not help, but only disturb the relationship once more, just when it had settled down again. After considering these arguments a bit further it becomes even more clear that police officers tend to think of woman beating as incidental, unintended, and unfortunate events that had better be forgotten about as soon as possible. Of course, if the relationship is not too bad and the parties are reconciled again, legal sanctions — especially when the proceedings take several months — may have bad effects. However, this does not hold for those women who have been living for years in a relationship that can hardly become worse than it is already. These women might be relieved when an authority such as the police sets limits to their husbands' violence.

Some officers thought that a harsher approach might have a deterrent effect in certain situations. That was when the man had not, or had not often, beaten his wife before and when there were no former police contacts. In other words, a basically 'decent' man might learn the lesson taught by the police. On the other hand it was considered useless to try to change a man's behaviour by a stiff warning or an arrest when he was incorrigible in his police contacts and in beating his wife. What these officers were actually saying was that they expected a more assertive police intervention to be more effective in situations where the police (including these officers) were least likely to take such action!

Not always did the police passively accept the possibility that a man would take revenge after being arrested. In two instances where the man was arrested, the police took measures to protect the woman after his release. In both situations all the conditions for initiating criminal proceedings (as described in the preceding sections) were met: in one case the woman was badly injured and in the other case the woman was attacked with a knife while she was lying in bed. She managed to fight off her assailant. Both women had signed a formal statement and both intended to end the relationship with the man. The detective dealing with the first case had warned the man not to come near where his wife lived and had seen to it that the area was more frequently checked by the community policeman. In the other case the man had announced to the police that he would kill his common-law wife after they let him go. He spent three weeks in custody and was released with a restraining order. However, when the police heard that the woman had taken the initiative in getting in contact with the man and had decided that she wanted to maintain the relationship, they were really fed up and told her that she should not call the police again the next time she was in trouble.

It was especially community policemen who would reassure the woman by saying that she could always call the police when she needed help, and by doing so frequently undermined a warning given earlier by their colleagues in other departments. A few of them had gone to great lengths to help the woman get out of a violent relationship.

The mere fact that in instances of woman beating the victim and the offender have an intimate relationship not only determines the assessment of the assaults, but also whether it is deemed useful (in terms of the woman's interests) or a waste of time (in terms of police work) to take legal action.

Police officers generally stated that they would arrest the man in serious cases or when assaults had happened before. Unfortunately, many such cases pass as just an argument, partly because violence in the home is by definition perceived as not so serious, but also because officers just don't know about previous assaults. One reason why they often have no idea how serious are the situations they encounter is that they respond to single incidents, and see them as such, rather than as fitting into a framework of ongoing violence. This means for instance that a man who locks his wife out is seen as a nuisance, rather than as somebody who probably also beats her up. This is reinforced by an apparent lack of communication within the police organization, which is, in turn, partly due to under-reporting of these incidents. One officer said that he would read through a note in the station diary if it was labeled as an assault, but not if it was labeled as a domestic dispute. Repeated calls from the same couple — where they are recognized as such — are seen not so much as an indication of the seriousness of the situation as much as an indication that these people don't want to be helped, unless the woman takes action by deciding to end the relationship.

Most officers tried to avoid taking sides in what they usually considered a domestic dispute. For some this meant in the first place that they would not believe the woman before they had heard the man's story, or that they tried to avoid being 'used' by one party against the other. For others this meant that both parties should get due attention. Although it was sometimes found difficult not to sympathize with the woman, this was seen as a weakness and as being 'emotional'. Such an impartial attitude presumes a certain equality of the parties involved in that they both bear responsibility for the situation they are in ('It takes two to make a fight'), and both can do something to bring about a change in that situation. The problem with this approach is that the parties do *not* have an equal share in the situation. In fact, it can implicitly (and probably unintentionally) have the effect of supporting the man as the stronger party. Only a few officers seemed to realize that. They tried to support the woman just because they presumed she was the 'weaker' party. One officer said that he assumed a more neutral (!) attitude than he used to do by taking the position of the woman more into account.

142

Generally, police officers tend to underestimate not only the seriousness of woman beating but also the possibility that they can intervene effectively. Although most of them saw it as a task for the police to respond to instances of woman beating, this task was limited in two ways. Only a few officers referred to the criminal aspect of the violence and considered it for that reason a police responsibility. Indeed, most officers saw a social role for the police, but were anxious to admit that they are not professional social workers and that other agencies are better equipped for this. By denying themselves a law enforcement role *and* a social work role the police seem to have manoeuvred themselves into the role of helpless witnesses.

Policing Woman Beating — a Woman's Point of View

Calling the Police

Whereas police officers often think that avoiding legal (or any other) action in order not to upset the man or to disturb the relationship is in the woman's best interest, women may expect something different from the police. It is likely that satisfaction with the police response is related to one's expectations. If women call the police with the expectation that they 'will do something about it', it can be very frustrating if they only 'calm down the situation'. If they expect in the first place understanding and support then the attitude of the police will probably be more important. For that matter it should be taken into account that many people don't have such clear-cut expectations when they call the police (Hogenhuis 1986). Why then do women call the police in the first place?

Those who consider woman beating as a 'marital problem' may wonder why women who need help go to the police instead of to another social agency. In fact, most women probably never call the police and try to cope somehow with their problems or manage to stop the violence with or without the help of people other than the police (Bowker 1984). Since battering is considered a crime here, a more appropriate question is why so many women do *not* go to the police. A survey of women who were staying or had stayed in shelters in the Netherlands showed that many of them did not call the police for help because of fear of reprisals and because they did not expect much of the police (Blijf van m'n Lijf 1984). It is obvious from women's experiences that the way the police often respond to calls for woman beating does not encourage women to enlist their help.

More than half of the twenty-two women interviewed had suffered assaults for many years before the police got involved for the first time. Only a few women called after the first or second assault or serious threat. Generally they tried first to solve their own problems. Besides, some women felt so ashamed that they kept it quiet for a long time from their neighbours, family, or friends. By threatening her, the man could also prevent her from talking about it with others, let alone asking the police for help. Fear, shame, and the feeling that they should be able to solve their own problems determined most of all at what stage in the history of abuse police assistance was enlisted.

It is obvious that the barrier against calling the police the first time could be very high. Apart from the factors just mentioned, accidental circumstances played a role. It could happen when the assault was more serious than before, or when the injuries were considerable, but this was not always the case. Often the incident for which the police were called was relatively less serious, but special circumstances such as the presence of a third party could turn the scale. It also happened that the woman, after having left the man, had lost her loyalty towards him and then eventually appealed to the police. Often others, such as neighbours or a child, called the police.

Where women requested police help more frequently after their first call, this was not necessarily because they found it much easier on subsequent occasions, or that they were satisfied with the initial police response. Rather, if they felt threatened or unable to cope, and there was no one else around who could help, calling the police was a last resort. One woman said that she felt it as a defeat every time she had to turn to the police. She saw it as her task to keep her marriage on the right track and she only called the police in emergencies ('Who else?'). Another woman who, in a very threatening situation, fled onto the steet in the middle of the night was not so pleased when other people asked for police assistance. For the police came *after* she had escaped, when the crisis was over.

Reasons for calling

Most of the women said that they called the police because they needed 'help'. This meant first of all that they wanted them to end the crisis and bring the situation back to manageable proportions, after which they often preferred to solve their own problems again. The 'help' that was wanted usually implied more than mediation and a referral to a social agency. This was made very clear by one woman, who was angry and amazed after the police had tried to mediate between her and her former lover. According to her they had been wrong in assuming the role of a social worker. If she wanted mediation, she said, she could just as well have asked the neighbours. She thought that the police should have sent the man away and should have offered her protection. Other women, too, who called the police for help appeared to appeal most of all to 'the strong arm' that would make the man leave the house or stay away from her door. Only one woman said she wanted help in the form of support and advice, and only that.

Some women said that they called the police to prevent what otherwise would just go on, or to impress the man after having previously warned him that this would happen the next time he made problems. Others called because they were angry and they felt that this was the only way to get their own back, or they wanted that he should be 'made to feel it'. They were among the eleven women who signed a formal statement. Of these women only two knowingly took into account the chance that the man would get punished. The other nine women hoped that this way the man could be forced to get some kind of treatment, or they hoped that the police could then finally do 'something' to make him stop harassing her, or they just wanted it to be registered so that the police would know about it. Five of these women explicitly said that they did *not* want the man to be prosecuted. In many cases, by signing a formal statement, the woman seemed to show the man (and probably also herself) that she was not going to take it any longer.

The chance that the man might be punished could also be a reason *not* to sign a formal statement. Others were afraid to take such a step, or they thought it was already bad enough that they had to call the police in the first place. In some cases women were discouraged by the police, who had said that it would be useless or that it was not a matter for the police.

In short, the women did not call the police only for immediate help and protection in a situation they could not cope with anymore. Several of them also had another purpose; they hoped that the police would somehow put a limit on the man's behaviour. They probably believed that the police could achieve a beneficial effect. Also, the women who wanted the man to get his just deserts seemed to expect some educative effect from a more assertive approach by the police. They apparently did not feel restrained by the fear that this might only make the situation worse.

What the women actually expected of the police is partly given in the reasons why the police were called. In a number of cases the woman expressed no clear expectations. Sometimes it was only expected 'that they would come'. More specific expectations concerned the actions the police would take (e.g. that they would send the man away) and the attitude of the police (e.g. that they would be understanding or would listen). Often the expectations expressed implied criticism of the police, for instance 'that they would come sooner', or 'that it would be less businesslike'. Some women did not seem to expect much, on the basis of earlier experiences. But they kept calling because they hoped that one time the police would be able to help.

Opinions about the police

The criticism that the police 'do nothing' has a great deal to do with the fact that the police seldom take legal action — even in serious cases or in situations that have been violent over a longer period. There are, however, other aspects of police performance that are important to whether or not women found that the police had been helpful. In several studies in which battered women have been asked about their experiences with the police, it has appeared that discontent with the police is related not only to the police unwillingness to arrest the man, but also to an indifferent attitude or a lack of involvement of the police officers concerned (Kennedy and Homant 1984; Brown 1984).

Also in the present study women were asked whether they were satisfied with the way the police responded *and* what it was that they appreciated or not. A few women could not say much about it, but others gave differentiated answers concerning the attitude of the police officers and what they had said and done, and what they achieved.

Results achieved. In most cases the police managed to calm down the situation — at least for the moment — and to reassure the woman. Yet only a few women were really happy with the result of the police intervention. Two women were given useful help by community policemen. In both situations the latter had contributed to a decision to finish the relationship. In one case he had organized a stay in a shelter in another town where she felt happier than she had been for a long time. In the other case the officer had helped the woman to find another place to live. Another woman was very content because the police achieved exactly what she had called them for: the man left the house. All three women were also very pleased with the attitude of the police officers concerned. Two other women said that they were not unhappy with the result, but the fact that they did not experience much understanding and support seemed more important in their opinion about the police.

The women who were not satisfied with the result and who thought that the poice had not done anything, had called before on several occasions, always with the same unsatisfactory result. One of them said, 'Every time I go to the police station I get the feeling that I am put off. And that is right from the beginning.' She nevertheless hoped that one day something could be done to stop her former lover from threatening her.

It appeared that the police don't want to miss an opportunity to make clear that 'they can't do anything here'. Some women seemed to resign themselves to that. Others tended to take the law in their own hands, but if they told the police this, it could recoil surprisingly fast against themselves. The police would then warn them that they might be arrested. Obviously such warnings meant an attack on the sense of justice in these women who could not reconcile this with the police lacking the power to take action against the man. One woman wondered indignantly what had happened to justice.in this country.

Police performance and attitudes. Whether or not the women found the police helpful was not only dependent on eventual results, but also on whether the officers concerned had been understanding and supportive. Unfortunately this was often lacking. Some police officers gave the impression that they wanted to get done with it as quickly as possible. Some women had the feeling that the police found it strange that they had called them for such a thing, or that they did not believe them. One woman who was locked out of the house by her husband was heard in the police car in front of all the neighbours while another policeman talked with the man in the house. This policeman told her that there was no problem at all, because her husband would have let her in anyway. In this case the police had to return five minutes after they left. The man had hit his wife, and this time he was taken to the police station while the woman was advised to make a formal statement. When she did this, somewhat dubiously, the officer taking the statement warned her so strongly of the negative effects of any legal action that she got the impression that it was a very strange thing to do to testify against your own husband. She did not sign the statement. The officer remarked afterwards, 'You see, this is what always happens in these cases. Well, at least she was able to tell her story.' During the interview the woman appeared to be of another opinion. Other women, too, who had come to the CID complained that they could not really tell their story because of the formal approach.

Police officers sometimes try to mediate in what they think is a dispute, with all the best intentions to bring about a lasting solution for what in their eyes would otherwise be a long-lasting problem. This happened to one woman who called the police after her former lover had forced his way into her house and had hit her. According to the police the problem was that the man wanted to see his child (the man agreed with that). According to the woman, however, the problem was that the man had beaten her over the years, and still harassed her every time he wanted to see the child. The woman said:

> Yes, I was really disappointed by the police. I think, even if they want to know how things came about, it was me who asked for help so they should have asked first who called them, and why, and I say he doesn't want to leave, and that they would put him outside. But they came here and asked what has happened and he started talking straightaway. I don't think this is a good system. If he wants to talk they could let him do that outside or somewhere else, and if they also want to talk to me, let them first put him outside and ask me what has happened and why I called them. And if there are two officers one can hear him, but not here in the kitchen for I feel in fact like a cat driven into a corner. Imagine that there was no community policeman — you wouldn't dare to

call the police anymore. You see, then he feels strong, he feels that he stands firm in his shoes because even when you call the police it doesn't help.

This was not the only time where the police tried to mediate in a situation where, according to the woman, there was nothing to mediate over. In another case it was a woman who after a long marriage, during which she had been brutally and regularly beaten, eventually got divorced, but was still threatened and abused by her ex-husband (who, as in the previous case, claimed that he wanted to see his children). Now she did not want to have anything to do with him anymore, but after repeated police interventions she was still asked to 'give him one more chance'. In a third case again the police thought that the problem would be solved if the man could see his children. It should be noted that for all of these three women the violence started long before any refusal to give the man access to his children became the 'cause' of it.

While in some cases police officers insisted on mediation far beyond the point where this could be considered appropriate, in other cases they advised legal proceedings and a divorce where the woman did not dare to do so or rather wanted to try once more. These women could hardly count on much understanding, but it was worse when they were put under pressure with the warning that they should not appeal again to the police if they did not follow the advice. One woman said that the police gave her the feeling that she could only be helped if she got a divorce. However, her husband, by whom she had been severely abused for many years, had made it clear to her that she had better not try to run away because he would know how to find her, wherever she was, and that would be the end for her. Since she was convinced that he would carry out his threat, a divorce was useless in her eyes. In fact, it would be 'safer' for her to stay at home. The police had said that they had warned her often enough and if she did not listen they would wash their hands of her, because they could not go on like this. The community police officer had been involved in this case for quite a long period. He felt unable to help and saw this as a hopeless case. He may have been right, in a way, but it is remarkable that the responsibility to bring about a change in the situation was assigned to the woman. The man, although recognized as 'not a very nice guy', was hardly held responsible.

For women who needed police assistance more than once it could be a real problem to follow the conflicting advice from different police officers.

In general, the women in this study were more positive about the community policemen than about their colleagues in other departments. Probably they met the expectations of the women better — that is they were not supposed to take (legal) action against the man but to listen, and that was what they mostly did: listen and find out what kind of help was needed. Some women said that it was easier to talk to police*women*, whom they found more understanding than policemen. One of them, however, felt safer with a police*man*.

The effects of police intervention

The effects of what the police do or don't do can be very divergent. An arrest or a stiff warning could make such an impression on the man that he would keep quiet or stay away for a while. A few women said that this would have no effect whatsoever on him, but then some of these men would not be impressed by any measure taken. It did happen that a man became aggressive after being arrested, but this was usually limited to verbal threats, or, as one woman said, he was angry but he kept quiet for a while. The man who announced to the police that he would kill his wife after his release was, according to her, nicer to her than ever before, and they could talk more easily. She thought that the time spent in custody had made him think things over.

Yet, two women said that their husbands had in the past assaulted them after they had been heard by the police. However, before they appealed to the police and afterwards, when they did not dare to do that anymore, they were also often and severely beaten. Given the fact that men who beat their wives can always find reasons, however trivial, for doing so, the importance of legal action as a 'trigger' should not be exaggerated. This is not to say that it is never risky or that the woman's fear of reprisals should not be taken seriously. However, it seems more approriate to take measures of protection such as a restraining order and frequent checks on the area concerned than to take no action at all in the hope that the man will not become violent. This obviously overlooks the fact that the man was already violent in the first place.

It appeared that it had only negative effects when the police put off the case, said that they could not do anything, or did not point out clearly enough to the man that his demeanour is not tolerated and constitutes a crime. In several cases where this happened it was the man who was most satisfied with the police; he did not object to his wife calling them because he knew that nothing would happen to him. Women with such experiences said that they lost heart and that they had the feeling that it was useless to call the police. If the police could not do anything it was expected that they at least could give some support. It could be frankly dangerous when warnings were given, such as, 'If you let him in again you needn't call the police anymore' or 'If you don't press charges we can't do anything.' Several women said that they indeed did not dare to call afterwards. For these and other women who did not feel supported the situation was rather hopeless. What could they do if they didn't let the man in, but instead were harassed in the street? What should they do when they got contradicting advice from different police officers? Or when the police said that *she* should keep him off her doorstep, otherwise they could not do anything? It is not likely that these women felt very helped by the police.

Fortunately there were police officers who, with an understanding of the situation, involvement, and good advice, provided an important contribution to a solution. One woman, who had finally decided to leave her husband after years of violence, said about a community police officer:

> During all those twenty years everybody kept saying, try once again. Go back and think about this and think about that, but never did anybody say, think also about yourself, you can go somewhere else [. . .] he was the first who helped me, who said you can go somewhere else [. . .] and not: wouldn't you give it another try?

Positive effects were often not that spectacular, but women felt reassured and safer if they knew that they could always call on the police if it was necessary. One woman said it had given her more self-confidence. Apart from actually putting a stop to a violent event, this may be the most important effect the police can have.

Conclusion

Whatever the police may think, it must have become clear from this study that the interests of the battered women are not very well served by a reserved approach. On the other hand it is not obvious that more arrest and a possible prosecution and conviction are what the women actually want. In fact, only a few women wanted their (ex-)husband or (ex-)lover to be prosecuted and punished. However, many women wanted more than mediation and a referral to some agency. First of all it was important that the immediate threat of the situation was removed and that protection was offered, but on top of that they hoped that the police would achieve what they apparently could not bring about themselves, namely to make the man understand that what he did was totally unacceptable, for example by telling him so, by sending him away with a warning or, if necessary, by arresting him. These are exactly the actions that the police try to avoid, because they deem it not in the woman's interest, or not in their own interest, and because they think that they should not take sides.

With mediation the police often appeal to the willingness of the woman to take steps that may bring about changes in the situation. According to both police officers and women, the man is usually less often prepared to make some effort. Moreover, advice often takes the form of conditions that have to be met by the woman in order not to lose the cooperation of the police in the future. Again, the man is not in the picture. Demonstrating that the police can't do anything will certainly confirm the man in his behaviour and make even more clear to the woman that she is in a fairly hopeless situation. The consequence of this approach is that the man gets the message that he can easily get away with it. The woman, however, is once again held responsible — not for the beating this time, but for finding a solution. The police therefore appear as supporters of the status quo.

In the police department where this study took place it appeared that since 1984 officers have tended to make use more often of their coercive power when dealing with battering cases. Those who would rather see a less prominent role of the criminal justice system generally may see this as a step in the wrong direction. Others may see it as a sign that, in spite of the negative experiences that women still report, woman beating is slowly being taken more seriously by the police. Nevertheless, it is argued that women should not pin their faith to a system that is designed to preserve the established social order rather than to change it and therefore is seen in itself as part of the problem.

It is true that seeking the solution through the police and the criminal justice system can be counter-productive in that instances of woman beating are treated as the individual crimes of some aggressive men. This is, in a way, not much different from the 'private quarrels' they were before. By focusing on individual 'deviancies', attention may be diverted from the fact that the origins of violence against women are to be found in the 'normal' (i.e. unequal) social relations between women and men. However, woman beating is not only a social phenomenon but also the experience of individual women, each of whom needs assistance and protection. Women who go to the police appeal not only for understanding and emotional support but also for the authority of the police and the fact that the police, in an acute threat, can offer protection. Even when it is an obvious truth that real changes can only be achieved by changes in the unequal power balance between men and women, there is nothing wrong with demanding in the meantime that the police do their job.

What can we expect in this respect in the Netherlands? Although in recent years the attention to the interest of victims of crimes has been growing, one still cannot say that they are generally well looked after. As long as battered women are not even seen as the victims of crimes, the chance that they will profit from the beneficial effects of victim support schemes set up by the government, or guidelines for the treatment of victims by the police and the judiciary, should not be exaggerated. Besides, to cut expenses in the police budget it has currently been suggested to shed police tasks when they are not in the public interest, or when the police are not the appropriate agency to deal with them. These include, among other things, services concerning family matters such as interpersonal disputes. Therefore it is even more important to ensure that woman beating is made a matter of public concern.

Notes

1 Since mid-1986 this possibility has been restricted. In accordance with the revised Constitution of 1983 it is now not possible to arrest

somebody without a criminal charge. However, there appears to be much uncertainty about whether or not an exception can be made in some situations. Instances of violence against women in the home have been mentioned in this respect. In the police department where the present study took place it was said that the new regulation did not much affect police practices.

2 For many of these women there is not only a language problem. They are entitled to an independent residence permit only after three years of marriage, of which at least one year has been spent in the Netherlands. If they want to leave their husband before the end of this period they face being sent back to their native country.

Chapter seven

The Legal Response to Woman Battering in the United States

Kathleen J. Ferraro

Overview of U.S. Legal Response to Battering

Introduction

Since the early 1970s, feminists in the United States have worked to raise public consciousness about the nature of male violence against women. Through organizing, lobbying, building alternative organizations, and rallying in the streets, feminists have demanded that male violence against women be recognized as the devastating and pervasive reality of a patriarchal culture. Women working against rape, battering, incest and sexual abuse of children, and sexual harassment in the workplace have demonstrated the significance of male violence for controlling women and maintaining their subordinate status (Hanmer and Maynard 1987; Schechter 1982; Stanko 1985).

While all these forms of violence are technically against the law in the United States, the actual protection afforded to women has been minimal. The chances of arrest, prosecution, and incarceration for acts of violence depend on the nature of the relationship between victim and offender (Black 1980). Violence that receives the most severe state sanctions is that which is committed by a subordinate against a superordinate in the social hierarchy, or by a

Earlier versions of this Chapter were presented at the Third International Congress on Women, Dublin, 1987, and the American Sociological Association, Washington, D.C., 1985. This research was supported in part by grants from the Arizona State Women's Studies Summer Grant program and the Arizona State University Research Fund. I would like to thank David Altheide, Kim Bauman, John Johnson, Nancy Jurik, Gerri Klein, and Kathy Seeley for their help in completing this research. I would also like to extend my appreciation to Chief Reuben Ortega and all the officers who generously allowed us to observe their work.

subversive group against the dominant political order. Thus, rapes are most likely to result in severe prison sentences when the woman is white and the man is black (LaFree 1980). They are least likely to result in any form of sanction when the rape occurs within marriage (Russell 1985). Male violence against women has been viewed legally through the lens of patriarchal hierarchies.

Notions of family privacy and male supremacy have informed the legal response to male violence against women in the United States. The physical, sexual, and emotional battering of women by men within the family has been viewed as external to the legitimate control of the state. It has taken extraordinary efforts on the part of feminist activists to challenge and alter this view. This essay will examine those efforts, with special attention to policing.

History

In the decade between 1977 and 1987, significant changes in the legal response to battering occurred in the United Staes. During this period, the grass-roots battered women's movement worked to change existing legislation and create laws specifically designed to provide government and legal support to battered women. Historically, efforts to control battering through the law were championed by early religious leaders, feminists, and retributivist politicians (Pleck 1987). In 1882 Maryland passed a law to punish wife beaters at the whipping post. A similar law was passed in Delaware and Oregon. Records indicate that very few men were actually whipped in public, and that the punishment was much more likely to be inflicted on black men (Pleck 1987). U.S. history also contains numerous accounts of vigilante efforts to control wife beating (Pleck 1979). During the latter part of the nineteenth century, racist mobs, such as the Ku Klux Klan and the White Caps, attempted to control wife beating through threats and beatings. According to Pleck, of the eighty targets of the White Caps in one Indiana county in the 1880s, nine were wife beaters (1987). Yet both the whipping post legislation and the vigilante responses were more attempts to control lower-class, black, and unconventional groups than to eliminate violence against women. The Ku Klux Klan focused primarily on slaves, and punished prostitutes and adultresses.

Progressive Era feminists, such as Elizabeth Cady Stanton,

worked against male violence, but relinquished the issue to concentrate on obtaining suffrage (Pleck 1983). During the present century, protection of women from male violence was an issue the legal system, along with the rest of the culture, chose to ignore.

In the early 1970s feminists again began to organize against battering. The first book published in the United States by Del Martin (1976) documented the official nonintervention policies of police departments, and the subsequent disastrous consequences for women. The battered women's movement began in the United States in 1970, with a keen awareness of the failure of the legal system to project victims of battering. It was informed by social science research, which documented the failure of police and courts to provide protection to battered women (Parnas 1967; Police Foundation 1976; Field and Field 1973).

Contemporary Critiques and Responses

One of the first responses of the legal system was the development of police crisis intervention teams (Bard 1969). These teams, however, did not alter the problems inherent in the policing of battering, and were criticised by feminists for failing to treat battering as a serious crime. In 1976, two lawsuits (*Scott v. Hart* and *Bruno v. Codd*) charged entire police departments in Oakland, California and New York City with failing to protect battered women. Both cases resulted in police departments agreeing to treat battering as a crime, to arrest in felony cases, to provide assistance to battered women when requested, and not to consider marital status in arrest decisions (Schechter 1982). These agreements, however, as we will see later, did not have a blanket effect on the behaviour of police toward battered women.

Legislative Efforts

There have been a variety of legislative approaches initiated to provide support to the movement and to individual women. As the state and federal governments became involved in the response to woman battering, the language and understanding of the problem have changed. Legislative language never refers to woman battering, but uses the more neutral (and misleading) terms 'domestic' or 'family' violence, or 'spouse abuse'. The language used is representative of the tension between the feminist analysis of battering, and the state understanding of battering as simply another form of deviant, criminal conduct. Bureaucratic and government langauge is also used to conceal the political nature of battering, and to ensure that condemnation of battering is not equated with condemnation of the patriarchal nuclear family.

In the early 1980s state legislatures throughout the United States passed laws that enhanced the power of police to arrest batterers. New legislation allowed officers to arrest for misdemeanor assaults on the basis of probable cause in domestic violence cases.[1] This legislation aimed to recognize the special conditions of battering, for in all other misdemeanor assaults, officers must either witness the assault or have a signed complaint by a citizen in order to arrest. By 1983, thirty-three states and the District of Columbia enacted legislation to enhance police power to arrest batterers (Lerman and Livingston 1983). Statutory changes also expanded police responsibility by requiring officers (1) provide information to women on legal options and services (eighteen states) and (2) transport women to hospitals or shelters (eleven states) (Buzawa and Buzawa 1985). Forty-three states also created new measures for obtaining orders of protection for battered women. These orders, depending on the state, require an abuser to leave the residence, refrain from contact with the woman, enter counselling, or make monetary payments to the woman. One study that has examined the effectiveness of orders of protection found little impact on serious offenders, although men committing less severe, first-time assaults seemed to be deterred somewhat by the presence of orders of protection (Grau et al. 1985). In general, despite legislated efforts to expand police protection, the law remains ineffective in protecting women or punishing batterers (Quarm and Schwartz 1984; Brown 1984).

One other form of legislation established surcharges on marriage licenses and/or divorce decrees which are used to support domestic violence programs. At least twenty-one states have marriage license or divorce surcharges (Lerman and Livingston 1983). The fees, ranging from $5 in Alabama to $20 in Oregon, are attached to the normal fee for marriage licenses and/or divorce decrees, and placed in a general fund which is dispersed among state programs. Some states have imposed limits on the number of programs that can receive funds, to ensure the monies are not splintered into trivial amounts. These surcharge funds generate between $150,000 (New

Hampshire) and $4,000,000 (California) each year (National Coalition Against Domestic Violence 1987b).

Federal Funding

At the federal level, attempts to fund services for battered women began in 1978 (Gelb 1983). After six years of political work, legislation was finally passed in 1984 under the Family Violence Prevention and Services Act. The Act appropriated $8.3 million for 1985 and 1986 and $8.5 million for 1987. Appropriations for 1988 will remain at the same levels as for 1987. Funding was used primarily for shelter services. Also in 1984, the Victims of Crime Act (VOCA) authorized use of fines for federal violations for state victim compensation programs. The Act specified that priority be given to victims of sexual assault, and spousal and child abuse (National Coalition Against Domestic Violence 1987a). A survey by the National Coalition Against Domestic Violence found that of the thirty-five responding state coalitions, only one state (Nebraska) had not received VOCA funding in 1986 and 1987. Amounts per state ranged from $85,000 in Utah to $2,800,000 in New York (NCADV 1987b). VOCA funds were cut to $35 million for 1988, and the Act must receive congressional reauthorization to continue.

These two pieces of legislation are specifically designed to provide funding for services to battered women. Thus, they are not as entangled with bureaucratic regulations as are other federal funding sources, such as the now defunct Law Enforcement Assistance Administration (LEAA). The linkage of battered women's shelters with federal and state funding agencies has both helped and hindered the movement. The financial support has permitted the development of physical facilities, hotlines, and training and education materials which would have been impossible otherwise. Yet government funds have direct and subtle effects on the manner in which services are provided (Ferraro 1981a). For example, LEAA funds were directed at improving law enforcement agencies. Shelters that made use of LEAA grants were required to work closely with police, and to have representatives of the police as members of their boards. Indeed, the notion of boards in itself implies a hierarchy of authority and power that is antithetical to the original feminist philosophy of shelters (Wharton 1987; Ahrens 1974). In addition to the direct impact on operations, dependence on federal funding has made shelter programs vulnerable to cutbacks. The elimination of social service programs and cutbacks in the 1980s has caused some shelters to pare staff and services to the minimum, and has prevented the expansion of new services.

Attorney General's Task Force

In 1984 a Task Force on Family Violence was appointed by the U.S. Attorney General. A panel of ten, primarily criminal justice professionals, heard testimony on all forms of family violence. The first recommendation of the Task Force for the justice system was that 'family violence should be recognized and responded to as a criminal activity' (Hart et al. 1984: 10). Law enforcement agencies were encouraged to "establish arrest as the preferred response in cases of family violence" (Hart et al. 1984: 17). Influenced by the federal government's promotion of police intervention, six states have passed laws requiring arrest under certain circumstances. In 1985, forty-seven cities with populations over 100,000 had police policies of mandatory or presumptive arrests for 'family fights'.[2] Still, 46 per cent of large cities surveyed by the Crime Control Institute in 1986 left the response to domestic violence to the officer's discretion.

Civil Suits Against the Criminal Justice System

Despite considerable change in written law at the state and federal levels, battered women continue to suffer from lack of protection. The failure of police, prosecutors, and courts to comply with laws and policies is reflected in the numerous lawsuits that have been filed individually and collectively by battered women (Woods 1986). Many of these cases have not been settled, but the content of the claims indicates women continue to be injured due to the non-responsiveness of the legal system. The most dramatic case to date, *Thurman v. City of Torrington*, resulted in the permanent scarring and paralysis of a battered woman after she had repeatedly requested police assistance. A federal court jury found police officers negligent and awarded Ms. Thurman $2.3 million (Woods 1986).

Impact of the Reagan Administration

Nationally, the battered women's movement has suffered under the conservatism of the Reagan administration. The federal Office of

Domestic Violence, created during the Carter administration, closed in 1980, along with the Clearinghouse on Domestic Violence, which it sponsored. The elimination of Comprehensive Employment and Training Act (CETA) and Law Enforcement Assistance Association (LEAA) funds also exacted a heavy toll on shelter progress. A recent survey by the National Coalition Against Domestic Violence found that 31 per cent of the states responding indicated a reduction in state funding for domestic violence progress (NCADV 1987b). In 1986 the U.S. Justice Department awarded a right-wing group headed by Phyllis Schlafly $622,905 to work on spouse abuse (*Aegis* 1986). Although the group (Task Force on Families) withdrew its grant application, they received the award as a political balance to the award given to the feminist NCADV. The NCADV returned their second year's funding due to excessive veto and control stipulations demanded by conservative Department of Justice officials (Neimann 1987).

Positive Growth

Although there has been opposition and cutbacks of funds, the battered woman's movement in the United States has grown in numbers and strength since 1970. The number of programs for battered women has increased from zero to over 1,200. The existing shelters house over 300,000 women and children annually. Programs for men who batter have also been developed and are being implemented around the country. Feminists have been active in limiting the funds that are diverted from women to abusive men. Some programs, for example DOVE in Phoenix, Arizona, are funded primarily by fees paid by men who enter the program. A national hotline opened in October 1987 which provides 24-hour access to women anywhere in the country (*Voice* 1987). After two months of operation, the hotline was averaging 120 to 150 calls per day. On days of national media attention, such as discussion on the Phil Donahue talk show, calls reached 1,000 for one day (*Voice* 1988). The movement has expanded its concerns to deal with battered elderly, rural, refugee, and disabled women. Recognizing that shelters do not meet women's needs on a long-term basis, resources are being committed to nonresidential advocacy and support systems. Public awareness is reinforced by frequent public service announcements locally. National attention is focused on battering during Domestic Violence Awareness Month each

October. National media presentations (such as the film, *The Burning Bed*), rallies, and educational presentations during October help to keep the public concerned and supportive of movement efforts.

In response to federal cutbacks, the national movement has created an innovative program, Shelter Aid. Private industry has agreed to donate a small percentage of retail sales on specified products to the National Coalition Against Domestic Violence. The campaign, begun in September 1987, was publicized by major national television stars Tyne Daley, Sharon Gless, and Lindsay Wagner. The support by private industry not only generates money, but also lends credibility to the work of NCADV.

Working in or Against the Criminal Justice System

It is still debatable whether the existing legal system can work in support of women's empowerment. Some have argued that this system is designed to maintain women's subordinate status within the nuclear family and the economy (Rifkin 1980; Grossholtz 1983). Thus, the creation of laws against domestic violence is limited as a tool for assisting women's escape from violent marriages (McMann 1985; Radford 1987). On the other hand, most U.S. writers argue that increasing legal sanctions against batterers will empower battered women and discourage male abuse (Walker 1985; Lerman 1984). The question of its implementation revolves more around who controls the use of the law and for what purposes.

Battered women need protection from violent men. The law may be able to provide this protection. But if it is to empower women, rather than reinforce their dependency, we must have knowledge of the behaviour of the law, its implementation in the criminal justice system, and the needs and desires of women.

Arrest as a Deterrent

An experimental study conducted in Minneapolis concluded that of arrest, separation, and mediation, arrest is the most effective deterrent for battering (Sherman and Berk 1984a). The results were partially supported by Berk and Newton (1985) and Tauchen et al. (1986). These findings, while not conclusive, have been incorporated into most of the U.S. discussions about the desirability of a pro-arrest stand. According to Marcia Neimann, executive director of NCADV, a pro-arrest stance is now the consensus opinion among U.S. activists. Differences continue over whether legislation, policymaking, training, or all three are the most appropriate strategies for increasing arrest (Neimann 1987).

Observations of Policing Battering

Rationale

In the spring of 1984 several colleagues and I conducted a study of the implementation of a 'presumptive arrest' policy in Phoenix, Arizona.[3] The study was initiated in response to the overwhelming publicity and support mandatory arrest was receiving. There were several rationales for the study. First, the literature on policing behavior in general demonstrates that discretion is an inherent component of police work (Brown 1981; Lipsky 1980; Aaronson et al. 1984). It is particularly embedded in police responses to disputes (Black 1980). The majority of police work involves order maintenance activities, rather than crime fighting, and arrest is the least used of options available for most offenses (Bittner 1967; Black 1980). The policing literature suggests that a mandatory or presumptive arrest policy for domestic violence would not be uniformly implemented (see Stanko, Chapter 3, this volume). Second, the assumption that arresting batterers would stop men from beating their wives is not supported by the literature on deterrence (Paternoster et al. 1983). Behavior that is interpersonal rather than strictly economic, and which is a pattern of living, is least likely to be altered by arrest.[4] Since most men spend less than seventy-two hours in jail, and the longest sentence most men who are arrested for battering receive is a week, the deterrent effect seems even less likely. Although the Sherman and Berk study found arrest to be the best deterrent, it seemed appropriate to gather more information.

We were interested in the *process* of implementation of a presumptive arrest policy in the context of ongoing police work. We also felt it was important to talk to battered women to learn whether they perceived the presumptive arrest policy as contributing to a genuine improvement of their situations, and if they would agree with the policy. Finally, the adoption of a presumptive arrest policy in our city provided the opportunity to conduct first-hand observations. The policy stated:

Officers should arrest domestic violence violators even if the victim does not desire prosecution. When probable cause exists, an arrest should be made even if a misdemeanour offense did not occur in the officer's presence. . . . Officers *will* arrest Order of Protection violators even if the victim does not desire prosecution. (Ortega 1984: 1)

Research Design

The police department provided arrest figures to the research team which indicated that the rate of arrest for 'family fights' had almost doubled in the first two months of implementation of the policy. 'Family fight' is the police category for any dispute or violence occurring between family members. Official arrest data, however, do not reflect the kinds of situations police encounter, the manner in which arrest and other interventions are conducted, or the factors that determine which intervention is implemented. The majority of calls are never reported on in any official way, so that the denominator in the arrest statistics is greatly reduced from the number of calls responded to.

For example, of the 21,000 calls to the police coded as family fights in 1984, about 2,000 resulted in detective reports and about 1,250 resulted in arrest. That leaves 17,750 calls unaccounted for. Given that only half, at most, of battered women call the police, the proportion of men arrested for battering is miniscule. This small proportion of arrests, however, is not inconsistent with the 'funneling effect' seen in other crimes against women (see, for example, Randall and Rose 1981).

In order to acquire a more complete picture of the process of policing battering, we conducted field observations and interviews. The first stage involved interviewing the police administrators most responsible for developing and disseminating information about the policy. The chief, three assistant chiefs, the lieutenant in charge of investigations, and two detectives assigned to domestic violence were interviewed. They were questioned about the development of the policy, the rationale behind it, the old policy, and expectations about officer implementation and effectiveness.

The research team, consisting of three women and two men, entered the field three weeks after the initial adoption of the presumptive arrest policy. Observers rode with officers on ten-hour weekend evening shifts for forty-four nights. Three police districts were observed, two low income and one middle class. Officers were told that we were studying domestic violence, and were instructed to respond to as many family fight calls as possible. On many evenings we were assigned to 'roving cars', which had no beat boundaries, enabling us to respond to family fight calls anywhere in the district.

During ten-hour shifts, we questioned officers about the new presumptive arrest policy, their experiences with family fights, and their opinions about the appropriate response. At family fight calls we observed the police intervention and spoke with those who were assaulted whenever possible. During the forty-four ride-alongs, police responded to sixty-nine family fight calls. In 1984 the police department recorded approximately 21,000 calls for family fights. With six districts, and six beats for each district, a given officer would receive approximately 1.5 calls each night. Of the calls observed, thirty involved married or formerly married couples, fifteen involved cohabitees or former lovers, thirteen involved neighbors or other relatives, seven were false reports, and four were resolved prior to police arrival. Narrative field notes were recorded for all aspects of the ride-alongs, including responses to other offenses.

We also conducted interviews with women who had called the police for assistance. The police detectives randomly selected 100 names and called women asking if they would be willing to be interviewed. Thirty-three said they would. Of these, seventeen resulted in completed interviews.[5]

Research Context

The study was conducted in Phoenix, Arizona. Phoenix is a large, rapidly growing area of the Southwest United States with a population of approximately 2 million people. It has one of the lowest minority populations in the country, although the districts observed have high proportions of Hispanic, Native American, and black residents. Arizona is relatively conservative politically compared with the rest of the country. It is dominated by the Republican party. It falls at the lower end of the spectrum in the United States in terms of financial support to social services. Arizona has a large population of Mormons, which is a conservative pro-family, antifeminist religious groups.

Although the area is not generally supportive of progressive issues, it has been the scene of considerable action in the area of domestic violence. One of the first and longest-lasting shelters, Rainbow Retreat, opened in Phoenix in 1972. Since that time eight more shelters have been established. There is a Maricopa County Task Force Against Domestic Violence, which is part of a state coalition. The Arizona Coalition is a member of the NCADV.

The Domestic Violence Act was passed in 1980, expanding police power to arrest and establishing orders of protection for those experiencing domestic violence to the second degree of consanguinity, or to first cousins. In 1986 the Act was expanded to include opposite-sex cohabitees. Arizona also has a surcharge on marriage licenses that is used to support domestic violence services.

The women's community in Phoenix is not very well organized. There is a strong pro-choice organization, a NOW chapter, and the County Task Force Against Domestic Violence. There was a small Take Back the Night organization, which held annual marches until 1986, when the march was postponed due to lack of participation. The shelters in the area are not feminist, although some are not opposed to feminism.[6] But the women's community is not united organizationally or ideologically.

Some parts of the country have strong women's communities which have provided the leadership for the battered women's movement. These cities include New York, Boston, Washington, D.C., Milwaukee, and San Francisco. All of the larger cities in Minnesota have organized groups that have implemented innovative domestic violence programs. Criminal justice reforms in cities with strong women's communities will probably be implemented differently from those without such groups, particularly in conservative areas. Reforms implemented without the input and continued monitoring of organized, unified women, will not be progressive. And unless these women include battered, low-income, minority, elderly, refugee, and disabled women, reforms will not reflect the needs of the entire population of battered women.

Police Perceptions of Woman Battering

The literature on police and woman battering cites a number of reasons why police do not like responding to calls to aid battered women (Bard 1969; Davis 1983; Buzawa and Buzawa 1985). These include danger to the police, concern about lawsuits against individual officers,[7] low rates of prosecution, wives' failure to follow through with complaints, and antipathy towards 'social work' versus crime fighting. All of these concerns were voiced by police officers we rode with. Most officers expressed frustration with 'family fight' calls, and believed there was little that law enforcement could do to stop wife beating. None of the officers liked to go to family fights, because they were perceived as no-win situations.

The mandate of the police, according to officers, is to maintain public order and peace. This mandate is consistent with responding to family fight calls only insofar as the 'fight' impinges on public peace and order. The police definition of the family is one of freely chosen association, the privacy of which should be guarded by the police against outside intruders. Battered women are viewed as voluntarily selecting a violent partner, and choosing to remain in an abusive situation. Their choice may be predicated on economic dependency and lack of viable alternatives, but the police view these problems as outside their area of expertise and control. Since it is assumed these adult women choose to live in violent relationships, police believe their involvement should be limited to situations where public peace and order are disturbed, that is, when the neighbors are complaining. Exceptions to this standard are cases of very severe violence, those involving lethal weapons, and those that endanger children. In cases observed where knives or guns were present on the scene, officers did make arrests. Such situations display characteristics that are known to lead to serious offenses, and therefore constitute legitimate concerns for police.

The belief that woman battering is not an appropriate arena for police work forms a background against which specific interactions are evaluated. The characteristics of women and their assailants are relevant to whether the fight is defined as 'a normal way of life for these people', or an exceptional occurrence that could be curtailed through police intervention. When violence is simply 'a way of life', police intervention is considered inappropriate. As several officers noted, 'One more arrest doesn't mean anything to these people.'

Normal versus Deviant Citizens

Officers tend to view the community as comprising dichotomous types of people: normal citizens and deviants. Normal citizens are people similar to themselves. They work, have families, live in nice, clean homes, do not use excessive amounts of alcohol or drugs, and speak English. Deviants do not work, have loose family structure or interracial marriages, are drunk and/or high most of the time, live in dirty, run-down homes, and sometimes speak foreign languages. The most frequently used term to describe such people was 'scum', but often the words 'these people' or 'those kind of people' were used to categorize people clearly defined as other. According to police knowledge of domestic violence, wife beating does occur among normal citizens. However, it is a rare occurrence, or for some officers, an understandable aspect of marital conflict. Woman battering in deviant families is viewed as part of the larger picture of pathology and vice.

The dichotomization of individuals into normal and deviant categories is certainly not unique to police officers. It is both a political and social-psychological mechanism for enhancing power and defining boundaries. Every officer recounted horror stories that justified this process, attempting to convince naïve researchers that some people were unquestionably different from us, that is, 'bad'. While the process is typically human and understandable, it organizes the manner in which officers define family fights. That is, there are family fights among normal citizens that are legitimate police concerns; there are family fights among deviants that the police cannot do anything about.

Even for family fights between normal citizens, however, the police stereotype of battered women is not conducive to the decision to arrest. The image most commonly held by police of the battered woman is that of an inconsistent complainant. Battered women are said to call the police for help, verbalize a desire for arrest, and later to recant. Every officer had personal or second-hand stories to document this stereotype. Some officers justified women's lack of commitment to prosecution by reference to economic dependency and fear of retribution. Regardless of the causes, however, an unwilling complainant resulted in a dropped case and, from the police perspective, a waste of time. Arrests took between three and four hours to complete. Officers later had to appear in court to testify, which usually meant going downtown during their time off. When women recanted their stories to detectives, failed to appear in court, or lied in court about the incident, officers felt betrayed.

The stereotype also led officers to be quite demanding of women's certainty about arrest at family fights. Officers asked women several times if they were sure they wanted an arrest, and explained they would have to testify in court and their husbands might go to jail. This questioning acted as a deterrent, sometimes apparently deliberately, to women to demand arrest. Given that women had just been physically assaulted by their husbands, and often had their homes torn up in the process, they were shaken and upset and needed time to recuperate. As one woman stated when asked if she desired arrest. 'Officer, that's very hard to answer right now.' In fact, in most cases observed, women stated that they did not desire prosecution, but simply to be left in peace for the night.

Both officer stereotypes about family fights and the ambiguity expressed by battered women were at odds with the department's mandate to arrest, creating a situation of dissonance for officers. The abstract policy ordered from above was thus interpreted on the street in light of these contradictory experiences.

Interpreting the Presumptive Arrest Policy

The initial presumptive arrest policy presented to officers required that arrests be made for all family fights, except in the most unusual circumstances. According to accounts by officers and police administrators, this hard-line approach produced a number of problems. Early examples include an instance where both husband and wife were arrested when neither had inflicted injury, because officers were unable to determine which party was at fault. One woman was arrested for tearing her own dress in an argument because officers had been instructed that destruction of community property was an offense and should result in arrest. The courts heard several cases where there was no evidence of any kind to substantiate arrest. A judge called the police chief to complain about the 'ridiculous' arrests being made. One month after the first policy was announced, officers were instructed that the policy did not override statutory requirements, and that probable cause must exist before an arrest should be made. The policy clarification did not soften the requirement to arrest, but only emphasised the need to establish probable cause.

The policy clarification, however, produced a variety of understandings among officers. Most officers told us that when the policy was first issued, they were required to arrest everybody. Some now believed that they were only to arrest when probable cause existed, which appears to be the intent of the clarification. Others, however, thought the change meant they were to increase their use of discretion, and only arrest when they thought it appropriate. Other officers perceived the clarification as a statement that things were 'back to normal', that is, that they were to continue handling family fights the way they always had, with rare use of arrest. These officers expressed the opinion that the first policy was either a political maneuver or an administrative mistake, and that the clarification was a directive to ignore the presumptive policy. A few officers did not know what the policy was.

An aspect of the presumptive arrest policy that opened the door to officer discretion was the requirement that probable cause be determined. This requirement is, of course, consistent with statutes designed to protect citizen rights. Individuals cannot be arrested for no reason, without evidence that an offense has occurred, and such arrests would waste the time of courts unable to prosecute for lack of witnesses and evidence. But officer interpretations of what constituted probable cause varied widely. According to the detective in charge of family fights, probable cause is established by the presence of visible injuries or property damage, weapons, or witnesses. For many officers, however, the existence of visible injuries to the complainant was required to establish probable cause. Property damage alone was never taken as sufficient evidence in cases we observed. In part, this was due to officers' perception that the law could not punish someone for damaging their own property in a community property state. In fact, the law and courts recognize that in family fights, men are damaging property that belongs in part to their wives, and thus are guilty of criminal damage. All of the officers we rode with were unaware of this, and did not arrest for destruction of property. Two women had their car windshields smashed in, one of these also had her tires slashed, one had her door kicked in and her apartment torn apart, and one had her water bed punctured by a knife. Men were not arrested for these acts. It was clear, however, that the women were terrorized and would have to replace their property at their own expense and inconvenience. Particularly when a woman is trying to escape from a violent husband, destruction of her vehicle is an effective method of immobilization.

Women who have been repeatedly beaten by their husbands know that threats of violence are usually not idle. In several cases, women called the police in fear after being threatened. These calls, however, did not constitute probable cause, and officers explained there was nothing they could do. This was true even when witnesses to the threats were present. Although threats technically fall within the boundaries of the domestic violence statute, they are not viewed as cases that could legitimately be pursued as criminal offenses.

The Arrest Decision

Arrests

Of the sixty-nine cases of domestic violence, only nine (13 per cent) resulted in arrest. This is a marked reduction from the 53 to 72 per cent rate reflected in the official police statistics. Of the nine arrests observed, six were of husbands. One man was arrested for possession of a concealed knife, one for discharging a firearm at his son, and the rest were arrested for assaulting their wives. Three of these men also assaulted one or more of their children. In all of these cases, the men were on the scene at the time, and in all but the knife incident, the wife desired an arrest to be made.

The other three arrests were of former lovers, one woman and two men. The woman was extremely upset that her former lover had a new woman friend. She put her own hand through a window and then stabbed the man in the neck. Although they did not fall under the domestic violence statute because they were not legally married, an assault with a deadly weapon does not require direct observation by an officer for an arrest to be made. The other two cases involved hitting bystanders.

In the first case, the man was enraged at the woman he was living with. She had previously reported him to child protective services for hitting her two-year-old son. They began arguing at Thanksgiving dinner, and he threw a glass of wine at her, spit on her, and locked her out of her home. Her male neighbour, who was eating Thanksgiving dinner with them, followed the woman out the house and they called the police. He walked back to the house and knocked on the door, and her former boyfriend opened it and punched him in the mouth, knocking loose his two front teeth. Then the police officer arrived, and as he walked to the door, the man moved toward him with a raised ball bat. The officer knelt and aimed his gun at the man. The man slammed the door in his face and escaped through the back window.

It is important to note that this was the only case observed in which the officer directly experienced danger. When men were not on the scene, or sat placidly on the sofa, police did not have the immediate experience of danger that the women felt. In this situation, the officer's observation and feeling of danger led him to an unusually aggressive response.

The officer chased the man, but could not locate him. At the woman's suggestion, the officer then hid his car in the alley and waited for the man to return. In a few minutes he burst through the door, and the officer threw him to the floor and tied his hands and feet behind his back. The woman was then instructed to place her foot on his back and say, 'I place you under citizen's arrest for assault.' This man was charged with two counts of simple assault, one for punching the neighbour, and one for spitting on the woman. After leaving the scene, the officer commented that the case 'wouldn't fly', because the couple was not married, and the neighbour could be considered a trespasser. In fact, our observer was called to court as a witness in this case, and the woman appeared to testify, but the man who was assaulted did not. The offender pled to one count of assault for spitting.

This arrest decision is interesting in several ways. First, the officer told the woman that she could initiate a citizen's arrest. Although this is always an option in assaults that are not covered by the domestic violence statute, it is rarely communicated. In this case, however, there was a second, more seriously injured victim, and the officer observed the man threatening with a ball bat. The seriousness of the injury, the presence of witnesses, the observed threat with a weapon, and the man's attempted escape in the presence of the officer led to an arrest. Two missing teeth, however, do not constitute a felony assault, and the officer did not witness the offense. Therefore, use of the citizen's arrest ensured the legitimacy of taking this man into custody.

The second unusual feature was the attempt to lure the offender back to the scene by hiding the police car. Although a number of women expressed fear that their violent husbands would return after the police left, in no other cases did officers attempt to conceal their presence, or return to make sure there was no further violence. In this case, the woman's suspicion that the man would return when the 'coast was clear' was taken seriously and acted upon. If the officer had left, it is almost certain that further violence would have occurred.

Finally, in this case, it was the male, unacquainted neighbour who failed to appear in court, and not the woman. Although the officer did not believe this case would result in prosecution, there was a conviction for spitting on a cohabitee. The case runs against police stereotypes of unwilling victims and the notion that nothing can be done when victims are unmarried.

Decisions Not to Arrest

In forty-five cases of domestic violence involving married and unmarried couples, thirty-six did not result in arrest. In many cases, the offender was not on the scene for the arrest to be made. Men who know the police have been called will usually leave the home until they know the police have been and gone. In one study, women who simply called the police were less likely to be assaulted than women who did not (Lanagan and Innes 1986). In others, there were no signs of physical abuse, deadly weapons, or property damage. In some cases, officers perceived the degree of violence as low (a single slap), and used discretion in employing alternatives to arrest.

In some cases, however, it was not clear that an arrest should not be made given the presumptive arrest policy. In these situations, a variety of rationales were used to explain decisions not to arrest.

One case involved a Native American couple from a reservation visiting relatives. The man was intoxicated. He broke the windshield on his wife's truck, slashed her tires, threw oil over it, and hit her in the face. When the officer arrived, the male relatives were sitting inside, the woman was outside, and the man was walking down the street. The man denied he was her husband and denied responsibility for destruction of the truck. He and his wife were both told that it was not an offense to destroy one's own property. The husband went back in the house, and the wife was told an arrest could not be made without visible signs of injury. She then expressed disinterest in prosecution, although she was given no indication that she had other options. The officer told her that it would be best for her and her children to spend the night somewhere else. She had four children, and this would have been a difficult course for her to follow, since her vehicle was immobilized and she was from out of town. The male relatives inside the apartment were not questioned about the incident. After leaving the scene, the officer said that there was no probable cause in this case, because there were no visible marks. Later that evening, however, this officer made the arrest for the spitting incident.

In another married couple incident, the woman displayed burn marks around her neck that were made when her husband choked her. She had fled with one child from her mother's home, where the assault occurred. She had walked to a friend's home and together they had used a pay phone to call the police. She wanted the officer to accompany her back to her mother's to get her other child, who was sleeping there. Her husband was still in the house. It was after 2:00 a.m. when we responded to this call. It was in the middle of a very run-down housing project. The woman was quite terrified, but the officer refused to assist her. The mother's house was two blocks away, but he said he did not have time to take her there and help get the child. He also said that the child was not in danger, and that the arrival of the police would serve to anger and upset her husband. He suggested she spend the night with her friend and that she call the police again if there was any further trouble. The woman was distraught and said that the officer she spoke with on the phone said someone would accompany her to the house. The officer was annoyed with her and told her to lock herself in her friend's apartment and get some sleep.

When we left, the officer explained that there was no point in involving the police in this situation, since everyone was out of danger. He drove by the mother's home to see if there was any sign of disturbance, and all the lights were off. The yard was strewn with ten to twelve beer cans. Although there were visible signs of injury, witnesses to the assault, and a terrified woman, and the location of the offender was known, this case was deemed inappropriate for arrest, since there was no apparent immediate danger involved.

The most serious injuries observed were inflicted on a young woman who was left standing on the sidewalk after being beaten by her boyfriend. No call was placed to the police on this incident, but she was observed by the officer, who stopped to ask her what happened. Her face was covered with cuts and blood, she had a large bump over her eye, and it appeared that her nose was broken. Her shirt was soaked in blood. The woman was somewhat intoxicated, but lucid. She said that her boyfriend had beaten her up, and asked to be given a ride to a bar a few blocks away. The officer asked if she wanted to press charges or have him look for her boyfriend. She said that she did not desire prosecution. She was told that police are not permitted to transport citizens, and was left standing on the sidewalk.

Although this assault was serious, it was not technically a felony assault. Since the woman was unmarried to her assailant, it was important to the officer that she did not want to press charges. The only avenue to arrest in this case would have been a citizen's arrest, and since she said she did not want to do anything, that option was not explained to her. The officer spent less than five minutes with this woman, did not file a detective's report on the incident, and provided no offers of assistance. Technically, however, he was following department policy.

In almost all cases where an arrest was made, it could be argued that there were legal or practical justifications for the decision, such as no suspect on the scene. However, in similar circumstances at other times, arrests *were* made, sometimes by the same officer who had declined to arrest earlier. The variety of police responses to these calls indicates the discretionary decision-making that took place, even in the face of a presumptive arrest policy.

Rationales for Police Decisions

Police described their reasons for implementing various options in terms of implicit and explicit rationales. Their ideas about woman battering and their occupational values and concerns formed background, implicit rationales for decision-making. The ideas that women can leave violent relationships if they want to or that violence is normal among certain groups were not consistent with a pro-arrest approach. Explicit rationales included legalistic, practical, client-oriented, and holistic considerations (Ferraro 1987). Officers invoked a lack of evidence (legalistic), the time

175

involved in tracking down offenders (practical), the belief that women did not want to press charges (client oriented), and the conviction that the case would not be prosecuted (holistic) as explanations for non-arrest decisions.

Although specific officers expressed racist attitudes in comments to the observers, they did not refuse to arrest men who assaulted women of colour, nor did they limit arrests to men of colour. In the sense of dichotomizing the community into normal and deviant populations, however, race was a relevant factor. It was only one factor, however, in the categorization process. Of overriding importance was the social class of victim and offender. Wife beating among lower-income couples was generally not taken as seriously as wife beating in middle-class homes.

The demeanour of the battered woman and the offender were also relevant criteria in decision-making. When women were ambivalent about arrest, were intoxicated or disorderly, or flatly stated a preference for non-arrest, officers did not arrest. When offenders were drunk and/or belligerent in the presence of the officer, an arrest was more likely to be made. When offenders were violent in the presence of officers, arrests were always made.

Officers did not blatently subvert the policy and tell women who pleaded for arrest that there was nothing they could do. Neither did they uniformly arrest in every case that legally met the criteria of the presumptive arrest policy. They employed rationales based on their own perspective on woman battering and policing to determine which intervention to employ in the context of a specific case. Officer evaluations of the dynamics of those cases, as well as the characteristics of the couple, determined whether arrests were made.

Battered Women's Assessments of Police

Of seventeen interviews with women who called the police, eight expressed negative evaluations of their response. The other nine women described the police as 'professional', 'very nice', or 'very helpful'. These evaluations are important, because they are not biased by the presence of an observer at the time of intervention. They are biased, however, by the selection process involved in volunteering and then actually completing the interview.

Two of the women were arrested. In the first case, the woman had heard a police interview on the radio encouraging women to call the police. She called when her husband was threatening her, and the police arrested both of them. She spent the night in jail, and it was an extremely traumatic experience. Her husband obtained an order of protection against her, and made her move out of the house. She described the police behavior towards her as 'professional', but disagreed with their decision to arrest her. She said she would tell other battered women to call a counselor, not the police.

The other woman was arrested for hitting her husband with an ashtray. They got into an argument while playing cards, and he began to choke her with his arm. A friend called the police. The woman hit her husband in the head with the ashtray as a way to break his choke hold. When the police arrived, the only visible injury was a cut on her husband's head, so they arrested her. This woman also described the police as 'professional', and thought they were probably only doing their job. She did not agree, however, with their decision to arrest her. She had a small daughter, and she was very concerned for her daughter's well-being while she spent the night in jail. She obviously did not think the arrest helped the situation.

Other sources of dissatisfaction involved rudeness, failing to follow through on their problems, and telling the woman they could not do anything. In one case, a woman called the police to accompany her to pick up her child from her ex-husband. The police left before the encounter was over, and the man punched her and broke a tooth.

In several cases the women described the police as 'very good', but of no help. These women expressed the opinion that nothing could stop their husbands' violence. In all of these cases, the husband was allegedly alcoholic. Their wives believed they were 'crazy', and nothing the police could do would stop them.

One woman reported that her husband leaves when she calls the police, hides, and returns when they are gone. On one occasion, in which he had bloodied her face, she explained this problem to the responding officers. They told her they would leave and return, but they did not. This same woman reported that the officers 'yelled at' her because she refused to press charges. She explained that her husband had recently obtained work after a long period of unemployment. She was afraid arrest would result in the loss of this job.

She finally obtained an order of protection, and thought that it would help to control her husband's violence. He had hit her, however, while the order was in effect.

Two other women said that the order of protection was not helpful. They reported that they were told they violated the order by seeing their husbands. The police therefore refused to enforce it.

Two women said that they did not want to press charges because they were concerned about losing their own or a relative's immigration status. Although none of the women in our sample expressed this concern, other women may be worried that their husbands will be deported if criminal charges are brought against them.

Finally, five of the seventeen women had only positive things to say about the police response. One woman said their intervention had shocked them both into getting help. The help this couple turned to was fundamentalist religion and prayer. She reported that they had experienced no further violence since they had both turned to Jesus. Three of the other women who were very pleased with the police divorced their husbands.[8] The other woman was divorced at the time of the assault. She got a second order of protection against her former husband, and he stopped bothering her.

The women were not united in what they wanted police to do about battering. Most said they would tell other women to call the police and have their husbands arrested if they were battered. Yet in their own situations, few felt that arrest was an answer. Some wanted their husbands to get counseling. Two said that they wanted counseling for themselves as well. Those who wanted counseling were married to alcoholics, and thought that dealing with the drinking was the only thing that would stop the violence. Two women married to alcoholics, however, believed that nothing would change their husbands.

Most of the other women either wanted the violence to stop, or wanted their husbands to stay away from them. Women who wanted to remain in their marriages just wanted the violence to stop, and were mixed in their emotions about involving the criminal justice system. Women who wanted their husbands to stay away from them wanted the police to be more helpful about enforcing orders of protection.

Discussion

This study of policing battering has found that decision-making criteria and rationales are not eliminated by the adoption of a pre-sumptive arrest policy. Officers will continue to respond to battering based on their implicit assumptions about battering and policing and their explicit evaluations of the characteristics of individuals and situations. The persistence of discretionary decision-making does not reflect disregard for administrative policy, or disdain for battered women. It reflects the realities of police work and the limitations of a criminal justice response to battering. A policy of nonintervention that encourages police to treat battering as a civil rather than a criminal matter has been the cause of much suffering and harm to battered women. This lack of protection cannot be tolerated if women are to escape violence. Immediate protection to individual women may be enhanced by more arrests. The data in this observational research suggest that some officers operating under a presumptive arrest policy are apt to take family fight calls seriously, and to arrest in some cases that are only marginally justifiable on strictly legal grounds. Still, the vast majority of family fight calls do not result in arrest. This is not only due to officer resistance to the policy, but also to the fact that family fight situations are not uniform and often lack clear-cut legal grounds for arrest, even when arrest power is expanded. The fact that most men flee when they know the police have been called, sometimes to return again when the coast is clear, also mitigates against immediate arrest.

It is also apparent that some women do not want their husbands arrested, but either want assistance in leaving with their children, or want their husbands to be taken somewhere to sober up. There may be very legitimate grounds for women's resistance to arrest, other than stereotypical conceptions of passivity or concern for the man. Arrest does not always mean detention. In the city where our research took place, most men are released within a few hours. Others are held overnight, but released the next day. Those who are actually prosecuted spend no more than a week in jail, or six weeks at a maximum. Such sentences, however, are a rare exception. While a week is not enough time for a woman to complete divorce proceedings, it is time enough for a man to lose a job. There is no guarantee that a man quickly released from jail will not return in an angry rage. While Sherman and Berk (1984a) found a 24-hour violence respite after release from jail in all of their follow-up interviews, it is not clear from their data whether all men were held for at least one day. One day is quite different from an hour or two, as it allows him to calm down and sober up and the woman to find transportation to a shelter or a friend's home.

For many women, involvement with the legal system is not a desirable outcome, for regardless of their fear of their husbands, their distrust of the legal system is greater (Radford 1987). This is particularly true for women holding marginal social status, such as women living on AFDC,[9] those with illegal immigration status, and those involved in illegal occupations.

On the other hand, arrest is a statement of wrongdoing, and provides symbolic support to women seeking to escape violent relationships. And, in the event of further violence, there is documentation that there have been previous assaults, and thus the possibility of lengthier sentences. This 'paper chain' of police intervention becomes critically relevant for battered women who eventually assault or kill their husbands in self-defense. Some women do want to prosecute their husbands, and so willingness of officers to follow their requests is desirable.

A policy should not only be evaluated in terms of its impact on specific individuals, however. Presumptive arrest policy should be examined within the broader context of social reality and its impact on that reality. There is a history of policy initiatives spurred by the actions of moral entrepreneurs attempting to rid society of particular evils. These include the purity crusade to eliminate prostitution (Musheno and Seeley 1986, Gordon 1976; Pivar 1973), Prohibition to eliminate alcoholism (Gusfield 1963), the child saving movement to eliminate delinquency and abuse of child labor (Platt 1969), and the series of efforts to control opiate and marijuana use (Becker 1963; Lauderdale 1983; Dickson 1968). Each of these endeavours has been founded on a moral condemnation of specific acts portrayed in a unidimensional, simplistic fashion. Policies developed from these movements emphasized social control of individuals to eliminate the offensive activities.

Implicit in these policies was the assumption of dichotomy between the pure and the impure, the deviant and the normal, which was amplified by the campaign to stamp out the problem. Historically, mobilization of social control over these acts has been intertwined with white, middle-class fears of immigrants, the working class, and racial and ethnic minorities. While the campaigns focused on specific problems created by capitalist expansion, patriarchy, and rapid urbanization, they all portrayed the 'impure' behaviors (prostitution, alcoholism, delinquency) as deviations from an inherently moral, 'pure' order. The ideology underlying these campaigns was the same: patriarchy and capitalism are sublime systems of social organization, which only need occasional purifications of deviant elements to maintain social harmony. The legitimacy of the state and the family were not at issue, but were held up as ideals that deserved protection from the threats of deviance.

The results of these crusades were the enhancement of social control mechanisms, deepening of the boundaries between deviant and normal populations, and limitations of free choice under the guise of protectionism. The purity crusade did not improve the economic or social position of women, but did contribute to the social ideology concerning the ideal woman's lack of sexual appetite (Smith-Rosenberg 1986). The child-saving movement established limits on the type and amount of work that could be demanded of children, but also created enormous discretionary state power to intervene in the lives of youths (Platt 1969).

A focus on increased policing of battering has the potential to divert attention from the sources of violence to its individual perpetrators. Earlier punitive efforts in the United States were characterized by an idealization of the nuclear family and mother-hood and were spearheaded by political conservatives (Pleck 1987). The intention of punishment was to strengthen the family and the traditional roles of men and women within it. In the 1980s official response to battering is subsumed under the neutral category of 'family violence'. A get tough, punitive approach is advocated by right-wing politicians who oppose reproductive choice, funding for shelters, and welfare benefits. This approach severs the social perception of woman battering from its roots in structured gender inequality, and elevates the criminal justice system as the appro-priate agency for eliminating violence against women. It is consistent with current conservative political imagery in which social problems are presented and treated as the manifestations of individual deficiencies. The political conservative's support for the criminalization of 'domestic violence' is couched in terms of the importance of the American family, and the danger battering presents to this institution. Their support belies the fact that the criminal justice system is not designed to empower women, but to maintain traditional family structures.

Still, women need protection from the male violence that permeates patriarchal cultures. In many cases, women want and need criminal justice agents to respond with swiftness and certainty to their assaults. Yet it is obvious that efforts to change police behavior apart from changes in the entire legal system and in the structure of society more generally lead to absurd contradictions. For example, it makes no sense to arrest men for battering and then to award sole or joint custody or liberal visitation rights to divorced men who have battered their wives (Chesler 1986). Similarly, if women want to divorce abusive men, they should be provided with the material resources to do so, rather than with a slim chance of staying in an overcrowded shelter for two weeks.

In the contemporary United States it is difficult to maintain efforts at social change without becoming incorporated into the existing system. While enhanced policing of battering cannot be rejected as a tool, it should never be forgotten whose hand controls that tool. The elimination of violence against women, like other women's issues, requires flexibility and wariness in utilizing existing structures, such as the criminal justice system. Strategies that are developed without appreciation of the structural features which support battering will be easily coopted.

Male violence against women in the United States is encouraged through militarism, competition, race, sex, and class inequality, and media glamorizations of violence. On the other hand, women are constrained by the structure of household labor, economic oppression, and fear of male violence. Enhanced police protection is one way of reducing this fear. It will not, however, change the structural conditions that perpetuate male violence and women's economic dependence on violent males.

Notes

1 Probable cause refers to legal criteria for determining whether it is legally reasonable to believe that an offense has been committed and a specific individual has committed the offense. In order to make an arrest for battering, an officer must have some evidence to establish probable cause. Acceptable evidence includes the woman's testimony,

testimony of witnesses, presence of physical injury, property damage or weapons. It is up to the officer to determine whether probable cause exists.

2   'Family fight' is a police department term, and I recognize that it is not an appropriate term for describing woman battering, since it masks the direction of violence from man to woman. We found that many types of disputes were coded 'family fight', by police dispatchers, including neighbor disputes. An analysis of how police dispatchers code incoming calls would be important for a complete understanding of policing battering.

3   Funding for this tudy was obtained through internal university grants. Applications were submitted to the National Science Foundation (NSF) and the National Institute of Justice (NIJ). NSF referees judged the proposal fundable, but did not allocate funds for the project. NIJ did not accept our proposal, but suggested we replicate the Sherman-Berk experimental study, for which nearly $2 million was allocated. We declined this opportunity.

4   The debate on deterrence is complex. It involves numerous attempts to apply statistical models to relationships between sanctions, behavior, and other variables. The statement here is a vast oversimplification of the deterrence debate. The point is, the question of the impact of arrests on battering relationships was of interest to us.

5   The seventeen interviews conducted represent only 17 per cent of the randomly selected sample drawn by police detectives. It should not, therefore, be considered representative of the entire population of women who called the police. The interviews with these women only describe the range of reactions and evaluations of police interventions.

6   The existence of non-feminist shelters may seem odd to those in other countries. In the United States shelter work is carried out not only by feminists, but by religious groups, traditional social service agencies, and drug and alcohol abuse groups. 'Feminism' is not a term that is comfortable to most of these groups. They view feminism as inherently anti-male and anti-family, and a dangerous label politically. In my survey of 127 shelters in 1978, only 46 per cent described themselves as feminist (Ferraro 1981b). In Wharton's more recent survey, she found six of twenty-five groups defined themselves as feminist, eleven saying they were not explicitly feminist, but agreed with feminist principles, and eight groups denying that they were feminist (Wharton 1987).

7   In the United States it is possible for citizens to sue police departments and individual officers for failing to conduct themselves appropriately. Police are sued for use of deadly force and for failure to provide protection, as in *Thurman v. Torrington* case, described on p. 160.

8   The fact that women who divorced their abusers were satisfied with the police response highlights the importance of legal and stuctural changes beyond the level of law enforcement. Those women with the

legal and practical resources to get out of the relationship appear to be the most satisfied with police intervention.

9 AFDC is Aid to Families with Dependent Children, and is a form of government supplement to single women with small children who do not earn enough money to survive. AFDC payments, however, are very low in most states. In Arizona in 1986 the monthly AFDC payment for a woman with two children was $248.

Chapter eight

Improving Policing for Women: The Way Forward

Jalna Hanmer, Jill Radford, and Elizabeth A. Stanko

Focusing on the policing needs on women that result from men's violence challenges the paradigms of both mainstream and radical criminologists. Contextualizing narrow questions concerning crime control or the protection of the community against crime raises fundamental political questions about the nature of the social order that the police are expected to protect. In societies like those addressed in this volume, the social order is characterized by power structures that divide and hierarchically structure the community into classes, races, and sexual groups and by gender. Because the police are accorded a front-line position in the maintenance of society as presently constructed their role is fundamentally political.

As the aim of policing is traditionally defined as the maintenance of public order, most analyses have focused on policing in the public arena. The police are seen to have a dual role: policing social relations in areas deemed public and preventing crime. The former is particularly well understood in the policing of public protest in relation to political struggles around industrial and economic issues and the consequent change in class relations. Recent examples from Britain include the policing of protest around industrial change in the mining and print industries, which involved large numbers of officers over extended periods of time and cost many millions of pounds. However, political struggles challenging existing social divisions based on race and imperialism, sexuality and gender are also characterized by inequality, exploitation, and oppression and consume considerable police resources. Recent examples from Britain include the policing of protest around attempts to restrict abortion, the rights of black people to remain in Britain, demands to end support for the racist regime in South Africa, and the expression of homosexuality and lesbianism as acceptable ways of life. Similarly, protests in the United States concerning access to abortion and military involvement in Central America have demanded considerable police time. The Australian bicentennial has been a focus of aboriginal demands for recognition.

The second arena of public order policing is located at the juncture of public order policing and crime prevention. In Britain for example, the inner city became a site of struggle when popular definitions of crime became associated with deprived and depressed black populations. Inner city residents, targeted for intensive surveillance and police action, responded by resistance and uprisings, converting a racist understanding of crime and crime prevention into a traditional public order policing scenario. In terms of resources and policing strategies, the focus is on the technical hardware required by officers for riot control, the increasing use of computers, and selective targeting and surveillance.

Defining the problem for policing in terms of the maintenance of public order is socially legitimated by the belief that the police can adopt a neutral social role. This is guaranteed by local or community accountability. Community accountability is often seen as a panacea, but it rests on an understanding of the community as a unified structure, one in which individuals do not have differential interests. For example, if racist and sexist ideologies predominate in a community, then community accountability cannot guarantee progressive change in police policy or practice. While issues around public order policing, crime prevention, and community accountability constitute the context in which practical policing is discussed, and mainstrean and radical criminologists analyse and debate, this context is genderless. A paradigm that focuses on the policing of gendered power relations is not included within this structuring of the issues and analysis of community need for policing and policing strategies. To include gender necessitates a new understanding of the public and the private.

Policing Private Arenas

The conceptual division of social life into public and private is a social construction that arises out of gendered social relations. Like the concept of the division of labour, that of the public and the private does not predate the social relations that give rise to it. Social relations characterized by subordination and superordination are named private and public and the labels become reified. This reification takes the following form: the private and the public, like the division of labour, are converted mentally into materiality where they appear to exist outside and prior to the social relations that make up the orderly patterns of hierarchically structured social life they describe. This way of understanding the concepts of the public and the private is socially necessary because the division of social life into these two categories is the major justification for a system of discriminatory policing in relation to gender.

The reification of the public and the private is an ideology that explains and justifies the decriminalization of men's violence against women. Viewed on the level of the individual, men and women act in the social world as gendered subjects. This means that not only are the police engaging in a world inhabited by gendered subjects in unequal power relationships, but the police also are gendered and constitute a part of, they are not above or outside, struggles around gendered relations. Identifying the police as gendered subjects provides insight into their public order and crime prevention activities.

The media surrounds us with reports of skyrocketing criminality, and constructs images of safety and danger that feed into public debates about the nature of crime, perceptions of public fears of crime, and how these issues are to be tackled. These media presentations generally lack a gender analysis. They are distorted through notions of neighbourhood safety and danger in the inner city, and the conflation of racist and classist ideologies. The result is to define certain areas as unsafe for women, and with each sexual murder or attack, the number expands. For example, Chapter 5 describes how the whole of West Yorkshire was defined as unsafe for women for the five years before the so-called Yorkshire Ripper, Peter Sutcliffe, was captured. The violence of men is being misrepresented as a geographical problem. This misrepresentation serves to control women by laying a geographical basis for the fear of crime, which limits our access to the community. Transforming the paradigm from a fear of men and male violence to geography enables men to be presented as our protectors.

The home can then be ideologically constructed as a safe haven in which women find love and security. This second link in the ideological chain serves to define the home, not only as woman's place, but as a safe and secure space (Stanko 1988). The ideology of hetero-patriarchy in part depends on a closely woven system of ideas about the security and safety of the family home for women in contrast to the dangerous crime-ridden and unsafe public world that women should only enter with male protection. The way police intervene in gendered interpersonal crime is essential to the continuing credibility of this ideology.

As a part of their crime prevention role, the police are accorded a formal responsibility for citizen safety that includes offering protection from violent crime. But most of the time the police cannot and will not provide pro-active protection to citizens, although it is accepted that Very Important People must be provided with round-the-clock protection. While 'citizen' is an apparently ungendered term, it would be a mistake to assume men and women are treated the same. Understanding about citizen safety is mediated by assumptions about gender. By and large men are regarded as capable of self-protection and women are protected through their dependency on men. Women outside of men's protection are then defined as deviant women, provocative women, undeserving of protection.

Crime prevention work increasingly draws on citizen participation. Citizens are instructed to use good sense in the fight against crime, which means making reasonable judgements about safety precautions. Our homes need converting into impenetrable fortresses and callers are to be scrutinized and identified before allowed entry. Through crime prevention policies the householder is made responsible for his, and his family (*sic*) safety. The police are not required to provide further protection.

A focus on women's experiences of violence can only lead researchers and theorists of policing to question and challenge the current understanding about strategies of public order and crime prevention policing. While the state, through the organization of the police and criminal justice system generally, is unable and unwilling to sustain a serious confrontation with men's violence directed at women, it is prepared to vociferously protect itself from terrorism or public disorder. The protection it offers women from violent men has been exposed as rhetoric (Hanmer and Stanko 1985) and the public face of this rhetoric is exposed most clearly in court trials of men for the rape or murder of women. A major focus is on the ways the victimized woman is not worthy of protection given her past or current behaviour (Jeffreys and Radford 1984; Radford 1984b).

The disjuncture between masculinist conceptions of policing and feminist analyses of violence against women which recognize men's violence as reflecting and securing women's subordinate status in hetero-patriachal societies is immense. This disjuncture is reflected in the language of policing and the courts, with socially constructed meanings and assumptions about the nature of 'crime', 'real crime', 'proper police work', 'sufficient evidence', and 'violence'. Because men hold greater social power, the largely male police and judiciary reflect their gendered knowledge and understanding in these definitions and the actions that flow from them.

In debates on policing male violence, feminist visions of women's autonomy are overshadowed by police visions of protection. A major task is to find a way by which feminists can promote the view that woman should be free of violence without compromising women's independence. This is not easy, but failure to engage in the debate on policing and to secure benefits for women will leave many women open to further abuse and even death. As previous chapters illustrate, the challenge for change has begun. Police in many Western countries today are under pressure from feminist activists and researchers to question the processes by which men's violence is policed. New police training inputs on rape, sexual assault, and the physical and sexual abuse of children are beginning to be added to officer education at all levels. New techniques are being introduced in the investigation of rape, sexual assault, and murder, including a review of the interviewing skills needed for women and children victimized by sexual violence.

These recent developments and 'reforms' are carried out in the name of women as a result of feminist criticisms. But do these reforms secure benefits for women? To be valid reforms must benefit *all* women irrespective of race, class, or relationship to heterosexuality. This is a principle in its own right, but are there also dangers for women in reforms that accord protection to only some women. Policies may benefit women more privileged in terms of divisions in societies around race, class, sexuality, age, or disability. Reforms, which on the surface appear to address violence against women, can cool out criticism through a redefinition of the problem and the appropriate response that excludes feminist analyses. With skillful public relations and media inputs the problem may be presented as solved; only women identified as irrational extremist feminists will be portrayed as dissatisfied.

The rise of the New Right in Europe and the United States, combined with the emergence of fundamentalist patriarchal religions worldwide, obviously has implications for women. Reforms introduced in this political climate require careful scrutiny. It is possible to envisage partial reform that ostensibly brings benefits to some women but serves only to secure women more firmly under family control. This would undermine the feminist goal of independence or autonomy for women. For example, a greater commitment to pursue, prosecute, and punish rapists who are strangers to women, while at the same time denying protection to women victimized by husbands, lovers, fathers, brothers, or other relatives and associates, obscures the unacceptable face of hetero-patriarchy. This process itself increases the power of men in the family over women by defining rapists as someone other than the men whom women live with and know. This is, of course, a traditional formula for the control of women, one discredited by the recent protests of women. In these changed times new packaging is required for the continuation of hetero-patriarchy in new forms.

The studies in this volume provide important insights into women's relationship to policing and the policing of male violence. Jill Radford's historical work alerts us to an initial recognition of the gendered nature of policing. The struggles for the establishment of women police in England earlier this century point to the extent of resistance to women police and the threat that women police, that is women with authority and power of arrest, posed for men inside and outside the police. Further, it demonstrates that when total opposition to the idea of women police was no longer politically viable, the men in charge found ways to undermine this feminist challenge. The women that were allowed into the force were those most accepting of male definitions and understanding about policing — that is those most accepting of male authority and priorities.

Radford further illustrates how a feminist-inspired campaign for a women's police force to control male violence without compromising women's independence was appropriated by the patriarchal state to simultaneously redress an obvious grievance and eliminate a site for struggle while achieving through the use of women a more effective and efficient policing of women. This history remains relevant today in several ways. First, women serving in the police forces of the countries referred to in this volume have neither the numbers nor the authority to effect major changes in policing practices that can benefit women. Second, history alerts us to the likelihood that women with this aim will be unacceptable to the police hierarchy and will be eased out long before they reach positions of influence.

The demand for women police comes from women in the community discussed in Chapter 5. Following an attack women may be reluctant to talk to male police officers. Some women prefer to speak to women officers because they assume they·will be more sympathetic. The assumption is that the shared gendered experience of life will make it easier for women officers to understand what has happened, but in practice some report that women police are even less sympathetic than their male colleagues (Radford 1987). The explanation for this lies in the power of masculinity within the organization of policing. Women who enter the force can be overshadowed by an institution that rigorously reinforces a gendered male view of policing and of men and women.

Women recruits enter a masculine bastion and, while change from within may be possible, it is likely to be slow and painful for its participants. As an individual a woman officer may have, and show, understanding and empathy with women victimized by male violence, but such attitudes run counter to the dominant ideology of her profession. There may be explicit or implicit criticism of her style of working and even a questioning of her suitability for police work. The presence of a small number of women in contemporary police forces cannot dent a male-dominated institution committed to securing the gendered status quo. The presence of a few women officers cannot alter the fact that in most policing situations police officers intervene as male gendered subjects.

In later chapters the focus is on the policing of violence against women in the home by men known to the women concerned. The police in the countries examined in this volume define home-based violence as 'domestic' and 'not real police work'. Despite these common sentiments, in recent years police authorities have introduced initiatives ostensibly to improve the policing of violence in the home. Elizabeth Stanko's article describes police forces as divided by conflicting interests that arise out of differential responsibilities within a hierarchical structure. As she points out it is the response of the officer on the spot, and not directives from policy making senior officers, that may be more influential in determining the outcome in any particular situation of violence against women. Relationships within the police are influenced by internal tensions and resistance to policy changes imposed from above.

Examining the police from an organizational point of view clarifies why changes in policy alone are insufficient to secure reforms. Stanko's point is that effecting change in police procedure is more complex and needs to involve police retraining progammes, alterations in the system of internal rewards or inducements for serving officers charged with the implementation of the new policy, and shifts in police attitudes and awareness so that violence against women is perceived as criminal behaviour. Further, policing is only one part of the criminal justice process. Other decision-makers from clerks to the court, the prosecution service, and judges influence the outcome of any case that reaches the courtroom. Resistance on the part of prosecutors provides further evidence that the legal system, its procedures, and rules of evidence are not favourable to women when adjudicating violence against women. The total criminal justice system is likely to concur that home-based violence is 'private' or 'domestic' and not properly the business of the criminal courts.

The general points raised in Chapters 2 and 3 are illustrated by specific studies in four separate nations. Identifying current practices in the policing of male violence in the home raises feminist strategies for the protection of women. Across national states and jurisdictions, a number of themes recur. Policing violence in the home makes a substantial demand on police time. While attending 'domestics' is a common experience for police officers, their responses to women's requests for assistance are not consistent. Guidelines for changes in police approaches lose much of their strength when not consistently applied (illustrated by the presumptive arrest policy, discussed in Chapter 7). Inconsistencies in the application of this policy have led to confusion and uncertainty for the women involved.

The chapters on the four countries demonstrate that women calling the police are demanding active intervention to bring the violent encounter to an end. Women are indeed active in 'crime prevention'. Achieving this fundamental first priority will vary depending on the circumstances of women. Some women may want transport for themselves and their children to a place of safety; some may want police assistance to exclude a man from their homes, or police assistance in securing court orders that achieve this end; some may want police assistance in returning to their homes following the granting of such orders; some may want police assistance to return home to retrieve their children, or their own and their children's belongings. Some women may need the temporary respite provided by presumptive arrest policies to facilitate their escape from the home, while others may want an arrest in the knowledge that this, in and of itself, will bring an end to the violence by clearly showing the man that 'society' supports the woman in her belief that violence is a criminal and not a socially sanctioned method of dispute resolution. Other women may judge an arrest as a way to escalate violence by adding to the grievances of the man with whom she intends to continue a relationship.

The police on the doorstep are not in the best position to make judgements regarding the longer-term consequences of their actions. While a woman may on occasion misjudge a man and, for example, remain in a life-threatening situation, officers who do not know her or him are much less likely to be able to accurately judge the future from a brief house call. Series or repeated violence is the most difficult situation for police officers to respond to success-fully, because their actions all too often are based on the mistaken belief that they should be able to predict future outcomes or that the future is of no concern, and only the present event is important.

Officers attending violence in the home are likely to encounter situations in which women are attempting to mediate the violence in their lives and have turned to the prefessionals as a last resort, that is when they no longer have any control over the situation. 'Calling the cops' may well be an extreme action reflecting a woman's feeling of powerlessness and desperation. This also may be the case when she cannot make the call herself, but sends a child to do so, or even when neighbours phone. In contrast, the police perception is of another family fight where identifying the aggressor and the victim is irrelevant. Both parties are assumed to be responsible for violence arising within the home as illustrated in Chapter 4. Presumptive arrest policies, however, attempt to provide the attacked or injured person protection in times of acute crisis during or following a potentially dangerous outburst. However, on occasion the police have drawn on their powers to either arrest both parties or even just the woman, who is most likely to be the target of violence.

Despite the educative work feminists in many countries are attempting with the police, there is a general lack of awareness and understanding of the power dynamics behind a woman's need for assistance. The police continue to bring to their work common-sense assumptions about the types of women likely to call them out. Particularly enduring is the ideology that divides women into 'deserving' and 'undeserving' of police attention. Undeserving women are those who somehow ask for, provoke, or entice their assailants into victimizing them. Broken bones, severe bruising, destroyed property, upset neighbours, and terrified children, according to these common-sense myths, are all due to a woman's nagging, discussing financial matters or child discipline, or being a 'bad' housekeeper. A man's suspicions of infidelity may be considered appropriate justification for a battering. By characterizing men's explanations as justifications, or at least as mediating reasons, police automatically reinforce 'appropriate' male behaviour within heterosexual relationships. The experiences of violence for many women are not seen as crime because the woman is accused of violating man's ideal of wife/lover/mother.

The category 'deserving' is as fluid as its opposite. Women who 'deserve' protection are seen to be behaving appropriately in their heterosexual relationships, yet the man fails to respect this or is defined as mentally ill or drunk and therefore not responsible for his behaviour. These categories are also informed by society's other power structures of race and class where typically more respect is accorded to women of status in these stuctures. The impact of these categories on behaviour, like all stereotypes, can be contradictory. For example, Zoomer (Chapter 6) records how police report more sympathy for Moroccan women than for white Dutch women, who are assumed to have all the benefits of race and class. Racist stereotypes regarding the violence the police attribute to Moroccan men underpin this judgement. Alternatively, Farraro (Chapter 7) notes that Spanish-speaking women and Native American women are more easily characterized by police as undeserving.

Underpinning the different perceptions of the situation between the officers called to the scene and the women concerned can be varying views on what are acceptable and unacceptable family relationships, what constitutes violence, and within that what constitutes criminal violence. Even more fundamental are beliefs about the essential natures of women and men, which include why men engage in violent behaviour and how women contribute to it, whether violence from men to women is understood as infrequent and limited to certain social groups or widely spread throughout society.

The police enter situations defined as 'domestic' with a different set of priorities and assumptions from those they bring to crimes against property. This is evident in their reactions to men who commit violence against women in the home. Police actions in situations defined as domestic are often constrained by their conception of men's violence as natural or typical expressions of male–female relationships. This fundamental assumption is a continuing source of unease for many feminists and central to difficulties women experience in dealings with the police. Rather than unambiguously defining these men as criminal the police may identify and see them as responding to the frustrations of the relationship. Men's feelings about the situation are taken into account by officers in their decisions on how to react, including decisions to arrest. Judges, too, take their perceptions of family relationships into account. Social workers or marriage guidance counselors also may identify the issue as family problems despite clear evidence of criminal violence, and entire families may be targeted for family therapy. Despite protests to the contrary such diversionary programmes can have the effect of decriminalizing violence and abuse within the home.

Strategies such as family therapy, mediation, and reparation schemes run the risk of removing responsibility for violence from violent men by creating contexts that effectively define the violated women and children as sharing, even if not completely, responsibility for the violence directed towards them. These strategies may serve to bind women more strongly to existing violent relationships or to create personal involvement where none previously existed. It is no wonder that women find it difficult to leave violent relationships when they are defined as attached to the man or part of the family unit, rather than as a woman with a right to inhabit a violence-free home. Characterizing battering as a relationship problem is a way of thinking that reflects and in turn reproduces women's dependency on men, that is the structural relationships of hetero-patriarchy.

Feminist expectations of the policing task are not centred on procedural issues around arrest or non-arrest, but on securing the present and future safety of women. Women who identify with the experiences of victimized women, at the very least, expect the police to provide information and necessary assistance to secure their safety. Depending on the circumstances and choices women make, this may involve arrest or assistance to find a place of safety with friends or relations or the women's aid shelter or refuge movements, or legal information about a woman's very limited rights to protection through civil law injunctions for exclusion from the home or restraint through non-molestation orders. In some circumstances an official warning, a caution, may be adequate.

Policing Male Violence and Women's Autonomy

In deciding on an appropriate response, what factors should inform the police use of discretion? This major question raises another basic disagreement between women and the police. In any police intervention their priority is to secure control over what is happening and bring it to what they define as a satisfactory conclusion. The only way a woman is satisfied by the outcome is if she achieves a degree of control over her life following the arrival of the police. It is *her* life that may be at stake. She may have experienced violence on other occasions the police know nothing about. She is likely to know of any patterns in the man's behaviour that lead to repeated violence. Because she knows the man and has experienced his behaviour previously, she is in the best position to know what is likely to happen when the police leave. She, and not the police, has to live with the consequences of any decision they take. She may need police assistance to gain sufficient control to ensure the violence is not repeated. She may need practical help in order to escape the violence together with her children, such as, for example, transport to a place of safety or help in gaining contact with a refuge or shelter. If the circumstances of the attack constitute a criminal offence she may think it is right for the man to be arrested. But it is only by allowing women to have this level of control that the police can provide protection or assistance that will be useful and consistent with respect for her autonomy as a woman.

Following a violent incident a woman may be in a state of shock and unable to make decisions that will shape her future life. In this situation the police role should be to facilitate short-term security and obtain medical attention, with a commitment to future involvement should she need it, for example to return home to collect clothing or other items, or the enforcement of an injunction or assistance at another time, possibly including the arrest of the man. Police records regarding each intervention must be readily accessible to other officers who may attend in the future. These records should be about the abusing man and not the victimized woman.

These priorities are not consistent with those the police in the four countries explored here bring to their work. Policing men's violence turns many existing police practices and procedures upside down. Police expectations about problem-solving need to be fundamentally changed when policing men's violence. Central to the development of a police policy that aims to offer assistance to women must include a respect for her autonomy so that she has some control over the process and outcome of intervention. This requires sensitivity and flexibility. The operation of presumptive arrest policy described in Chapter 7 points to the problems that arise when introducing a reform but not taking into consideration the need for essential policing skills and attitudes.

Presumptive arrest is procedurally limited. It can only be used in relation to an immediate event and does not involve additional resources to secure women's safety. This may mean a woman is in the same situation when the arrested man returns to the home after being, more likely than not, released on bail. The benefit may only be a brief respite from violence, although this can be of decisive value when women use the interval to leave the home and man. Further, presumptive arrest policies seem to be implemented in a contradictory manner. The police seem confused about what they are supposed to be doing. The success or failure of the policy is linked to police notions of successful intervention, which as we have seen are interwoven with a masulinist world view. The policing problems posed by men's violence against women are more fundamental than the limited decision about whether or not to arrest a man responsible for violence against a woman he is or has been in a relationship with. The issues about the nature of policing in general and the role of the police in societies divided by gender, race, and economic circumstances are more complex than perceived in the so-called rationality of public policy.

Some contemporary criminologists in Britain look to police accountability as a solution to policing problems in contemporary societies. Persuading the police to be accountable to local communities is advocated as a way of alleviating the problem of over-policing in the inner city. Negotiations between community representatives and the police are seen as the way to achieve agreed policing priorities and policing levels. This would, it is argued, result in the establishment of sufficient trust between the police and the community. But in addition to the problem of identifying who constitutes the community, issues remain of how the community is to be represented, and what levels within the police are to be accountable.

There are fundamental conflicts of interest in communities. For example, police accountability in communities that are not characterized by a commitment to anti-racism and anti-sexism may mean policing simply reflects their racism and sexism. On an individual level there is a fundamental conflict of interests between the parties in a 'domestic'. Community accountability in situations of conflict, whether between individuals within the community or between sections of the community, are likely to result in the police incorporating the interests of the dominant group in any strategies that emerge from accountability programmes. Where there is a gendered conflict of interests, the interests of the dominant sex class, men, will be shared by the police as a gendered institution. Police accountability could result in further legitimation for existing police practices. To call simply for police accountability offers no solution to the policing of violence against women.

Our argument is that effective policing of violence against women requires a deeper understanding of the power structures of hetero-patriarchy and the role of men's violence in reinforcing these power inequalities. Police protection for women requires that the police understand and respond to the needs of women. The most fundamental need of women is an end to the violence. The form of intervention that restricts or eliminates future attack allows the woman some control over the outcome. The police should facilitate the woman's control by ending the violence, by providing any necessary information about legal rights and community resources, and by assisting the woman to achieve the outcome she defines as most workable. This may not be achieved on the spot, as the expectation that women in situations of violence should immediately take possibly life-changing decisions is not always appropriate. Rather, the police role must be to provide initial action that permits women to obtain safe space in which options can be considered.

The type of policing we are advocating throws existing police conventions and procedures into an uproar. It may not provide officers with an instant 'result'. Arrest and court proceedings may or may not be relevant in any particular incident. But the major issue is the mistaken belief that this would restrict police discretion or make policing irrelevant. Professional work that reaches a high standard always treats the client with respect, knowing that her involvement and understanding of the situation is the basis for professional intervention. This is as true for doctors as it is for accountants, lawyers, and the police. To deny or threaten a woman that she will not receive protection in the future unless she responds in the way the police think appropriate (described in Chapter 5) is to deny both her legal rights and any control in the organization of her future life. We argue that this response is as irresponsible and unprofessional as the traditional police response of 'Sorry, love, it's a domestic. We can't help.'

The demand that the police give the protection of women a central priority also will be criticised as overturning their 'neutral' or objective approach. We have agreed that in situations of gender conflict and violence an 'objective' approach is supportive of the status quo. In the societies described in this volume the dominance of men is deemed 'normal', thereby in practice the use of violence in the control of women is condoned. The situations in which women will receive protection are very limited. Further, giving abused women a central priority need not compromise the legal rights of violent men.

Women's controlling what happens after the police arrive is not accountability in the masculinist sense that has dominated the discussion of this concept so far. First, a focus on the community, the neighbourhood, borough, or city level excludes women as a group defining for themselves their needs in terms of policing or community resources. Second, a focus that does not include accountability to victimized individuals excludes women and the women's support networks that may be assisting those who are kept from control over their lives. The most liberal policy stance to emerge from previous debates is the presumptive arrest policy. We label it liberal because implicit within it is the recognition that violence against women is a crime. But it is a policy change without reference to the context in which it is based.

The context in which policy intervention about men's violence takes place is mediated by an ideology that defines women's existence always, and only, in relation to men. This is the context in which violence against women is understood. Time and again, as the previous four chapters illustrate, police officers do not accept that women have a right to leave violent men. They may feel sympathy with particular women involved with very violent men, but the idea that a woman can live autonomously from men is not part of their understanding of the world. Sympathy may be expressed in terms of financial constraints, as the police may know that women are one man away from poverty. But they are more likely to perceive violence in the apparently gender-free context of 'family squabbles', by definition situations that are not appropriate in their eyes for any intervention. They do not want to challenge heterosexual relationships, so they seek to avoid defining practices as unacceptable.

Women, too, are influenced by dominant ideologies and may not perceive that women can live autonomously from men. But the response of the police may condone behaviours that women perceive as violent. This means that the interests of men predominate in actual policing practices. Policemen are attuned, consciously or unconsciously, to the needs of the man the woman is complaining about. This is an issue of both perception and current procedures. It is the challenge to these gendered perceptions and procedural practices that makes the approach we are outlining both radical and feminist rather than liberal. Power imbalances in our societies are acknowledged and prioritized over liberal concerns with individual intentionality of violent men, at least until the safety of the woman is secured. Policies, such as presumptive arrest, which are not located within a recognition of gendered power relations, can result in the further oppression and even arrest of women under the guise of even-handedness or equality.

Without an understanding of gendered power relationships, the view that either party is equally likely to be at fault and the role of the police is to find out who is innocent and who is guilty seems fair. 'It's six of one and half a dozen of the other', sums up common police attitudes, which can justify policing practices of inaction on one hand and arresting of all parties on the other. The commitment to a concept of family as consisting of one male and one female adult, with or without children, as the 'normal' and desirable way to live further justifies these strategies. The core belief that women only exist in relation to men explains the persistence of the view, despite evidence to the contrary, that women do not want or it is not in women's interests to leave violent men.

Policing men's violence against women is located within the structures of hetero-patriarchy. If policing is to provide protection it can only do so in a limited way in social systems that are founded on men's use of violence. If we are searching for a protection that allows women some control in their lives, some rights to decide their own futures, then it is necessary to alter the terms of the debate from a consideration of current shifts in police policies or discussions of police accountability. It is necessary to include wider social questions about the effect on the police of gendered power relations in societies dominated by the interests and concerns of men, and how these can be altered, in order that a truly fair, and therefore helpful, service can be offered to all women.

Bibliography

Aaronson, David E., C. Thomas Dienes, and Michael C. Musheno
(1984) *Public Policy and Police Discretion*, New York: Clark
Boardman.

Abel, E. M., and E. K. Suh (1987) 'Use of police services by battered
women', *Social Work* 32(6): 526–28.

Acker, N., and N. Rawie (1982) 'Seksueel geweld tegen vrouwen en
meisjes', Report of the Conference on Sexual Violence Against
Women and Girls, June 1982, The Hague: Ministry of Social Affairs
and Employment.

Adler, Suzanna (1987) *Rape on Trial*, London: Routledge & Kegan
Paul.

Aegis (1986) 'NCADV nemesis gets Justice Department grant', 41: 30.

Ahrens, Lois (1974) 'From collective to coopted', *Aegis* 1: 5–9.

Allen, Mary (1925) *The Pioneer Policewoman*, London: Chatto &
Windus.

Attorney General's Task Force (1984) 'Report on family violence: final
report', Washington, D.C.: Department of Justice.

Bains, Surinder (1987) *Manchester's Crime Survey of Women for
Women*, Police Monitoring Unit, Manchester City Council.

Baker, Michael (1985) *Our Three Selves: A Life of Radclyffe Hall*,
London: Hamish Hamilton.

Balgarnie, Florence (1894?) *A Plea for the Appointment of Police
Matrons*, London: White Ribbon Co. Ltd, for the British Women's
Temperance Association.

Banton, Michael (1964) *The Policeman in the Community*, London:
Tavistock.

Bard, Morton (1969) 'Family intervention police teams as a community
mental health resource', *Journal of Criminal Law, Criminology and
Police Science* 60(2): 247–50.

——— (1974) 'Training police as specialists in family crisis intervention', in
R. W. Kobetz (ed.), *Crisis Intervention and the Police*, Chicago, Il:
Dayton.

Bart, Pauline, and Patricia O'Brien (1985) *Stopping Rape: Successful
Survival Strategies*, New York: Pergamon.

Becker, Howard S. (1963) *Outsiders: Studies in the Sociology of Deviance*, New York: Free Press.

Bell, D. J. (1984) 'The police responses to domestic violence: a replication study', *Police Studies* 7: 136–43.

(1985) 'Domestic violence: victimisation, police intervention and disposition', *Journal of Criminal Justice* 13: 525–34.

Berk, Richard A., S. F. Berk, and P. J. Newton (1984) 'An empirical analysis of police responses to incidents of wife battering', unpublished paper, Santa Barbara, CA: University of California, Department of Sociology, and the Social Process Research Institute.

Berk, Richard A., S. F. Berk, P. J. Newton, and D. R. Loseke (1984) 'Cops on call: summoning the police to the scene of spousal violence', *Law and Society Review* 18(3): 479–98.

Berk, Richard A., and P. J. Newton (1985) 'Does arrest really deter wife battering? An effort to replicate the findings of the Minneapolis spouse abuse experiment', *American Sociological Review* 50: 253–62.

Berk, Sarah F., and D. R. Loseke (1980–81) ' "Handling" family violence: situational determinants of police arrest in domestic disturbances', *Law and Society Review* 15: 317–46.

Beyer, A., F. Hermans, D. Paridaens, and I. Speek (1983) *Vrouwenmishandeling en Politie-optreden*, Utrecht: State University.

Binney, Val, Gina Harkell, and Judy Nixon (1981) *Leaving Violent Men: A Study of Refuges and Housing for Battered Women*, London: Women's Aid Federation, England.

Bittner, Egon (1967) 'The police on skid row: a study of peace keeping', *American Sociological Review* 32: 699–715.

Black, Donald (1970) 'Production of crime rates', *American Sociological Review* 35(4): 733–48.

(1976) *The Behaviour of Law*, New York: Academic Press.

(1980) *The Manners and Customs of the Police*, New York: Academic Press.

(1983) 'Crime as social control', *American Sociological Review* 48: 34–45.

Blair, Ian (1985) *Investigating Rape: A New Approach for Police*, London: Croom Helm.

Bland, Lucy (1985) 'In the name of protection: the policing of women in the First World War', in J. Brophy and C. Smart (eds), *Women in Law: Explorations in Law, Family and Sexuality*, London: Routledge & Kegan Paul.

Blijf van m'n Lijf (1978) *Speerpuntenonderzoek Vrouwenmishandeling en Julpverlening in Amsterdam*.

(1984) *Thuis geslagen meyrouw, dan kunnen wij niets doen* (Blijf m'n' Lijf Amsterdam about police, justice and the government), Amsterdam.

Borowoski, Margaret, Mervyn Murch, and Val Walker (1983) *Marital Violence: The Community Response*, London: Tavistock.

Bowker, Lee H. (1982) 'Police services to battered women', *Criminal Justice and Behavior* 9(4): 476–94.

(1984) 'Battered wives and the police: a national study of usage and effectiveness', *Police Studies* 7(2): 84–93.

Boyle, C. Nina (1983) 'The male peril', *The Vote* (27 August).

Brittan, Arthur, and Mary Maynard (1984) *Sexism, Racism and Oppression*, Oxford: Basil Blackwell.

Brown, Michael K. (1981) *Working the Street: Police Discretion and the Dilemmas of Reform*, New York: Russell Sage.

Brown, Stephen E. (1984) 'Police responses to wife beating: neglect of a crime of violence', *Journal of Criminal Justice* 12: 277–88.

Burris, Carol Anne, and Peter Jaffe (1983) 'Wife abuse as a crime: the impact of police laying charges', *Canadian Journal of Criminology* 25: 309–18.

Buzawa, Eva, and Carl C. Buzawa (1985) 'Legislative trends in the criminal justice response to domestic violence', in Alan Jay Lincoln and Murray A. Straus (eds), *Crime and the Family*, Springfield, IL: Charles C. Thomas.

Cain, Maureen (1973) *Society and the Policeman's Role*, London: Routledge.

Casey, Maeve (1987) *Domestic Violence Against Women*, Dublin: Social Organisational Psychology Research Unit, UCD, Dublin 4, Ireland.

Chambers, Gerry, and Ann Millar (1983) *Investigating Sexual Assault*, Edinburgh: HMSO.

Chambers, Gerry, and Jackie Tombs (1984) *The British Crime Survey: Scotland*, London: HMSO.

Chatterton, Michael (1983) 'Police work and assault charges', in Maurice Punch (ed.), *Control in the Police Organisation*, Cambridge, MA: MIT Press.

Chesler, Phyllis (1986) *Mothers on Trial*, New York: McGraw-Hill.

Clark, Lorenne, and Debra Lewis (1977) *Rape: The Price of Coercive Sexuality*, Toronto: Canadian Women's Educational Press.

Clarke, Anna (1987) *Women's Silence, Men's Violence: Sexual Assault in England, 1770–1845*, London and New York: Pandora.

Cobbe, Francis Power (1878) 'Wife torture in England', *Contemporary Review* (April): 55–87.

Coveney, Lal, Margaret Jackson, Sheila Jeffreys, Leslie Kaye, and Pat Mahoney (1984) *The Sexuality Papers: Male Sexuality and the Social Control of Women*, London: Hutchinson.

Cowlin, Mabel, H. (1937) 'Women police past and present', *Women Citizen* (July).

Crime Control Institute (1986) 'Police domestic violence policy change', *Response* 9(2): 16.

Critchley, T. A. (1978) *A History of Police in England and Wales*, rev. ed., London: Constable (first published 1968).

Davis, Nanette J., and Karlene Faith (1985) 'Women and the state: crisis in social control', a paper presented to the annual meeting of the American Society of Criminology, San Diego, California.

Davis, Phillip W. (1981) 'Structured rationales for non-arrest: police stereotypes of the domestic disturbance', *Criminal Justice Review* 6(2): 8–15.

(1983) 'Restoring the semblance of order: police strategies in the domestic disturbance', *Symbolic Interaction* 6(2): 216–74.

Dickens, Alison, and Sara Scott (1988) 'Controlling with kindness', *Trouble and Strife* 3: 40–45.

Dickson, Donald (1968) 'Bureaucracy and morality: an organizational perspective on a moral crusade', *Social Problems* 16 (Fall): 143–57.

Dobash, Rebecca Emerson, and Russell Dobash (1979) *Violence Against Wives: A Case Against Patriarchy*, New York: Free Press.

(1980) *Violence Against Wives: A Case Against Patriarchy*, London: Open Books.

(1984) 'The nature and antecedent of violent events', *British Journal of Criminology* 24(3): 269–88.

Edwards, Susan S. (1985) 'A socio-legal evaluation of gender ideologies in domestic violence assault and spousal homicides', *Victimology* 10(4): 186–205.

(1986a) 'Police attitudes and dispositions in domestic disputes: the London study', *Police Journal*: 130–41.

(1986b) *The Police Response to Domestic Violence in London*, London: Polytechnic of Central London.

(1987) ' "Provoking her own demise": from common assault to homicide', in Jalna Hanmer and Mary Maynard (eds), *Women, Violence and Social Control*, London: Macmillan.

(1986) 'Police attitudes and dispositions in domestic disputes: the London study', *Police Journal*: 230–41.

Ekblom, Paul, and K. Heal (1982) *The Police Response to Calls from the Public*, London: HMSO.

Ellis, D. (1987) *Policing Wife Abuse: The Contribution Made by Domestic Disturbances to Deaths and Injuries among Police Officers*, unpublished paper, Department of Sociology, York University, Toronto.

Ellis, J. W. (1984) 'Prosecutorial discretion to charge in cases of spousal assault: a dialogue', *Journal of Criminal Law and Criminology* 75(1): 56–102.

Emerson, Robert (1983) 'Holistic effects in social control decision-making', *Law and Society Review* 17(3): 425–55.

Enlow, Cynthia (1983) *Does Khaki Become You? The Militarisation of Women's Lives*, London: Pluto Press.

Estrich, Susan (1987) *Real Rape*, Cambridge, MA: Harvard University Press.

Fekete, Liz (1988) 'Policing of black women', *Spare Rib 1986* (January): 8–10.

Ferraro, Kathleen J. (1981a) 'Processing battered women', *Journal of Family Issues* 2: 415–38.

(1981b) 'Battered women and the shelter movement', Ph.D. dissertation, Tempe, AZ: Arizona State University.

(1987) 'Policing woman battering', unpublished manuscript, Tempe, AZ: School of Justice Studies, Arizona State University.

Field, Martha H., and Henry F. Field (1973) 'Marital violence and the criminal process: neither justice nor peace, *Social Service Review* 47(2): 221–40.

Fielding, Nigel (1984) 'Police socialisation and police competence', *British Journal of Sociology* 35(4): 568–90.

Ford, D. A. (1983) 'Wife beating and criminal justice: a study of victim decision-making', *Family Relations* 32(4): 463–75.

Geddes, Sir Eric Campbell (1922) *First Interim of the Committee of National Expenditure* (known as the *Geddes Report*).

Gee, P. (1983) 'Ensuring police protection for battered women: the *Scott v. Hart* suit', *Signs* 8(3): 554–67.

Gelb, Joyce (1983) 'The politics of wife abuse', in I. Diamond (ed.), *Families, Police and Public Policy*, New York: Longman.

Gordon, Linda (1987) *Women's Body, Women's Right*, New York: Grossman.

Grau, Janice, Jeffrey Fagan, and Sandra Wexler (1985) 'Restraining orders for battered women: issues of access and efficacy', *Women and Politics* 4(3): 13–28.

Green, C. (1986) *The Metropolitan Police Task Force on Domestic Violence*, unpublished manuscript.

Grossholtz, Jean (1983) 'Battered women's shelters and the political economy of sexual violence', in I. Diamond (ed.), *Families, Politics, and Public Policy*, New York: Longman.

Gusfield, Joseph (1963) *Symbolic Crusade: Status Politics and the American Temperance Movement*, Urbana, IL: University of Illinois.

Hall, Ruth (1986) *Ask Any Woman: A London Inquiry into Rape and Sexual Assault*, Bristol: Falling Wall Press.

Hanmer, Jalna (1978) 'Violence and the social control of women', in Gary Littlejohn, B. Smart, J. Wakefield, and N. Yuval-Davis (eds), *Power and the State*, London: Croom Helm.

Hanmer, Jalna, and Mary Maynard (eds) (1987) *Women, Violence and Social Control*, London: Macmillan.

Hanmer, Jalna and Shiela Saunders (1984) *Well Founded Fear*, London: Hutchinson.

—— (1987) *Women, Violence and Crime Prevention*, West Yorkshire County Council, England,

Hanmer, Jalna, and Elizabeth A. Stanko (1985) 'Stripping away the rhetoric of protection: violence to women, law and the state in Britain and the U.S.A.', *International Journal of the Sociology of Law* 13: 357–74.

Hart, William., J. Ashcroft, A. Burgess, N. Flanagan, C. Meese, C. Milton, C. Narramore, R. Ortega, and F. Seward (1984) Attorney General's Task Force on Family Violence, Washington D.C.: Department of Justice.

Hatty, Suzanne E. (1986) 'On the reproduction of misogyny: the therapeutic management of violence against women,' in S. E. Hatty (ed.), *National Conference on Domestic Violence*, Canberra: Australia Institute of Criminology.

—— (1987a) 'Women battering as a social problem: the denial of injury,' *Australian and New Zealand Journal of Sociology* 23(1): 36–46.

—— (1987b) 'The criminalization of women battering: an apparent alliance between feminists and the state,' *New Zealand Journal of Social Work* 12(1 & 2): 6–11.

Hatty, Suzanne E., and R. A. Knight (1986) 'Violence against women in Canberra,' Australian Law Reform Commission Domestic Violence Reference, research paper.

Hatty, Suzanne E., and J. E. Sutton (1986a) 'Policing violence against women,' in S. E. Hatty (ed.), *National Conference on Domestic Violence*, Canberra: Australian Institute of Criminology.

    (1986b) 'Children of battered women: the attitudes of intervening police officers,' paper presented to the Sixth International Congress on Child Abuse and Neglect, Sydney, August 11–14, 1986.

Henderson-Livesley, A. H. (undated, post-1924) *The Woman Police Question*, with an introduction by Ashley Brown, London: Social Services Ltd for the League of Womanhood.

Hepburn, John (1978) 'Race and the decision to arrest,' *Journal of Research in Crime and Delinquency* 15: 54–73.

Hes, J. (1984–85) 'Het straatverbod in kort geding als "ultimum remedium",' *Nemesis* 1(3): 130–39.

Hogenhuis, C. (1986) 'U belt . . . wij komen. Reacties op de assistentie-surveillance,' *Algemeen Politieblad* 135(14): 326–28.

Home Office (1987) *Violent Crime: Police Advice for Women on How to Reduce the Risks*, Central Office of Information, London: HMSO.

Home Office Circular 25/83, London: Home Office.

Home Office Circular 69/86, *Violence Against Women: Treatment of Victims of Rape and Domestic Violence*, London: Home Office.

Home Office Circular 96/194 (1944, 30 March).

Home Office Departmental Committee on the Employment of Women on Police Duties, 1920, Cmnd 877, London: HMSO (Sir John Baird (chairman), known as the *Baird Report*).

Home Office Departmental Committee on Women Police: The Bridgman Committee 1924, London: HMSO, Cmnd 2224.

Home Office Statutory Regulation for Policewomen, 7 October 1931.

Hough, Mike, Pat Mathew (1983) *The British Crime Survey*, Research Study 76, London: HMSO.

    (1985) *Taking Account of Crime: Key Findings from the 1984 British Crime Survey*, Research Study 85, London: HMSO.

Hunt, Jennifer (1984) 'The development of rapport through the negotiation of gender in fieldwork among police,' *Human Organization* 43(4): 283–96.

    (1985) 'Police accounts of normal force,' *Urban Life* 13(4): 315–41.

Jaffe, Peter, and Carole A. Burris (1981) *An Integrated Response to Wife Assault: A Community Model*, Ottawa: Solicitor General of Canada.

Jaffe, Peter, P. Wolfe, A. Telford, and G. Austin (1986) 'The impact of police charges in incidents of wife abuse,' *Journal of Family Violence* 1: 43

Jeffreys, Sheila, and Jill Radford (1984) 'Contributory negligence or being a woman? The car rapist case,' in P. Scraton and P. Gordon (eds), *Causes for Concern*, Harmondsworth: Penguin.

John, I. D. ' "The Scientist" as role model for "The Psychologist",' *Australian Psychologist* 21(2): 219–30

Jones, Sandra (1986) *Policewomen and Equality: Formal Policy v. Informal Practice?* London: Macmillan.

Junger-Tas, J. (1977) 'Hulpverlening en opleiding,' *Justitiele Verkenningen* 447–53.

Kalmus, Debra S., and M. A. Straus (1982) 'Wife's marital dependency and wife abuse,' *Journal of Marriage and the Family* 44: 277–86.

Kelly, Liz (1987) 'The continuum of sexual violence,' in Jalna Hanmer and Mary Maynard (eds), *Women, Violence and Social Control*, London: Macmillan.

Kelly, Liz, and Jill Radford (1987) 'The problem of men,' in P. Scraton (ed.), *Law, Order and the Authoritarian State*, Milton Keynes: Open University Press.

Kennedy, D. B., and R. J. Homant (1984) 'Battered women's evaluation of the police response,' *Victimology, an International Journal* 9(1): 174–79.

Kinsey, R., J. Lea, and J. Young (1986) *Losing the Fight Against Crime*, Oxford: Blackwell.

Klaus, P. A., and M. R. Rand (1984) *Family Violence*, special report of the Bureau of Justice Statistics, Washington, D.C.

——— (1987) 'Theoretical and methodological perspectives on domestic violence: implications for social action,' *Australian Journal of Social Issues* 22(2): 452–64.

Knight, R. A., and S. E. Hatty (in press) 'Violence against women in Australia's capital city', *Victimology*.

Kocan, P. (1986) *The Treatment and the Cure*, Sydney: Angus & Robertson.

LaFave, Wayne R. (1969) 'Noninvocation of the criminal law by police,' in D. R. Cressey and D. A. Ward (eds), *Delinquency, Crime and Social Process*, New York: Harper & Row.

LaFree, Gary D. (1980) 'The effect of sexual stratification by race on official reactions to rape,' *American Sociological Review* 45: 842–54.

Lanagan, Patricia A., and Carol A. Innes (1986) *Special Report: Preventing Domestic Violence Against Women*, Washington, D.C.: Bureau of Justice Statistics.

Lauderdale, Pat (1983) 'The creation and growth of opiate regulation,' in J. Inverarity, with contributions by P. Lauderdale, and B. Feld (eds), *Law and Society, Sociological Perspectives on Criminal Law*, Boston: Little, Brown.

Law Reform Task Force on Violence Against Women and Children (1987) *Consultation Paper*, Sydney: Women's Co-ordination Unit.

Lea, John, and J. Young (1984) *What Is to Be Done About Law and Order?* London: Penguin.

Lerman, Lisa G. (1984) 'Mediation of wife abuse cases: the adverse impact of informal disputes resolution on women,' *Harvard Women's Law Journal* 7: 57–113.

Lerman, Lisa G., and Franci Livingston (1983) 'State legislation on domestic violence,' *Response* 6(5).

Lipsky, Michael (1980) *Street-Level Bureaucracy: Dilemmas of the Individual in Public Services*, New York: Russell Sage.

Lock, Joan (1979) 'It's a fair cop,' *Sunday Times Magazine* (London), November 5.

  The British Policewoman: Her Story, London: Robert Hale.

  (1986) 'Grantham's other first,' *Police Review* 6.

London Rape Crisis Centre (1984) *Sexual Violence: The Reality for Women*, London: Women's Press.

London Strategic Policy Unit (1986) *Police Response to Domestic Violence*, Police Monitoring and Research Group Briefing Paper no. 1, London: LSPU.

Loving, Nancy (1980) *Responding to Spouse Abuse and Wife Beating: A Guide for Police*, Washington D.C.: Police Executive Research Forum.

Mackinnon, Catherine A. (1983) 'Feminism, Marxism, method and the state: toward feminist jurisprudence,' *Signs* 8(4): 635–58.

  (1987) *Feminism unmodified: discourses on life and law*, Cambridge, MA: Harvard University Press.

MacLeod, L. (1986) 'Policy as chivalry: the criminalisation of wife battering,' in S. E. Hatty (ed.), *Domestic Violence*, Canberra: Australian Institute of Criminology.

Macready, Nevil (1924) *Annals of an Active Life*, London: Hutchinson and Co.

Malcolmson, R. W. (1977) 'Infanticide in the eighteenth century,' in Cockburn, J. S. (ed.), *Crime in England*, London: Methuen.

Manning, Peter (1978) 'The police: mandate, strategies and appearances,' in P. Manning and J. Van Maanen (eds), *Policing: A View from the Street*, Santa Monica, CA: Goodyear Publishing.

Marsh, J. C., A. Geist, and N. Caplan (1982) *Rape and the Limits of Law Reform*, Boston, MA: Auburn House.

Martin, Del (1976) *Battered Wives*, San Francisco, CA: Glide.

McLeod, Maureen (1983) 'Victim non-cooperation in the prosecution of domestic assaults,' *Criminology* 21(3): 395–416.

McMann, Kathryn (1985) 'Battered women and the law: the limits of legislation,' in J. Brophy and C. Smart (eds), *Women in Law: Explorations in Law, Family and Sexuality*, London: Routledge & Kegan Paul.

Meredith, Eileen (1979) 'Some possibilities and problems in the proceedings used in cases of abuse of women in the family,' in Jalna Hanmer (ed.), *Battered Women and Abused Children: Intricacies of Legal and Administrative Intervention*, Issues Occasional Paper no. 4, University of Bradford.

Merry, Sally E. (1981) *Urban Danger: Life in a Neighborhood of Strangers*, Philadelphia, PA: Temple University Press.

Millett, Kate (1970) *Sexual Politics*, New York: Doubleday.

Morgan, Robin (ed.) (1970) *Sisterhood Is Powerful: An Anthology of Writings from the Women's Liberation Movement*, New York: Vintage.

Morrell, Caroline (1980) *Black Friday: A Study of Violence in the Suffragette Movement*, London: Women's Research and Resources Centre.

Muir, William K. (1977) *Police: Streetcorner Politicians*, Chicago, Il: University of Chicago Press.

Musheno, Michael, and Kathryn Seeley (1986) 'Prostitution policy and the women's movement: historical analysis of feminist thought and organization,' *Contemporary Crises* 10: 237–55.

Myers, Martha, and J. Hagan (1979) Private and public trouble: prosecutors and the allocation of court resources, *Social Problems* 16(4): 439–51.

National Coalition Against Domestic Violence (1987a) *Legislative Update*, Washington, D.C.: NCADV.

(1987b) *Survey of State Coalitions Against Domestic Violence*, Washington, D.C.: NCADV.

Neimann, Marcia (1987) Telephone interview.

Nott-Bower (1914) 'Women police officials,' *The Vote* (19 June).

Oppenlander, Nan (1982) 'Coping or copping out: police service delivery in domestic disputes,' *Criminology* 20(3): 449–65.

Ortega, Reuben B. (1984) *Operations Digest*, nos. 84–85: 1–2.

Pagelow, Mildred D. (1981) *Women Battering: Victims and Their Experiences*, California: Sage.

Pahl, Jan (1978) *A Refuge for Battered Women: A Syudy of the Role of a Women's Centre*, London: HMSO.

(1982) 'Police response to battered women,' *Journal of Social Welfare Law* (November): 337–43.

(ed.) (1985) *Private Violence and Public Policy: The Needs of Battered Women and the Response of the Public Services*, London: Routledge & Kegan Paul.

Parliamentary Select Committee on Violence in Marriage (1975) *Vol. I, Report (with Proceedings of the Committee); Vol. II, Evidence; Vol. III, Apendices*; London: HMSO.

Parnas, Raymond I. (1967) 'The police response to the domestic disturbance,' *Wisconsin Law Review* 2: 914–60.

(1972) 'The police response to the domestic disturbance,' in L. Radnowitz and M. E. Wolfgang (eds), *The Criminal in the Arms of the Law*, New York: Basic Books.

Paternoster, Raymond, L. E. Saltzman, G. P. Waldo, and T. G. Chiricos (1983) 'Perceived risk and social control: do sanctions really deter?' *Law and Society Review* 17(3): 457–79.

Pivar, David J. (1973) *Sexual Morality and Social Control, 1868–1900*, Westport, CT: Greenwood Press.

Platt, Anthony M. (1969) *The Child Savers*, Chicago, IL: University of Chicago.

Pleck, Elizabeth (1979) 'Wife beating in nineteenth century America,' *Victimology* 4(1): 60–74.

(1983) 'Feminist responses to "crimes against women", 1868–1896,' *Signs* 8(2): 451–70.

(1987) *Domestic Tyranny: The Making of Social Policy Against Family Violence from Colonial Times to the present*, New York: Oxford University Press.

Police Chronicle (25 March 1944).

Police Foundation (1976) 'Domestic violence and the police: studies in Detroit and Kansas City,' Washington D.C.: Police Foundation.

Punch, Maurice (1975) 'Rayonagent: Politieman ais maatschappelijk werker,' *Algemeen Politieblad* 124(3): 51–54.

(1979) *Policing the Inner City: A Study of Amsterdam's* Warmoesstraat, London: Macmillan.

(1985) *Conduct Unbecoming*, London: Tavistock.

Quarm, Daisy, and Martin D. Schwartz (1984) 'Domestic violence in criminal court: an examination of new legislation in Ohio,' *Women and Politics* 4(3): 29–46.

Radford, Jill (1984a) *Violence Against Women – Women Speak Out Survey*, Wandsworth Policing Campaign.

(1984b) ' "Womanslaughter": a licence to kill? The killing of Jane Asher,' in P. Scraton and P. Gordon (eds), *Causes for Concern*, Harmondsworth: Penguin.

(1987) Policing male violence – policing women,' in Jalna Hanmer and Mary Maynard (eds), *Women, Violence and Social Control*, London: Macmillan.

Radford, Lorraine (1987) 'Legalising woman abuse,' in Jalna Hanmer and Mary Maynard (eds), *Women, Violence and Social Control*, London: Macmillan.

Radzinowicz, L. (1956) *A History of English Criminal Law and its Administration from 1750*, Vols 2 and 3, London: Stevens.

Randall, Susan, C., and Vicki M. Rose (1981) 'Barriers to becoming a "successful" rape victim,' in L. Bowker (ed.), *Women and Crime in America*, New York: Macmillan.

Raymond, Janice (1986) *A Passion for Friends: Towards a Philosophy of Female Affections*, Boston, MA: Beacon Press.

Reiner, Robert (1985) *The Politics of the Police*, Brighton, Sussex: Wheatsheaf Books.

Report of the City of Ottawa Task Force on Wife Assault (1984) Ottawa, Ontario.

Report of the New South Wales Domestic Violence Committee (1985) Sydney: Women's Coordination Unit.

Rhodes, Dusty, and Sandra McNeill (eds) (1985) *Women Against Violence Against Women*, London: Only Women Press.

Rich, Adrienne (1980) 'Compulsory heterosexuality and lesbian existence,' *SIGNS: Journal of Women in Culture and Society* 5(4): 631–60.

Rifkin, Janet (1980) 'Toward a theory of law and patriarchy,' *Harvard Women's Law Journal*: 83–95.

Rose, Vicky M., and S. C. Randall (1982) 'The impact of investigator perceptions of victim legitimacy on the processing of rape/sexual assault cases,' *Symbolic Interaction* 5(1): 23–26.

Rowbotham, Sheila (1975) *Hidden from History: Three Hundred Years of Women's Oppression and the Fight Against It*, Harmondsworth: Pelican Books.

Royal Commission on Police Powers and Procedure (1929) Cmnd 3297, London: HMSO.

Rubenstein, Jonathan (1973) *City Police*, New York: Ballantine.

Russell, Diana (1982) *Rape in Marriage*, New York: Macmillan.

    (1984) *Sexual Exploitation: Rape, Child Sexual Abuse and Workplace Harassment*, Beverly Hills, CA: Sage.

Sacks, Harvey (1972) 'Notes on police assessment of moral character,' in D. Sudnow (ed.), *Studies in Social Interaction*, New York: Free Press.

Sanders, Andrew (1987) 'Prosecuting "domestic" and non-domestic violence,' paper presented to the British Criminology Conference.

SANE (1987) 5(1): 3–6.

Sarachild, Kathy (ed.) (1975) *Redstockings: Feminist Revolution*, New York: Redstockings.

Schechter, Susan (1982) *Women and Male Violence: The Visions and Struggles of the Battered Women's Movement*, Boston, MA: South End Press.

Scraton, Phil (1985) *The State of the Police*, London: Pluto Press.

Shapland, Joanna, and D. Hobbs (1987) *Policing on the Ground in Highland*, Oxford: Centre for Criminological Research.

Sherman, Lawrence W., and Richard A. Berk (1984a) 'The specific deterrent effects of arrest for domestic assault,' *American Sociological Review* 49: 261–72.

    (1984b) *The Minneapolis Domestic Violence Experiment*, Police Foundation Reports 1, Washington D.C.

Sherman, Lawrence W., J. Garner, and E. Cohn (1986) 'The impact of research on police practice,' in S. E. Hatty (ed.), *National Conference on Domestic Violence*, Canberra: Australian Institute of Criminology.

Skolnick, Jerome H. (1975) *Justice Without Trial*, 2nd edn, New York: Wiley.

Smart, Carol (1986) 'Feminism and the law: some problems of analysis and strategy,' *International Journal of the Sociology of Law* 14: 109–23.

Smith, David J., and J. Gray (1983) *Police and People in London*, London: Policy Studies Institute.

Smith, D. A., and J. R. Klein (1984) 'Police control of interpersonal disputes,' *Social Probelms* 31(4): 468–81.

Smith, D. A., C. A. Visher, and L. A. Davidson (1984) 'Equity and discretionary justice: the influence of race on police arrest decisions,' *Journal of Criminal Law and Criminology* 75: 234–49.

Smith-Rosenberg, Carol (1986) 'Writing history: language, class and gender,' in T. deLauretis (ed.), *Feminist Studies, Critical Studies*, Bloomington, IN: Indiana University.

Spender, Dale (1982) *Women of Ideas — and What Men Have Done to Them*, London: Routledge & Kegan Paul.

Stang Dahl, T. (1986) 'Women's law: method, problems, values,'
Contemporary Crisis 10(4): 361–71.
Stanko, Elizabeth A. (1977) 'These are the cases that try themselves,'
Ph.D. thesis, CUNY Graduate Center, New York.
        (1981) 'The arrest versus the case,' *Urban Life* 9(4): 395–414.
        (1982) 'Would you believe this woman?' in N. H. Rafter and E. A.
Stanko (eds), *Judge, Lawyer, Victim, Thief: Women, Gender Roles
and Criminal Justice*, Boston, MA: Northeastern University Press.
        (1985) *Intimate Intrusions: Women's Experience of male Violence*,
London: Routledge & Kegan Paul.
        (1987) 'Typical violence, normal precaution: men, women and
interpersonal violence in England, Wales, Scotland and the USA,' in
J. Hanmer and M. Maynard (eds), *Women, Violence and Social
Control*, London: Macmillan.
        (1988) 'Fear of crime and the myth of the safe home,' in K. Yllö and
M. Bograd (eds), *Feminist Perspectives on Wife Abuse*, London: Sage.
Steedman, Caroline (1984) *Policing the Victorian Community: The
Formation of the English Police Forces, 1856–1880*, London:
Routledge & Kegan Paul.
Steinmetz, C. H. D., and H. C. Van Andel (1985) *Mishandeling en
hulpverlening*, The Hague: Staatsuitgeverij.
Storch, Robert D. (1975) 'The plague of blue Locusts: police reform and
popular resistance in Northern England, 1840–1857,' *International
Review of Social History* 20.
Straus, M. A. (1977–78) 'Wife beating: how common and why?'
Victimology, An International Journal 2(3–4): 443–58.
Strube, M. J., and L. S. Barbour (1983) 'The decision to leave an
abusive relationship: economic dependence and psychological
commitment,' *Journal of Marriage and the Family* 45(4): 785–93.
Struder, M. (1984) 'Wife beating as a social problem: the process of
definition,' *International Journal of Women's Studies* 7(5): 412–22.
Tancred, Edith (1951) 'Women police, 1914–1950,' pamphlet published
by the National Council of Women.
Tauchen, George, H. Tauchen, and A. Witte (1986) 'The dynamics of
domestic violence: a reanalysis of the Minneapolis experiment,'
unpublished paper, Wellesley, MA: Department of Economics,
Wellesley College.
Taylor, Bernard (1979) *Cruelly Murdered*, London: Souvenir Press.
Times (13 October 1914).
The Vote: The Organ of the Women's Freedom League, C. Despart
(ed.) 10 February 1912; 13 March 1912; 21 September 1912; 25 July
1913; 19 June 1914; 24 July 1914; 1 January 1915; 8 January 1915; 15
January 1915; 19 February 1915; 27 August 1915.
Toner, Barbara (1982) *The Facts of Rape*, London: Arrow.
Ursel, E. J., and D. Farough (1985) 'The legal and public response to
the new wife abuse directive in Manitoba,' Winnipeg Area Study
Report no. 4, Department of Sociology, University of Manitoba,
Winnipeg, Canada.

Van der Zee-Nefkens, A. (1975) *Onderzoek assistentieverlening Gemeentepolitie*, The Hague: Ministry of Justice.

Van Lierop, J. (1985) *Vrouwenmishandeling en politie*, Apeldoorn: Netherlands Police Academy.

Van Maanen, John (1978) 'Observations on the making of policemen,' in P. Manning and J. Van Maanen (eds), *Policing: A View from the Street*, Santa Monica, CA: Goodyear Publishing.

Van Straelen, F. W. M. (1978) 'Het seponerings — en strafvorderings-beleid van het Openbaar Ministerie,' in L. Gunther Moor and E. Leuw (eds), *Beslissingsmomenten in het strafrechtelijk systeem*, Utrecht: Ars Aequi Libri.

Voice (1987) 'National hotline and promotion planned,' (Spring): 1.
    (1988) 'NCADV Notes' (Winter): 7.

Vredeveld, G. (1978) 'Gezinsinterventie door de politie,' *Algemeen Politieblad* 127(1, 2, 3).

Walby, Sylvia (1986) *Patriachy at Work*, Cambridge: Polity Press.

Walker, Lenore (1985) 'Psychological impact of the criminalization of domestic violence on victims,' *Victimology* 10(1–4): 281–300.

Walters, J. D. (1981) 'Police in the middle: a study of small city police intervention in domestic disputes,' *Journal of Police Science and Administration* 9(3): 243–261.

Wambaugh, Joseph (1970) *The New Centurions*, Boston, MA: Little, Brown.

Wasoff, Fran (1982) 'Law protection from wife beating: the processing of domestic assaults by Scottish prosecutors and criminal courts,' *International Journal of the Sociology of Law* 10: 187–204.

Wharton, Carol S. 61987) 'Establishing shelters for battered women: local manifestations of a social movement,' *Qualitative Sociology* 10(2): 146–63.

Women's National Commission (1985) *Violence Against Women*, London: Cabinet Office.

Woods, Laurie (1986) 'Resource list: battered women: litigation,' New York: National Center on Women and Family Law.

Worden, Robert, E., and A. A. Pollitz (1984) 'Police arrests in domestic disturbances: a further look,' *Law and Society Review* 18(1): 16–34.

Wöstmann, M., and H. van de Bunt (1987) 'Verbaliseren van politie-optreden'bij vrouwenmishandeling,' in G. Bruinsma, E. Leuw, E. Lissenberg, and A. A. van Vliet (eds), *Vrouw en Criminaliteit*, Meppel/Amsterdamn: Boom.

Young, Vernetta (1986) 'Gender expectations and their impact on black female offenders and victims,' *Justice Quarterly* 3: 305–27,

Zoomer, Olga J. (1979) 'Female victims of crimes and how the criminal justice system reacts to them,' paper presented at the conference of the International Sociological Association, The Hague, August 1979.
    (1984) *Het politie-optreden in probleemsituaties: de behandeling van gevallen van vrouwenmishandeling*, The Hague: Ministry of Home Affairs.

Zoomer, O. J., and R. M. M. Vossen (1986) 'Politie-optreden bij vrouwenmishandeling; enkele "harde" cijfers over over een gevoelig onderwerp,' *Algemeen Politieblad* 135(23): 515–19.

Index

Note: organizations etc. are British unless stated otherwise.